TEN MOST WANTED

THE NEW WESTERN LITERATURE

BLAKE ALLMENDINGER

ROUTLEDGE   NEW YORK AND LONDON

Published in 1998 by
Routledge
29 West 35th Street
New York, NY 10001

Published in Great Britain in 1998 by
Routledge
11 New Fetter Lane
London EC4P 4EE

Copyright © 1998 by Routledge

Printed in the United States of America on acid-free paper
Design: Jack Donner

Library of Congress Cataloging-in-Publication Data

Allmendinger, Blake.
    Ten most wanted : the new western literature / Blake Allmendinger.
        p.   cm.
    Includes bibliographical references (p.   ) and index.
    ISBN 0–415–91462–0 (hardbound). — ISBN 0–415–91463–9 (pbk.)
1. American literature—West (U.S.)–History and criticism.   2. American
literature—20th century—History and criticism.   3. Western stories—History and
criticism.   4. West (U.S.)—In literature.   5. Canon (Literature)   I. Title.
PS271.A44   1998
810.9'3278—dc21
                                                            97–37577
                                                            CIP

FOR CINDI, TAYLOR, AND MATT

Contents

Acknowledgments

Two sources at the University of California, Los Angeles, funded this project. The Academic Senate provided annual grants that supported my research and covered the cost of the book's illustrations. The Center for Seventeenth- and Eighteenth-Century Studies awarded me an Ahmanson–Getty Fellowship in 1993–94. As a Fellow, I participated in a yearlong conference held at the William Andrews Clark Memorial Library. The conference, entitled "American Dreams, Western Images: Mapping the Contours of Western Experiences," attracted scholars from different regions and disciplines. As individuals and as members of an intellectual "western" community, they influenced my thinking enormously. I would like to thank the other Fellows I met while in residence, as well as Valerie Matsumoto, one of the organizers, who asked me to join her in editing a volume of conference essays entitled *Over the Edge: Remapping Western Experiences* (Berkeley: University of California Press, 1998).

I would also like to thank Rose Mary Allmendinger, my mother, for reading everything that I write and for serving as my ideal audience; William Handley and Kris Fresonke, former graduate students and research assistants, who have moved on to successful careers of their own; and my editor at Routledge, William Germano, who said that he wanted this book because it sounded "delightfully mad."

Introduction

It's lonely being me.

That's what I thought, as an assistant professor, teaching my first course on nineteenth-century American literature. Professors who taught the course generally focused on New England writers. Instead, I took the East as a starting point, moving West as we progressed through the syllabus. Beginning with essays on nature, written by New England philosophers, the class then read works by members of the eastern establishment, who had tested and revised their conceptions of the wilderness on the western frontier. The class also read translated works by Native Americans, who offered radically different perspectives on "civilized" contacts, white conquest, and settlement.

The class wasn't happy. Like consumers, some undergraduates demanded their money's worth—not that they necessarily wanted to read better-known canonical works, but they expected certain "representative" texts to automatically appear on the syllabus. Even students who liked my course seemed to think they were slumming. In their evaluations at the end of term, they praised my commitment to teaching "regional" literature. How had students come to believe that an introverted poet such as Emily Dickinson, or a resident of tiny Walden Pond, was somehow "American," while anyone who took as his or her subject the whole western half of a continent was a regionalist, a local color writer, or a miniature portraitist?

There are two reasons why literature of the American West seems insignificant. First, it has never had the literary equivalent of a frontier hypothesis, a unifying theory that argues that the entire corpus of American literature stems from a fascination with the nation's frontier. (The works of Henry Nash Smith and Richard Slotkin are too discriminating to make such wide-sweeping claims.) However, Frederick Jackson Turner's belief—that westward movement, the concept of free land, and the process of settlement, have fundamentally shaped all Americans—legitimized the study of western history in the late nineteenth century and continues, more than one hundred years later, to influence scholarship. (Witness the revisionist work of the "new western historians," whose responses to Turner have received great acclaim.) Second, in addition to failing to put forth a theory that lays claim to dominance, western literature has evolved along more than one line, leading to the question: What *is* western literature? The most popular genre within the field is the formula western, which is what members of the general public assume I teach when I tell them my field. But the western is also the most intellectually ridiculed genre within western literature. What can you say about a tradition that has dwindled rather than developing in artistic stature—that begins with James Fenimore Cooper and ends with Louis L'Amour?

A lot, apparently. For although formula westerns are often regarded as lowbrow, they nevertheless receive a disproportionate amount of serious scrutiny. The reason for this, as Jane Tompkins and Lee Mitchell suggest, is that early westerns were written by members of the eastern establishment with the intention of explicating a set of eastern concerns. Tompkins argues that the western developed in response to the sentimental literature of the mid-nineteenth century. Owen Wister inaugurated the genre, she claims, erecting the cult of the phallus to challenge the cult of true womanhood. Subsequent westerns rejected Christianity, the home, and the family, glorifying male exploits, violence and death, the outdoors, and freedom from social constraints. Although he writes with more erudition and insight about the way in which westerns construct masculinity, Mitchell, like Tompkins, defines westerns as literary responses to contemporary urban social affairs. According to Mitchell, for example, *Riders of the Purple Sage* should be read within the context of the debate over the New Woman at the turn of the century.

I am less interested in the merits of these various readings and more concerned with the way in which they position the West (and the western) in relation to the rest of the nation. Scholars study the western, while at the same time apologizing for their interest in such a debased form of literature,[1] either because they read the western as a response to canonical literature or because they interpret the western within the context of non-western events. Reenacting the course of empire (the process of subordinating the West to a central intelligence), scholars colonize and demote western literature, defining it as an adjunct of the dominant culture, reducing it to a footnote in history. People interested in the West might as well ask: Why read westerns at all, if they're written by easterners in order to gloss eastern aesthetic, political, and social developments? One comes away from such studies, no matter how convincing they are, feeling somehow unsatisfied.

It's no wonder that the field seems to be languishing when the most popular genre within western literature, instead of focusing our attention on the West, redirects it back East. Although other texts and traditions within western literature tell us more about the West than the western does, the very wealth of material makes it difficult for scholars to arrange these works conceptually within one single discipline. For critical and pedagogical reasons, it is even more difficult to center the field on any one of several competing traditions. Although there are many possible ways of organizing material, as various western anthologies illustrate, for the sake of convenience there are five categories into which much (though not all) of western literature falls. As opposed to the formula western, which is discussed and dismissed, there is what I think of as "canonical" western literature, which is revered but ignored. To be included in this group, you must have written something that everyone agrees is important but no one much wants to read (anything by Bret Harte, Frank Norris, Jack London); or you have to be a non-western writer, such as Mark Twain, whose one western work (*Roughing It*) lends prestige to the field; or you have to be Willa Cather, a crossover artist whose work is admired by both mainstream critics and westernists.

In a third category we have the literature of discovery, which at some point in the nineteenth century, during the course of western settlement, turns into the travelogue. (A hybrid of the two is the immigrant or pioneer autobiography). The problem with teaching this literature doesn't derive from the fact that Euro-American "discovery" is now regarded as a discredited enterprise, but from the perception that these texts are personal narratives, glosses on history, not really art. Most students I know believe that *The Journals of Lewis and Clark*, one of the masterpieces of nineteenth-century American literature, would be easier to follow and more entertaining if it just had more maps.

Unlike the literature of discovery, which is concerned with empire-building and nation-formation, regional literature has more modest goals: to capture the landscape and setting, the people and customs, of a particular area. This category includes subsets as general as "southwestern" literature (Mary Austin, Barbara Kingsolver) and as specific as "Montana" literature (Thomas McGuane, Ivan Doig). If the problem with the formula western is that it reflects eastern rather than western concerns, the problem with regional literature is that it focuses on the West exclusively, so minutely, that anyone uninterested in or living outside the area in question might ask: Who cares? Anyone working in western literature faces the challenge of reconciling two conflicting imperatives: the desire to claim importance for the work that one does by relating it to larger theoretical constructs, national literary movements, outside historical and political forces, and external trends; and the need not to lose sight of what makes a work distinctive, "western," unique.

Trying to group all ethnic literatures into a fifth and final category might be like trying to squeeze an aging hippie into a pair of blue jeans that no longer fit. Chicana/Chicano, Asian American, and Native American literature have developed into their own separate fields in the last several decades, having outgrown western literature. Until these fields achieved prominence, it was easy for western scholars to ignore nearly all ethnic literature. Now, with the partitioning of departments and the politicization of fields, combined with the inherent movement toward specialization within academia, the temptation once again might be to avoid ethnic works, leaving them in the hands of qualified specialists. Westernists must resist this temptation, attempting to understand the complex interactive roles ethnic traditions have played within a larger group western history.

Instead, westernists have put writers such as Wallace Stegner on a critical pedestal. Stegner was a leading conservationist, a Pulitzer Prize-winning author, and for many years the head of Stanford's creative writing program, which produced Ken Kesey, Larry McMurtry, and others. He was also an admittedly old-fashioned artist whose stories about decent people, coming to terms with themselves and the West, deserve a certain regard. But his gentlemanly novels present only one view of the West, one that sometimes seems blandly homogenized. According to one recent critic, Stegner justified not writing about Native Americans because he mistakenly believed that they had "vanished" from the West almost one hundred years ago.[2] But Stegner excluded more than one group of people from his artistic purview. In one of his own essays, aptly named "Born a Square," Stegner acknowledged that because he grew up in provincial surroundings, certain people were invisible to him (including blacks, Jews, and "faggots") and some forms of behavior seemed alien (including homosexuality—an "unfortunate illness," he claimed).[3] Leaving aside the question of whether Stegner should be condemned for his ignorance, rather than praised for writing about what he knew best ("western settlement and the legitimate inclinations of the sexes"[4]), one still has to wonder why the field continues to embrace his work so uncritically.

The leading journal in the field exists in a time warp and reflects an intellectual state of stagnation. Founded in 1966, *Western American Literature* publishes scholarship, book reviews, and professional notices. A bibliography, appearing in each winter issue, provides an annual list of current and ongoing research. A sponsoring association holds a convention for members each year. (Western literature is less popular than western history because it is considered a less sexy discipline. Members of the Western History Association outnumber their counterparts by a ratio of about three to one.[5]) The journal's editor, Thomas J. Lyon,[6] is sometimes acknowledged as the field's representative, its senior spokesman and taste-maker. Case in point: When the editors of *The Oxford History of the American West* needed someone to "sum up" western literature, they asked Mr. Lyon to provide a chapter in which important writers, traditions, and trends were identified.

Mr. Lyon has enjoyed an almost uninterrupted reign at *Western American Literature* since 1974. (In one recent issue, the lead review praised a new book coedited by Mr. Lyon himself.[7]) Although the yearly bibliography points to changing trends in the field, the journal itself publishes the same kind of articles on pretty much the same group of authors year after year. Here, writers who were big in the 1950s and 1960s—Walter Van Tilburg Clark, Vardis Fisher, A. B. Guthrie, and Robinson Jeffers—are still names to be reckoned with, along with Jean Stafford, Wright Morris, and a small host of others. Remember when eco-criticism was cool and Edward Abbey was king? The editorial motto at *Western American Literature* reads: "Edward Abbey is dead. Long live the king!" A benevolent dictatorship occasionally sees to it that contemporary, minority, and avant-garde writers are spared execution, but the odd pieces on Cormac McCarthy, Tony Hillerman, Ruth Lum McCunn, and Sam Shepard pose little in the way of seditious threats to the ancien régime.

Furthermore, renowned scholars from major research institutions have rarely published articles in *Western American Literature*. Look at the institutional affiliations of the journal's contributors. I've been in the profession for almost ten years, yet even with a map I couldn't tell you where some of these people are coming from. Raise your hand if you've heard of Chadron State College. Quinnipiac College? Radford University? (Radford's my Waterloo. People from Radford publish in the journal with great regularity. Or maybe it's the same person, reappearing over and over again.) Then again, some scholars come from places whose schools offer helpful directions, as if they're trying to get you to visit (Northwest Missouri State University). And then there are the amateur western enthusiasts—the layperson who became interested in the West because his grandfather once hiked a leg of the Oregon Trail, or the nature lover who boasts no recognized ties to society. (I guess the contributor from "San Juan Mountains, Colorado," must like his space.)

In one sense, getting published in the journal represents a tremendous accomplishment. Given the fact that approximately half of each issue is earmarked for book reviews, and that one out of every four issues is devoted almost entirely to bibliographies, each average issue therefore has room for only two or three brief, scantily footnoted essays. Hence the phenomenon that a journal that obsessively documents books and articles, dissertations and theses, at the same time produces no noteworthy scholarship. Wouldn't it make more sense to free up the space that is reserved for reviewing books by third-rate presses and publishing arcane bibliographies, then using that space to present longer, more numerous, and more interesting articles? The primary purpose of *Western American Literature* should be to inspire, solicit, and publish the work of the best intellectuals.

Instead, graduate students don't enter a field that they perceive to be dead, and because they don't enter the field it never has a chance to revive. At most institutions, except for a few western state universities, assistant professors aren't hired to teach western literature (on the average, the MLA Job List advertises one or two such positions each year). They're hired to teach some other field in American literature, and "do" the West on the side. Career-minded academics don't send their work to western publishers since there's no prestige in doing so. They give it to mainstream presses and hope that reviewers who don't know the field and who may not be qualified to judge their work choose to publish it anyway. Most of their scholarship—on the formula western or on "canonical" literature—is concerned with finding new ways to read old traditions, not with animating and enlarging the field by finding new texts to read.

Guess what I want to do?

II

Answer: Locate and investigate a "new" western literature, first, by resurrecting several western works from obscurity, and second, by claiming as western certain well-known but seemingly non-western works. The first part of my book is entitled "Discovery." I use this term somewhat ironically, unlike frontier explorers who believed they had "found" a New World that was already there. Some of the books I discuss in this section were first discovered by readers upon publication; others faced almost instant oblivion. But they all escaped scholarly scrutiny—and some of them lapsed out of print—because they were written by marginal members of society (women and children, people of color, and religious minorities); because the writing was crude and the ideas were unpopular; or because the narratives dealt with topical historical issues that now seem irrelevant. However, all of these works, I will argue, reflect important frontier aesthetic traditions, pivotal historical moments and cultural shifts in the West, or political debates concerning the region's significance during a period of national expansion in the mid- and late nineteenth century.

The first two essays indicate how the treatment of race can contribute to a book's unpopularity. Although thousands of blacks worked as cowboys in the late nineteenth century, only one man, Nat Love, published his autobiography. Perhaps because he was writing for a mainly white readership, Love denied having been the victim of prejudice. Instead he described his kind treatment at the hands of white bosses, his acceptance within a color-blind cowboy fraternity, and his subsequent rise to fame in a nonracist frontier environment. Whether he subtly critiqued (as certain passages indicate) or sincerely approved white society, the author failed to draw interest, admiration, or sympathy. On one hand, because Love was black, his work may have alienated white audiences accustomed to reading (white) frontier autobiographies. On the other hand, because Love preferred apolitical subject matter and adopted a placating tone, his work may have appeared increasingly distasteful to blacks with the passage of time. In the 1960s, during the Civil Rights era, Love's conciliatory writings finally fell out of print.

The Life and Adventures of Joaquín Murieta, the first novel published by a Native American, also failed to satisfy two separate constituencies because it dealt with race problematically. The book tells the story of Joaquín Murieta, a Mexican outlaw who, in revenge for having been persecuted during the Gold Rush, organizes a gang and terrorizes frontier communities. The author, John Rollin Ridge, who was half white and half Cherokee, partially sympathized with his mestizo character. Having been dispossessed of tribal land by the government, Ridge identified with Murieta as a disenfranchised minority. But having relocated and invested in mainstream society, Ridge also disapproved of Murieta's indiscriminate attacks on the populace. A self-contradicting and confused work of art, the novel is also a cultural document whose schisms perfectly parallel California's own shaky status in the mid-nineteenth century. Because of his mixed ethnic heritage and conflicting allegiances, Ridge was well qualified to write about the state's instability—its internal divisions, generated by racial hostilities, and its conditional footing, caused by the political tug-of-war between the United States and Mexico.

For a variety of reasons, the remaining texts in this section, all of them written by women, have failed to earn recognition or to regain their lost popularity. Since the Mormon Church no longer condones plural marriages, nineteenth-century anti-polygamy literature (including propaganda tracts, novels, and exposés) now seems antiquated and no longer relevant. It is easy to forget that the nation once was enthralled by alleged first-hand accounts, as-told-to reports, and fictional narratives describing the horrors of frontier polygamy. Only by reading these works as versions of Indian captivity narratives can we understand their visceral appeal at the time and their continuing relevance as part of a mythic frontier tradition within western literature. The fact that Mormons had a lengthy and well-documented history of dealing with Indians—combined with the fact that the popular media caricatured both groups as polygamous, bloodthirsty savages—made it easier for readers to equate Mormon marriage with sexual enslavement and barbaric servitude.

Like the women writers who condemned Mormon polygamy, Louise A.K.S. Clappe (better known by her pen name "Dame Shirley") suffers from decreased visibility—not because she embraced a cause that now seems obscure but because another writer has since overshadowed her. *The Shirley Letters*, a series of personal sketches describing life in a mining camp, provided Bret Harte with information for his first successful short story. Although Harte never acknowledged having reworked some of Dame Shirley's material, in "The Luck of Roaring Camp" he came to terms with his deed. By claiming that the miners of Roaring Camp passively accepted gold that a bountiful earth-mother offered them, Harte suggested the compliance—even the complicity—of a "female" source, thus indirectly excusing his own artistic theft.

The final essay in the first section, dedicated to works that have seldom if ever been studied, devotes itself to one of the most bizarre texts in twentieth-century American literature. *The Story of Opal*, purportedly written at the turn of the century, narrates the adventures of a girl who allegedly lived in a logging camp when she was six and seven years old. The unorthodox "journal" filters real life through fantasy, concentrating on Opal's dreamy trips through the forest and on her unique interactions with animals. On one hand, because of doubts concerning the author's veracity, her work is no longer believed to be factual. (Opal's claim, that she was a literary prodigy as well as a daughter of the French aristocracy who had been orphaned and adopted by lumberjacks, continues to test the book's credibility.) On the other hand, because her work reads like nonsense, her "fiction" is never taken that seriously. Therefore it comes as something of a surprise to note that, instead of being a self-absorbed piece of preciousness, *The Story of Opal* actually engages the same themes and common concerns found in most frontier literature.

Unlike this first section, which "discovers" neglected texts that are clearly western in emphasis, the second part revisits well-known but seemingly non-western materials. The goal of "Discovery" is to expand the field from within. The purpose of "Rediscovery" is to introduce works from outside western literature, expanding the field by extending the region's parameters. The first three essays in this part examine works set in foreign locales. (Unlike scholars who diminish the West when they view it through a non-western lens, I seek to magnify the role that the West plays in literature, using the enlarging end of a far-sighted telescope.) First, I argue that the bestselling novel, *Ben-Hur*, although set in the Far East, should be read in the context of events that occurred on the U.S. frontier. Lew Wallace wrote the novel while he governed New Mexico in

the late 1880s. While he was making the new territory "safe" for white settlement (forcing Indians onto reservations and arbitrating range wars between ranchers and cattlemen), Wallace was completing the story of
Ben-Hur, a Jew who converts to Christianity and fights pagan Rome. The
epic pitted members of an enlightened "civilization" against Roman "savagery," prefigured the formula western, and offered an allegory on empire during the period of U.S. Manifest Destiny.

While Wallace resituated New Mexico in a far distant land, Robert
Louis Stevenson transformed California into a place of fantastic make-
believe. Stevenson wrote *Treasure Island* after visiting the remains of a
mining camp in the late nineteenth century. Environmental devastation and human decay—the consequences of a boom-bust mining
economy and a resultant migrant society—suggested to Stevenson that
the pursuit of wealth was a hollow and misguided enterprise. Although
he was sobered by the ghostly scene that confronted him, he was also
seduced by the camp's haunting atmosphere. Thus *Treasure Island*,
inspired by Stevenson's western experience, captured the risk and
excitement of searching for treasure while demonstrating the destructive effect that greed and ambition had on its characters. If frontier
events provided the key to Wallace's biblical narrative, they also sup-
plied inspiration for Stevenson's romantic parable.

After revisiting ancient Rome and the English high seas, we travel to
the plains of north China in the late 1920s. Here, during this period,
Pearl Buck helped her husband, an agricultural missionary, teach Chinese peasants new farming techniques. Gradually Buck began to doubt
the usefulness of U.S. technology at the same time that overseas agricultural enterprise, speculation, and intensive application of modern
machinery were combining with poor weather conditions to devastate
the U.S. Great Plains. Her novel, *The Good Earth*, was published in the
same year that the first dust bowls appeared. The story of Chinese
farmers who weather a plague of vicissitudes—not always triumphing
over poverty, family hardships, and natural catastrophes—inspired
audiences during the Depression who were waging their own war with
environmental disasters, famine, mass unemployment, and homelessness. *The Good Earth* offered solace while at the same time proposing an
anachronistic alternative, critiquing U.S. practices that had led to the
Dust Bowl by romanticizing "primitive" Chinese rural traditions.

In the last two essays in the second part, we return to the West, tracing works with popular appeal, national stature, and broad visibility

back to their forgotten yet distinct western origins. *In Cold Blood*, Truman Capote's 1960s' bestseller, has been viewed from so many angles (as a treatise on capital punishment, as the first nonfiction novel, as a self-serving stunt intended to add to the author's celebrity) that it might seem impossible at this point to study the novel from some new perspective. I argue, however, that the work frames itself within the tradition of "queer" frontier literature. *In Cold Blood* eroticizes homosocial desire, which is present but latent in the formula western. It explores the nature of interracial same-sex relationships, which D. H. Lawrence and Leslie Fiedler have identified as a recurring dynamic in American literature. It associates homosexuality with criminality, as other books and films do, especially in the 1940s and afterward. And, indirectly, it reflects the author's narcissistic attraction to one of the work's central characters.

The book ends on a contemporary, nonliterary, and whimsical note (for those of you who don't already think that all of my choices are whimsical) with a reappraisal of *Twin Peaks*, the television series and brief cult phenomenon. The essay explains why daytime soap operas tend to be set in the East and Midwest; why nighttime soap operas, beginning in the late 1970s, were located out West instead; and why shows such as *Dallas* and *Dynasty*, with their ongoing narratives, simulated the process of exploring an unclosed frontier. Unlike nighttime soap operas, which featured the exploitation of the West's seemingly unlimited resources (i.e., cattle, oil, vineyards, and real estate), *Twin Peaks*, which took place in a northwestern logging town, viewed nature from multiple, conflicting perspectives. Alternately, the parodic soap opera represented the forest as part of nature's ecology, as the dwelling place of some dark psychic entity, as raw material for the production of kitsch wooden artifacts, and as the object of mystical reverence, never being so dull and predictable as to have an ideological agenda or a confirmed point of view.

III

In an essay published six years ago, Annette Kolodny suggested that we reconceptualize frontier American literature by redefining the frontier as "a locus of first cultural contact,"[8] as any place where two or more groups of people converge. Such a model would privilege "no group's priority and no region's primacy."[9] Eskimo legends, Icelandic versions of Norse sagas, European immigrant narratives, and accounts of Spanish conquistadores—all of these and more would fall under the heading of frontier or first–contact literature. In order to "establish a truly compre-hensive frontier literary history," Kolodny notes in her article, "both geography and chronology must be viewed as fluid and ongoing, as a continuously unfolding palimpsest that requires us to include Old Norse, Papago, Nahuatl, Quechua, Spanish, Yaqui, Tewa, Gullah, French, Dutch, Chinese, Japanese, German, Yiddish, and so on—as well as Eng-lish—within our textual canon."[10]

Kolodny's frontier points in more directions than one single scholar can follow. (I haven't even heard of some of the fourteen foreign lan-guages Kolodny says I should know. And I'm too old to learn how to conjugate irregular verbs in Tewa or Quechua.) So, although I share Kolodny's interest in other cultures, I'm confined in this study to work-ing with English–language materials; and although I search for the frontier in places as far–flung as China, I'm also content to stay home, looking for new frontiers within the West where I was born and raised and now work. My "new" western literature moves across geographical borders and spans several centuries. It includes obscure works and famous ones. It represents multicultural, transnational, queer, and mes-tizo experiences. It reports on such occupations as ranching, dust–bowl farming, mining, and forestry, but also chronicles such strange events as chariot races, locust plagues, and battles with pirates at sea. It intro-duces a motley cast of characters, including Brigham Young's nine-teenth wife, a black cowboy, the Log Lady, and an alleged member of the French aristocracy who named her pet pig Aphrodite.

I'm not interested in proposing an alternative canon but in partially reconstituting the existing field by exploring new works. The texts I've chosen are wide–ranging, have little in common with each other, and seem far from definitive. Anyone reading these essays might think of alternative choices that would work just as well. But that's the point of these essays: to suggest new possibilities. If I privilege works that seem tangential to the field, improbably "western," eccentric, or marginal, it's because I'm responding to a field that is intellectually conservative and, what is worse, unimaginative, one in which *Unforgiven* is considered a "revisionist" western (Clint Eastwood kills people, but this time he's sorry). If I don't include enough fresh and under–represented material, then I look forward to someone else nominating other new works for study.

Just as you won't find a complete list of works, so you won't find a thesis that ties the whole book together. Gradually, I've come to the conclusion that there are two kinds of books one can write: a definitive tome, in which a master thesis attempts to explain the existence of all western literature, or a less ambitious project that, regardless of whether or not it succeeds as a monograph, lacks the heft and importance, the universal applicability, the instant "classic" stature, of the definitive tome. In the first instance, one looks (somewhat grudgingly) for cracks in the monument, for "evidence" that has been forced unconvincingly to conform to the thesis or else left out entirely. (Why doesn't Henry Nash Smith include Mormons in his discussion of the West as symbol and myth? Where are the women in the last two volumes of Richard Slotkin's groundbreaking trilogy?) In the second case, although one admires the dissertation or monograph that expertly manages its selected material, one isn't likely to reserve for that work a central place on one's bookshelf. Here, within a brief space, I have sought to cover as much ground as possible. Yet I have resisted the impulse to transform ten separate essays into installments or "chapters" in one master narrative, believing that it is important to (re)discover and document diverse works by men and women, people of all ages, western and non-western writers, blacks and whites, queers and straights, Mormons and Native Americans, even if one can't make those works fit neatly in one thematic formula. Instead of organizing a broad range of material into a framework that makes simple sense, I aim to demonstrate that the West, with the largest land mass of any region in the United States and the fastest growing segment of the nation's population, has an equally substantial and expanding body of literature.

If you've read this far, you probably don't expect me to claim that I'm committed to a particular theory or a pure methodology. I believe that an assortment of texts calls for shifting approaches and flexible attitudes. You may have guessed that western literature isn't exactly the most theorized field in the world. It's an un-p.c. region where people know more about fur coats than Foucault. So I'm indebted to criticism, both inside and outside my field, that has helped me understand such diverse works as ex-slave narratives, children's literature, soap operas, and Mormon theology. Where there already exists a significant body of scholarship—on formula westerns, for instance—I've elected to sample various theories rather than settling for one of them. (Since *Ben-Hur* and *In Cold Blood* are generic mutations rather than "westerns" per se, one must regard them as hybrids, not as the offspring of one critical formula.) In the process of expanding the field, the new western literature incorporates heterogeneous materials and overlaps disciplines.

* * *

I'm not good at making closing remarks. For once, however, that may be appropriate. The redefinition of western literature should be an ongoing process, as I've suggested above. My desire to facilitate that process explains why I resist the temptation to tie up loose ends or to have the last word. But I also have less high-minded reasons for not wanting to finish what is, and must always be, an incomplete work. The introduction may be the first thing one reads, but for an author it's more like a conclusion since it's often the last thing one writes. As I withdraw from a process of researching, thinking, and writing, which has lasted almost five years, I hope that readers, who pick up where I leave off, encounter the same pleasures exploring this book that I had while charting it.

PART ONE

DISCOVERY

ONE

The White Open Spaces

In his famous essay, "The Significance of the Frontier in American History" (1893), Frederick Jackson Turner defined the frontier experience as a process that transformed Anglo–Europeans into one distinct race. Hunters and trappers, ranchers and farmers, miners, railroad men, and entrepreneurs: According to Turner, those who explored and settled the West were collectively defined by the process of finding new land. Paradoxically, through the act of taming the wilderness, frontiersmen were freed. Turner believed that they were liberated by a democratizing process that enabled all people, regardless of background or class, to share equally in the struggle as well as the benefits of Manifest Destiny. While they appropriated land for the nation, people at the same time were assimilating themselves into one whole society. "In the crucible of the frontier," Turner explained metaphorically, individuals collected and came together as a "mixed race" of men, creating a "composite nationality" that united them, in spite of their differences, and that identified these men as uniquely "American."[1]

In Turner's essay, however, this new race of Americans excluded women and people of color. White men were leaders of westward progress and enterprise; subservient characters (family members, indentured slaves, and natives) were helpmates, servants, or foes. While there would seem to be no significant role for a black man to play in this narrative, one man—whose autobiography perversely embraces Turner's frontier hypothesis—suggests that there is.

The Life and Adventures of Nat Love, Better Known in the Cattle Country as "Deadwood Dick" (1907), written by "Himself," is a work that almost no one has read. The book has remained out of print until recently.[2] The neglect of *The Life and Adventures* by both western historians and African American critics suggests that the awareness level for the book has always been low.[3] On one hand, this isn't surprising since, out of thousands of blacks who worked as cowboys in the late nineteenth century, Love is the only one who published his autobiography. On the other hand, even if his book lacked aesthetic value as literature, it at least ought to merit attention as a unique and noteworthy document.

Illustrating the efforts of a former black slave to transform himself imaginarily into one of Turner's white men, *The Life and Adventures* offers a rare firsthand account of racial perceptions on the early frontier. Writing for a largely white readership, Love claims affiliation with whites in order to assume a western hero's position. At the turn of the century, western narratives featured white male protagonists almost exclusively. In keeping with that tradition, Love describes himself as a mythic adventurer who, like other (white) cowboys, found fame and glory out West. Unlike other autobiographies that were written by slaves and ex-slaves, Love's book is distinctly western in emphasis, differing in degrees, not in kind, from stories that white cowboys wrote. If one looks for a "black" point of view—for a critique of white ranchers, white cowboys, and white western communities that oppressed black men like Love—one searches almost in vain. For Love, if not Turner, black and white cowboys were indistinguishable members of the same western melting pot.

I

The narration of Love's early life as a slave and ex-slave comprises the first section—merely a quarter—of Love's autobiography. This part of *The Life and Adventures* takes place on a plantation near Nashville, where the hero's family labors in bondage to a white man named Love. Nat Love's father supervises slaves who work in the fields; his mother manages the house's domestic staff.[4] When the slaves are emancipated, Love's father rents twenty acres from his ex-master and begins growing and selling his own tobacco and vegetables (18). But his family's plans for self-support are jeopardized when Love's father, older sister, and brother-in-law die within the space of a year or two (21, 23).

Now, while his mother and siblings continue to farm, Love leaves home and takes two part-time jobs, performing unspecified work for a white man named Brooks and breaking stock for a white man named Williams, who pays Love ten cents for each horse he trains (28). In this first section of the autobiography, the author envisions his early training as preparation for becoming a cowboy out West. One almost forgets that Love is a black adolescent working down South. For the first section of *The Life and Adventures* functions as frontier typology: The labors of the slave and ex-slave are interpreted as meaningful only insofar as they confer on Love the skills for dealing later with western livestock and men. In chapter 3, for example, Love writes, concerning working for Brooks: "I learned true usefulness and acquired the habit of helping others which I carried with me all through my life and that trait perhaps more than any other endeared me to my companions on the range" (25). Chapter 4 ends with the flourish of a like-minded moral. Referring to breaking horses for Williams, Love notes that the experience prepared him for his later profession (32). *The Life and Adventures* seconds one of Turner's most provocative arguments, illustrating that the story of slavery constituted only an "incident" in the larger, more important narrative of western conquest and settlement.[5]

In 1869, Love achieves his "sweet" freedom (37). An uncle's agreement to manage the farm enables Love to go West. He arrives in Dodge City, Kansas, on February 10, at the approximate age of fifteen, with the intention of becoming a real working cowboy. "[T]he wild cow boy, prancing horses of which I was very fond, and the wild life generally, all had their attractions for me" (40). According to the author, the "wild life" constitutes the West's main appeal. Remembering his years spent in an unfenced, open environment, Love describes a lifestyle that was "free and wild" (43), "wild and free" (45), and "wild, reckless and free" (70). Like a slave who escapes from the South to the North, Love represents his migration West as an exodus. However, while many ex-slaves used their freedom to help other blacks fight for equality, Love strives not to relieve group oppression but to further his personal quest for adventure on the western frontier. Love claims a white genealogy in nineteenth-century American literature. In his eagerness to light out for the territory, he resembles Huck Finn and Tom Sawyer rather than Jim, the ex-slave.

The second part of *The Life and Adventures*, recounting Love's career as a cowboy, takes up more than half of the story, by far the largest part of the narrative. In Dodge City, Love signs on with an outfit run by a man named Duval. Operating mainly in the western Texas panhandle, he rides herd for three years (41). In 1872, he switches employers, moving to Arizona to work for a man named Pete Gallinger (43). Love protects Gallinger's stock from raiding rustlers and Indians and sometimes transports cattle to markets up north. Beginning in 1874, Love hires on with a succession of outfits. Afterward, in the autobiography, if the names of Love's employers and the dates of his employment sometimes seem fuzzy, one fact becomes clear: working outdoors turns Love into a "bronze hardened dare devil cow boy" (70). In photographs that illustrate his autobiography, Love appears extremely dark–skinned. But his words make Love seem tanned (turned "bronze") by the sun. Love represents himself as being like any (white) ranch hand whose skin slowly weathers, turning from tenderfoot pink to light burnished bronze. In accordance with the conventions of white western literature, the archetypal cowboy attributes his heritage to Caucasian origins.

Identifying himself with the dominant culture in his autobiography, Love frequently opposes himself to other people of color. When Indians raid a herd of horses, for instance, Love and his companions quickly give chase. "[W]e were unable to follow them, although we had the satisfaction of knowing we had made several good Indians out of bad ones," he adds, hinting broadly that they managed to kill a few "savages" (42). As a result of their success on the battlefield, Love and his followers "became heroes of the range, and we received unstinted praise from our boss" (64).

This notion of Cowboys and Indians—of "us" versus "them"—seldom gives way to a more problematic perspective, an understanding that Love has as much (and as little) in common with one race as he has with the other. Although Love identifies Indians as "blood thirsty" savages (95),[6] in one scene he shares with his enemies the same crude/heroic propensities. Stranded on the plains, in one particularly harrowing episode, Love survives by killing a calf, slitting its throat, and drinking its blood (114). Other resemblances to "blood thirsty" savages are due more to race than to circumstance. During a raid on a herd, on October 4, 1876, Indians capture Love and take him back to their camp. (The Indians, never identified as members of a particular tribe, are referred to generically as "red skins" and "savages." Love calls the chief of the tribe that captures him "Yellow Dog," but this name may be Love's mocking epithet since both words denote cowardice.) He suspects that the Indians spare him because Love is black. "Yellow Dog's tribe was composed largely of half breeds, and there was a large percentage of colored blood in the tribe, and as I was a colored man they wanted to keep me, as they thought I was too good ... to die" (99). However, Love doesn't share an allegiance with Indians because of his color. During an adoption ceremony, in which the tribe recognizes Love as an honorary blood brother, the cowboy steals a horse and escapes (101).

Love identifies with white men, not with half-breeds or full-blooded Indians. His loyalty to the dominant race forces white men to notice him. For example, after getting drunk at Fort Dodge, Love lassos a cannon and tries to abscond with it. When a sentry arrests him, Love demands to see the sheriff, Bat Masterson. Love tells the sheriff that he needed the cannon because he wanted to wage war with the Indians; "then they all laughed." (107) Although Love is drunk, he may also be shrewd. His obsequious loyalty to white civilization and frontier authority may constitute a sincere form of flattery. But it also enables him to escape serious punishment. "Bat said that I was the only cowboy that he liked," Love recalls, adding that the sheriff then set him free (109). Elsewhere, his friendship with whites, and their joint war on Mexicans, indicates Love's racist tendencies. In a saloon on the Texas–Mexico border, Love orders a "fat wobbling greaser" to pour free drinks for everyone. Then he and his friends escape before the local authorities (the "Mexican bums") can give chase (75). Words like "red skins" and "greasers" appear frequently in white frontier literature. Rather than rejecting this language, Love accepts western custom, adopting the same racist rhetoric.

Love seems as alienated from blacks as he is from other racial minorities. Historians speculate that blacks represented one-fifth to one-fourth of all working cowboys by the late nineteenth century.[7] In the late 1860s, when Love first appeared, blacks gathered mainly in Texas and Kansas—especially in Dodge City, where cowboys often met at the end of the trail.[8] Love meets black cowboys when he first visits Dodge City (41). But never again does he mention having black friends, mentors, or role models.

The Life and Adventures reads less like an ex-slave narrative and more like a cowboy autobiography. Some cowboys, who retired at the turn of the century, when the cattle industry began to decline, later wrote books in which they capitalized on the public's love for western nostalgia.

Claiming to have known legendary western figures, these cowboy romancers boosted the sales of their books while expanding the annals of frontier mythology. In the tradition of western autobiographers, Love asserts his own bragging rights, advertising alleged friendships with Bat Masterson, Buffalo Bill (97), and William H. Bonney (118–22).

In addition, cowboy autobiographers often recalled their initiation into a western fraternity in an archetypal scene in which the authors lost their status as "tenderfoots." Even non–cowboy writers, such as Teddy Roosevelt, Owen Wister, and Mark Twain, made use of such moments, in which cowboys fooled a novice or easterner into riding an unbroken horse. In this case, the "tenderfoot" scene takes place at the beginning of the second section of Love's autobiography, when the aspiring cowboy first arrives in Dodge City. Duval's employees attempt to trick Love into riding a bronc, unaware that the black man has previously made a living breaking rough stock down South. "This proved the worst horse to ride, ... but I stayed with him," he claims (41). The southern ex–slave assumes the role of the white eastern dandy, who proves himself worthy of becoming a "real" western man. Initially, Love says that he must have seemed as silly "as any tenderfoot from the *east* could ... be" (123, emphasis added).

The reputation of the "tenderfoot" doesn't haunt Love for long. After he tames the bronc in Dodge City, herds cattle, and shoots a few Indians, Love gains new credibility. Employers and peers think of him now as a "king" who enjoys the "trust" and "homage" of men, "many of whom were indebted to me on occasions when my long rope or ever ready forty–five colt pistol had saved them from serious injury or death," he steadfastly maintains (70). A centennial Fourth of July celebration in Deadwood, Dakota,[9] showcases his skills. First, Love wins the calf-roping competition (93), then hits the bull's eye when he enters the sharp-shooting contest (95), and finally earns the nickname "Deadwood Dick" in honor of the town in which his triumphs take place (97). From this moment on, the author replaces his slave name with a new name that recognizes his mastery, western independence, and reinvented identity.

In one sense, the third section of Love's autobiography marks the end of his hard–earned autonomy. In 1889, realizing that railroads that ship cattle are negating the need for trail drives and thus making cowboys expendable, Love quits his job, gets married, moves to Denver, and takes a job as a Pullman car porter (130). The final section occupies the briefest percentage of space in *The Life and Adventures*. But, like previous portions

Deadwood Dick, king of the cowboys, posing with his scepter and throne.
(From the author's collection.)

of Love's autobiography, this new account elaborates the book's "cowboy" narrative. In a transitional scene, shortly before Love quits his job, the cowboy gets drunk, rides out to the railroad tracks, and waits for a train. As one passes by, he lassos its smokestack, falls off his horse, and is dragged on the ground when the rope—still attached to the smokestack—pull him out of his saddle (123, 125). Writing in retrospect, Love might have suggested that this unfortunate episode forecasts his fall: His freedom as a cowboy is gone and his fate as a porter is now tied to railroads, the new frontier industry.[10] But instead of symbolizing the end of an era, the railroad represents an optimistic new start. Exchanging his seat in the saddle for a place on the "iron horse" allows Love to continue "to see the world" (131), just as he once did when he crisscrossed the country with cattle herds. The Pullman coach even resembles the set of *The Great Train Robbery*, America's first western film. As if on cue, Love's archenemies—"those greasers"—return in this new setting, give an encore performance, and try to rob the train's passengers. Not to be upstaged, Love gets his "forty-fives in active operation" and shoots the villains in "true western style" (150).

One never senses, as Richard Slatta has claimed, that frontier democracy was a "myth" for black cowboys—that "the livestock industry developed clear, discriminatory color lines."[11] Nor does Love suggest that color lines separated black Pullman porters from white conductors and passengers. In the 1860s, when George Pullman first started building luxury sleeping cars, he hired black porters to pamper white passengers. As his business expanded, Pullman hired more and more men, becoming the nation's largest private employer of black men by the mid–1920s.[12] Pullman helped create a black middle class, offering decent pay and respectable status to underprivileged minorities. At the same time, however, porters earned less money than white men who performed comparable jobs. To supplement their salaries, black porters received gratuities—working overtime and staying up nights shining customers' shoes, going into bathrooms to sleep for three or four hours, then getting up before dawn to perform their required routines. Although they were technically free men who improved their social and economic positions by working in a theoretically free open market, they were essentially slaves who reenacted the slaves' legal servitude, taking orders and executing menial chores. Although porters performed well in their posts, they were never promoted to the rank of conductor, a better paying position of authority that was held by white men.[13]

Nat Love, in later years, as a proud Pullman porter. (From the author's collection.)

Love never comments on the Pullman Company's discriminatory hiring and promoting practices. In addition, he seldom complains about disadvantages that go with his job. One critic notes that a shared oral culture enabled porters to cope with life's daily indignities. Stories about spoiled white customers and cheap–tipping travelers helped porters lighten their load. "Talk was their entertainment, and narratives (stories of personal experiences or stories that they heard and passed on) were essential" to communicating with each other and forming a "black" group identity.[14] In his autobiography, Love doesn't repeat jokes that porters told at the expense of white passengers, although he does recall anecdotes that he told to entertain customers. Love jests with people in order to get on their good side and earn bigger tips. He doesn't admit to laughing at his captive white audience. "Laugh and the whole world laughs with you," he says (141). Instead of critiquing it, laughter sustains the white status quo.

In spite of the fact that Love appears apolitical, he belonged to one of the most militant organizations of black men in the country during this period. In the late nineteenth century, in response to lack of promotions and low pay at work, black porters rallied. In 1925, they formed America's first black labor union, the Brotherhood of Sleeping Car Porters. In 1937, after a long legal battle, the Pullman Company recognized the right of porters to unionize. Love acknowledges neither the black labor movement nor the improved job security, benefits, and pay that black protesters won. Instead he accuses his peers of impeding the progress toward racial equality. In his autobiography, he describes presenting George Pullman with his plan for building "The Porter's Home," a community for retired employees. Love offers to raise money to buy one thousand acres if Pullman donates funds to build a home on the purchase site. When Love asks his fellow workers to contribute to the project, however, the black men refuse, suspecting that Love wants to scam them and abscond with their money (152). Love suggests that blacks distrust each other because of stupidity and low self-esteem. As a result, they sabotage efforts to improve conditions for the black middle class. The fact that black porters were struggling to unionize—to achieve even more compensation than their white employer was willing to grant—remains unacknowledged in Love's autobiography.

The first section of *The Life and Adventures* deals superficially with the author's life as a slave and ex–slave. The second portion more substantively addresses race relations on the western frontier, although not necessarily in ways that one might expect. Here, Love identifies not with blacks but with whites, sharing the dominant culture's contempt for minorities. Hence, in the final part of the autobiography, Love's sympathy for white employers and passengers, not for black Pullman porters, seems ideologically consistent with the rest of the narrative. If contemporary readers expect critiques of plantation life, frontier racism, and discriminatory practices in the trains where Love worked, then—as a cowboy might say—they are looking for Love in all the wrong places. *The Life and Adventures* doesn't reward that kind of search.

II

Love seems reluctant to identify with blacks in his autobiography, just as his book resists theories for reading black literature. One critic, for example, argues that slave narratives functioned "as an early form of protest literature, whose purpose was to expose the nature of the slave system and to provide moral instruction through the vehicle of autobiography."[15] *The Life and Adventures* generally fails to provide such instruction and thus, in its refusal to protest at length against the institution of slavery, lacks affiliation with other slave narratives.

Love addresses the subject only once in his autobiography, noting that "the dominant race" used involuntary slave labor to transform the South (11). Whites accomplished this feat by denying blacks legal rights, by exploiting their labor, by refusing to pay decent wages, and by splitting up families, auctioning off individuals, and treating blacks as disposable pieces of property (13). But by claiming that the Emancipation Proclamation abolished the evils of slavery (13), Love argues that prejudice and inequality no longer existed by the late nineteenth century. By confining himself to criticism of the pre–Civil War period, Love clears the way, in the rest of the narrative, to dwell on his success as a cowboy and train porter, in a world free from bigotry.

In traditional slave narratives, a slave's escape from the South leads to freedom. In addition, it often enables a slave to receive certain advantages, including a good education.[16] Love achieves freedom and literacy by migrating West. In the South, Love learns to read and write English at home, since "there was no school a black child could attend" (18); in the West, however, Love has to learn a new alphabet. In the process of learning to read and write cattle brands, he becomes so proficient that ranchers elect Love to supervise the roundups at branding time (47, 55, 129). Love's acquisition of western language empowers him.

The cowboy co-opts the language of slavery, achieving mastery over the brand, which slave owners once used to claim blacks as their property. Now Love controls other men's property, determining ownership of livestock based on his ability to read western brands.

Henry Louis Gates Jr. has demonstrated that many black writers trope on traditions in Caribbean, African, and African American literature.[17] Love tropes instead on the language of white southern slaveowners, interpreting brands in the tradition of white western cattlemen. He empowers himself through language not by extending the traditions of black folklore and literature but by appropriating and subverting white signs of power. Love's book only dimly resonates with the rest of black literature. Unlike *Yellow Back Radio Broke-Down* (1969), Ishmael Reed's postmodern comedy, which rewrites the western by having its black cowboy hero use voodoo to hex his white enemies, [18] *The Life and Adventures* invokes white traditions—not black ones—and masters them, assimilating its protagonist within a conventional framework of power.

Love conforms to existing ideals of white western manhood. Like Francis Parkman and Richard Henry Dana, Owen Wister and Theodore Roosevelt, and other (white) men who treated the West as a testing ground, Love enacts a familiar rite of passage in the course of his narrative. He toughens himself in the process of living outdoors, surviving sandstorms and blizzards, stampeding longhorns, encounters with outlaws, and rampaging Indians. Performing the same manual labor and participating in the same frontier adventures that white cowboys do, Love develops into a frontier icon of manliness.

One critic has explained why black men in nineteenth-century American literature so often seemed to lack stature and dignity. Because they were slaves, they were perceived as unmanly; if they rebelled against bondage, they were viewed as violent and bestial.[19] Faced with an equally perplexing dilemma, Love tries to have it both ways. He boasts about his life and adventures, attempting to transform his cowboy alter ego, "Deadwood Dick," into a figure of near mythic proportions. But in order not to intimidate his largely white audience, which otherwise might be distressed by the author's triumphs over white men in contests and rodeos, and in unstaged events requiring courage and skill, Love reminds readers that, as a black man with power, he revenges himself not on the white race but on the white race's enemies. Contemporary white readers, who might have felt threatened by a black man's freedom, boldness, and violent streak, could rest easy knowing that Love confines himself to attacking "red skins" and "greasers." By comparison, he seems manly—not savage—because he attacks even more "savage" racial minorities.

Moving from the unfenced range to the confined space of the Pullman car narrows Love's opportunities. Although working for the railroad permits him to shoot Mexican bandits when they hold up the train, it gives the resourceful quick-draw few other chances to practice his marksmanship. Once free to roam the prairies and plains, Love now travels by rail, afoot and unarmed, serving wealthy white passengers. In the beginning, Love admits, a life of service "disgusted" him. Initially he resigned from his job and returned to it only after failing to find other work. Love writes that he began to enjoy himself only when he learned to take satisfaction in pleasing his customers (132–33).

This cheerful resignation may explain why critics have paid scant attention to Love's autobiography. During the Civil Rights era, revolutions were taking place in black literature. In the 1960s, the conciliatory writings of Booker T. Washington began to lose favor. At the same time, the rebellious writings of Frederick Douglass started gaining more credibility. Eldridge Cleaver, Malcolm X, Angela Davis, and other black writers published their autobiographies in this decade as well, adding radical new chapters to the history of black protest literature.[20] In 1968, near the end of this period, Love's book dropped out of print. The decision not to reissue *The Life and Adventures* may have been due to the perception that Love's autobiography didn't speak for the times; that an expanding black readership, during a period of increasing political consciousness, had no interest in an old Uncle Tom.

While *The Life and Adventures* was in the process of vanishing, new works about Love were beginning to surface. *The Adventures of the Negro Cowboys* (1965), a children's book by Philip Durham and Everett L. Jones, included one chapter on Love. *Nat Love, Negro Cowboy* (1969), a children's book by Harold W. Felton, devoted itself exclusively to a study of the black pioneer. Both books, published during the Civil Rights era, were intended to offer children positive role models and to teach them little-known facts about black western history. Interestingly, the lack of tension between blacks and whites, in his autobiography, seems to have contributed to a consensus that Love was a nondivisive role model for boys of all kinds. As a successful but nonthreatening black man, Love seemed to realize the hope for racial integration and color-blind harmony. Durham and Jones, and Felton as well, take their cues from prompts in Love's book. Durham and Jones dramatize the hero's emancipation from slavery and his freedom as a cowboy out West. The authors chart Love's rise to success, but don't trace his fall. They omit the humbling account of Love's later years on a train, shining shoes. For his part, Felton hurries through a description of Love's final years, stating in passing that serving as a Pullman porter filled Love with "great" pride.[21] These ellipses mimic the suppressive strategies in Love's autobiography. Because it trivializes and homogenizes the black frontier experience, *The Life and Adventures* was easy for children to translate at the same time that it was tempting for adults to dismiss.

When blacks read "The Significance of the Frontier in American History," according to Houston A. Baker, they feel "no regret over the end of the western frontier." The "frontier," he claims, represented the geographical end point, the political prize, and the mythic embodiment of Manifest Destiny. By definition, the western United States—a site of conquest and plunder, removal and genocide—couldn't guarantee freedom, success, or advancement for blacks.[22] *The Life and Adventures* tacitly proves this hypothesis. By disguising himself as one of Turner's white men, Love demonstrates that there is no conceptual place, no affirming identity, for blacks on the U.S. frontier. In order to heighten his stature in his autobiography, Love has to emulate existing white heroes in western history, legend, and literature.

By doing so, he refutes Turner's argument. In patterning *The Life and Adventures* after cowboy autobiographies, Love appropriates a distinct literary tradition and makes it his own. But his book also has a unique ambiguity. Is it sincerely naive; does it accept certain racist assumptions and swallow them whole? Does it critique them subversively, presenting Love as a trickster–narrator who mocks whites while appearing to curry their favor? Or does the book seek to compromise, heralding the author's acceptance in frontier society while at the same time suggesting the extraordinary effort it takes for a black man to achieve recognition, respect, and equality?

If he sought to achieve popularity by striking this compromise, Love failed with *The Life and Adventures* to attain immortality. The absence of popular or scholarly references to the autobiography suggests that the book lacks a place in black cultural history. Only *Posse* (1993), the black western film, mentions Love's name in passing—more as a gesture, it seems, than as a sign of indebtedness. *The Life and Adventures* remained out of print until recently, and seems likely to reside in obscurity, because it can't be easily synthesized. Due to its western subject matter, regional setting, and placating tone, the book, unlike southern slave narratives, seems too "western" as well as too apolitical to attract an eager black readership. Because the author is a foreign ambassador of sorts, representing an unfamiliar black world, the book seems unlike most frontier autobiographies and thus takes its place outside the canon of predominately white western literature. Failing to meet the demands of two separate constituencies—one that expects a conventional slave autobiography and one that requires a generic adventure tale—Love pioneered a work that resists classification; that ventures beyond the borders which limit discussions of genre, region, and race.

TWO

Less Than Zorro

John Rollin Ridge deserves recognition not because he was the best but because he was the first of his kind. Ridge was the first Native American to earn his living by writing professionally.[1] During his lifetime he published poems, newspaper articles, and one novel. *The Life and Adventures of Joaquín Murieta* (1854) was the first and, until the end of the nineteenth century, the only novel published by a Native American.[2] In sensational pulp–fiction style, the book tells the story of Joaquín Murieta, a Mexican immigrant who joins the California Gold Rush, seeking his fortune as a gambler and prospector in small towns and mining camps. Experiencing racism and injustice instead, he organizes a Mexican gang that retaliates by indiscriminately terrorizing members of frontier society. As the first English–language novel dealing with California's Mexican community in the aftermath of the Mexican War,[3] *The Life and Adventures of Joaquín Murieta* merits at least a footnote in history. But as a work about California's first famous outlaw, the book also contributes to the creation of a western mythology and to the development of a national literature in the mid–nineteenth century.[4]

In spite of its importance, *The Life and Adventures of Joaquín Murieta* initially failed to attract much attention. The novel might have achieved notoriety if its author had been a full–blooded Indian, writing fiction that thinly disguised his own life experience. But Ridge was an "invisible" Indian, educated by whites, assimilated within frontier society, and determined to write a novel that had seemingly nothing to do with his native culture and history. While Black Hawk, also in the mid–nineteenth century, collaborated with white men to write his autobiography and thus reached an audience interested in reading about frontier warfare and tribal life, Ridge, a professional author who was half–white and half–Cherokee, sought to entertain readers by marketing legends about stand offs between white men and Mexicans. As subject matter, the story of the U.S. containment of Mexican "savagery," like accounts of triumphant military encounters with Indians, had the potential to engage a receptive white readership. But because he felt ambivalently about Joaquín Murieta, Ridge was unsure how to represent the initial success and ultimate defeat of the book's central character. Having been dispossessed of Cherokee land by the government, Ridge identified with Murieta as a member of a persecuted racial minority; but having relocated and invested in mainstream society, Ridge also disapproved of Murieta's repeated attacks on white frontier communities.

The Life and Adventures of Joaquín Murieta is an early example of "borderland" literature. Like other works in this tradition, the text represents the artistic endeavor of a mestizo/mestiza, or mixed blood, to find his or her place on the border between two or more different worlds; to express a state of transition, a shifting identity, and many allegiances.[5] Having created a violent and anarchic hero, Ridge both exalted and censured him. The author's complex response to his biracial identity seemingly confused his work and kept it from selling well. However, his mixed ethnic heritage also made Ridge sensitive to issues within the novel that are more problematic and interesting than a one–dimensional Mexican hero or villain would be today. Living in his own personal borderland, Ridge was well suited to write about a border hero who experienced the tensions that characterized California in the early and mid–1850s. Representing the new western state as a politically contested, multicultural frontier society, Ridge used Murieta as a test case to discuss ethnic inter–rivalries and racial hostilities during a period of frontier nation-formation in which the U.S. government had recently seized California from Mexico.

I

The discovery of gold in the Cherokee Nation in the late 1820s led to efforts by the U.S. government to purchase the homeland of John

Rollin Ridge. Fear of dispossession split the tribe into two distinct groups. The Patriot Party, composed mainly of full-blooded Cherokees, was led by Chief John Ross, who opposed the sale of Indian lands to the U.S. government. The Removal Party, consisting of half-breeds and mixed-bloods, favored negotiating with white politicians and moving West to relocate the tribe. In 1835, after Ross and elected representatives of the tribal council refused to meet with the U.S. government, members of the opposition group, including Ridge's father and grandfather, signed a treaty in which they exchanged the tribe's land for approximately $5 million and territory on the border between Oklahoma and Arkansas. Over the next several years, members of the Removal or Treaty Party moved West voluntarily. Indians in the Patriot Party, feeling betrayed by the Ridge family and by other "traitors" who had sold out to the U.S. government, fought relocation. In 1838–39 the government marched these protesters off their land and onto their new reservation. Four thousand Cherokees died on the Trail of Tears, including John Ross's wife.[6]

In the summer of 1839, when Ridge was just twelve years old, his father, grandfather, and first cousin were murdered by members of the Patriot Party, who had formed execution squads to punish the Ridge family for doing business with the U.S. government. Ridge's mother, a white woman, escaped with Ridge and his siblings to Fayetteville, Arkansas. Shortly afterward she sent Ridge back East, enrolling him in an academy in Great Barrington, Massachusetts, near where her parents lived. Ridge studied there throughout the early and mid-1840s and then came back to Arkansas. In 1847 he married a local white woman, and for a short while thereafter the two lived in peace. But in 1849 Ridge killed David Kell, his neighbor and one of John Ross's supporters, in a dispute over property. Although he claimed self-defense, Ridge was convinced that he wouldn't receive a fair trial as long as the Cherokee Nation was controlled by Ross and his followers. After escaping from Arkansas, returning home, and then drifting aimlessly, in the spring of 1850 Ridge joined the Gold Rush, deciding to start life over on the western frontier.[7]

When he failed to strike it rich in the mining camps, Ridge began writing for local newspapers, journals, and magazines. Historically, the early 1850s in California constituted a transitional period of flux and uncertainty. On one hand, Mexicans were unsure whether California would honor the articles of protection, written into the Treaty of

Guadalupe Hidalgo (1848), which were intended to protect Mexican citizens and their property in the aftermath of the Mexican War. They felt further intimidated by the influx of immigrants, especially Anglo–Americans, who swarmed into California over the course of the next several years. If Mexicans feared disenfranchisement, U.S. citizens, on the other hand, felt justified in claiming legal and economic entitlements. Many Americans believed that the treaty that had ended the Mexican War was unfair, especially Article VIII, which stated that Mexicans living in postwar California could continue to claim Mexican citizenship and thus retain title and rights to their property.[8] In the late 1840s the arrival of fortune hunters from south of the border convinced white Californians that even more wealth was being seized and stolen by foreigners. Hence in 1850 the California legislature passed the Foreign Miners' Tax Law, which financially penalized certain individuals who worked in the mining camps by forcing them to pay stiff monthly fees. In effect, the law spared white Europeans—who were defined by consent as "Americans"—and punished, in particular, Peruvians, Chileans, and Mexicans, many of whom had experience in their home countries working in copper and silver mines.[9]

Economically discouraged—if not legally prohibited—from making an honest living in mining camps, some discontented, unemployed Mexicans resorted to banditry. In *The Life and Adventures of Joaquín Murieta*, John Rollin Ridge based his hero on a composite of some of these criminals.[10] In the novel, Murieta immigrates to California in 1850, at the age of eighteen. While panning for gold, he encounters a group of white miners who view Mexicans as "conquered subjects of the United States, having no rights which could stand before a haughtier and superior race."[11] The men brutally beat Murieta, rape his girlfriend, and leave the two young lovers to die. Instead they survive and go north, only to endure further insults and bigotry. After being tied to a tree and publicly whipped, forced to give up his mining claim, and made to witness his half brother's lynching, Murieta declares that he will live "henceforth for revenge" (12–13). Leading a gang of renegade Mexicans, Murieta goes on a murder spree. His reign of terror ends only when the California legislature appoints Captain Harry Love, a veteran of the Mexican War, to track down the feared desperado. Love and his mob of deputies capture and kill Murieta, cut off his head, and preserve it in alcohol. Finally they return with their trophy, in order to prove the dead man's identity, and claim a large cash reward.

Because there are similarities between the two men, it has often been suggested that Joaquín Murieta was the dark alter ego of John Rollin Ridge. Driven from his homeland once gold was discovered there, and persecuted not only by the U.S. government but also by a faction of his own native tribe, Ridge, who allegedly killed one man in self-defense, according to some critics dreamed of inflicting mass revenge on his enemies.[12] Although he was educated, professionalized, and able because of his light skin to pass for white in society, Ridge didn't completely assimilate, these critics theorize. Having experienced what it was like to be a member of a persecuted tribal as well as racial minority, Ridge identified with Mexicans in California and thus abhorred frontier bigotry. Although Murieta sometimes killed those who were innocent as well as those who were guilty of bigotry, his supporters believe that Ridge nonetheless generally agreed with the principle of ethnic retaliation and therefore privately cheered on his character. Interpreting the novel in this fashion, one might conclude that *The Life and Adventures of Joaquín Murieta* is not only "autobiographical" but also in some spirit "Indian." For, as Arnold Krupat has stated, "defeat is the enabling condition of Indian autobiography."[13] Whereas the subjects of white western histories—such as Daniel Boone and Kit Carson—advertised themselves as victorious heroes in order to gain noteriety, Indian warriors—such as Black Hawk and Black Elk—could attract a large and sympathetic white readership only by pretending that they were racially inferior in some crucial sense and hence doomed to fail. Like Indians, who feigned capitulation for the sake of white audiences, only to argue subversively against defeat within the texts of their autobiographies, Ridge only seemed on the surface to conform to the expectations of frontier society. Instead of accepting the death of his character, as he seemed to do, Ridge shared vicariously in Murieta's resistance and in his brief, early victories.

Undermining this interpretation of the novel is the fact that Ridge's identification with Murieta, instead of being subversively hinted at, was originally publicly advertised. The cover and title page of the first edition listed John Rollin Ridge by his tribal name, "Yellow Bird" (the literal translation of his Cherokee name, "Chees–quat–a–law–ny"[14]). The "Publisher's Preface," announcing that "Yellow Bird" was a "Cherokee Indian," claimed that he was familiar with all that was "thrilling, fearful, and tragical." Having witnessed "the tragical events which occurred so frequently in his own country, the rising of factions, the stormy controversies with ... whites, the fall of distinguished chiefs, family feuds, individual retaliation and revenge, and all the consequences of that terrible civil commotion which followed the removal of the Cherokee Nation from the east to the west," the author seemed qualified to portray the equally "fearful" scenes that were related in the subsequent narrative (2). Given this information, a contemporary reader would have been surprised to discover not that John Rollin Ridge, a.k.a. "Yellow Bird," sympathized with his Mexican character but that the author, to some extent, reserved his enthusiasm for Murieta and withheld his sympathy.

Some critics, troubled by the author's mixed feelings, have contended that Ridge's real sympathies rested with oppressed individuals, especially racial and ethnic minorities.[15] Hence his association with white frontier society was a survival tactic, merely a pragmatic necessity. These critics have argued that Ridge chose not to write directly about his life or about the plight of the Cherokees because public interest in Indians had begun to wane by the mid–1850s. Instead Ridge intended to write a serious work about California's racist treatment of Mexicans. But because Ridge was a professional writer who depended on the income produced by his literature, he was ultimately forced to turn his work into a potboiler—to demonize Murieta in order to sensationalize the book and thus make it popular.[16]

By choice or necessity, Ridge and his family had been gradually conforming to white expectations and customs for at least three generations. As one of the Five Civilized Tribes, the Cherokees had slowly transformed themselves into farmers and artisans, into tradespeople and small manufacturers. By the mid–nineteenth century they had drafted and adopted their own constitution; formed executive, legislative, and judicial branches of government; welcomed Christian missionaries into their culture; created a public school system in which English was taught; and founded one bilingual newspaper.[17]

Assimilation, however, brought with it changes that were not always positive. Beginning in the late eighteenth century, some tribal members, including those who were part white and part Cherokee, sought to distinguish between Indians and blacks, and to prevent whites from ranking Indians in the same group as their colored "inferiors," by instituting the practice of slavery.[18] At Ridge's Ferry, the farm where Ridge's grandfather raised livestock, grew crops, and had orchards, there were indentured servants and laborers; at Running Waters, the homestead where Ridge's father lived, eighteen slaves tended more than four hundred acres. (When Ridge's father, grandfather, and first cousin were murdered, Ridge inherited two family slaves, "ten dollars in hogs, one yoke of oxen, four cows, one colt and wagon & etc."[19]) In later years, as a Douglas Democrat, Ridge maintained that states should decide for themselves on the question of slavery. He himself believed that certain signs of "progress," such as advances in technology and Manifest Destiny,[20] proved that the United States as a country was evolving toward the highest plateau. In accordance with scientific racism, which held sway in the mid-nineteenth century, Ridge felt that Anglo-Saxons were superior to other races and thus destined to take the inland frontier from the Indians and California from Mexico. The southeastern Cherokees, having evolved to almost the same position as whites, were entitled to the same rights and privileges. Like the other "civilized" tribes (the Choctaws, the Chickasaws, the Creeks, and the Seminoles), the Cherokees were more assimilated than western "savages," who ought to be put on reservations, if necessary, until they learned to adopt modern ways.[21]

It isn't surprising then that tensions and contradictions appear throughout Ridge's borderland literature. In *The Life and Adventures of Joaquín Murieta*, fissures occur on the fault lines of race and ethnicity, social science and culture, national politics and personal autobiography. While the author, a half-breed, may have partially identified with his mestizo character, Ridge shared the prejudices of other upper-class mixed-bloods, believing in Manifest Destiny, Anglo-Saxon supremacy, and the innate inferiority of racial and ethnic minorities. His instincts and experience may have urged him to advocate Murieta's rebellion against frontier society; but his "civilized" upbringing also caused him to view the hero's acts problematically. Rather than arguing that his ideas were "complexly reinforcing," as one critic has stated,[22] it seems more accurate to say that Ridge's opinions were divided and sometimes self-contradictory.

This is not to say that one can't form conclusions about Ridge's work simply because the text contradicts itself. But because criticism regarding the novel is scarce and not always useful, it is necessary to look elsewhere for help in interpreting the novel's significance. Arnold Krupat, for example, has studied nineteenth-century Native American autobiographies coproduced by Indian subjects and white translators, authors, and editors. These "bicultural composite compositions,"[23] as

Krupat phrases it, literarily graphed western boundary lines. Here whites transcribed, translated, edited, amended, and thus altered narratives told by Native Americans; here speaking subjects experienced white mediation, resisted representation, and in some instances subverted attempts made by outsiders to wrest away artistic authority. As "the textual ground on which two cultures [met]," early autobiographical collaborations forced contact between Native American storytellers and white interventionists. As "the discursive equivalent of the frontier," these texts articulated the porous western boundaries separating "civilization" from "savagery." Here whites and Indians assembled not to fight but to write and tell separate stories.[24]

Because Murieta's story to some extent parallels Yellow Bird's own life experience, Ridge's work—although not an oral text or a collaborative autobiography—in essential ways fits Krupat's critical paradigm. Like the bicultural confrontations that led to the production of nineteenth-century Native American autobiographies, the writing of a novel by Ridge led to the creation of an autobiographically informed fictional narrative with two distinct points of view. Instead of facing off with a translator, coauthor, or editor, Ridge confronts only himself in the narrative, debating how to represent both whites and Mexicans. A series of profound inconsistencies make for a novel that is flawed though complex. With its intellectual boundary lines in dispute and in jeopardy, this "borderland" literature constitutes a true "frontier" text.

II

At stake in the work are questions concerning the origins and influences of written language and speech, the relationship between words and issues of ethnic identity, the affect that literary genres have on the representation of race, and the cultural and political purposes of Ridge's fiction and poetry.

Several critics have identified characteristics of Ridge's prose style as "Indian," referring vaguely to the "aboriginal oratorical tradition," to the "histrionic quality" and the "wild eloquence" allegedly present in much of his literature.[25] In these rhapsodic analyses, the exact nature of Ridge's rhetorical influence or stylistic indebtedness remains unspecific, perhaps because, as Arnold Krupat has confessed, "traditional Cherokee oratorical practices, like those of most of the indigenous people of the Americas, are very little known" to contemporary non-native scholars.[26] What would seem more apparent is the extent to which the author and his Mexican character have both mastered English. Ridge's third-person omniscient narrator employs a form of expression that is emotive, ornamental, and sometimes archaic. Because it seems self-conscious and theatrically stylized, this kind of language suits the showy and sensational narrative. It also energizes the speeches of Joaquín Murieta, who typically halts the action just long enough to declaim against racial injustice and to call for further acts of revenge on society.

Perhaps, as one critic has theorized, Ridge's mastery of the English language enables him not only to assimilate into but also to subvert white society, to write a novel in which he critiques the dominant culture's treatment of racial and ethnic minorities.[27] This would also seem to be the intention of the author's main character. Because he passes as white, Murieta can insinuate himself into the world of his enemies. In one instance the light-skinned bandit, who looks more Castilian than Indian, testifies as a white man in court. Bringing with him a packet of letters that indicate his literacy and thus "prove" his Anglo identity, Murieta rescues one of his gang from a jail cell, claiming that the Mexican is a wayward employee who belongs in his white master's custody (94–96). His fluency in English suggests that Murieta is not only equal to whites but even in some sense superior. In one comic scene on a city street, next to a misspelled "For Sail" sign, a "Wanted" poster advertises a $5,000 reward for the renegade. Murieta uses the English language to mock white California authorities. At the bottom of the "Wanted" poster he offers to double the reward, writing in grammatically perfect graffiti: "I will give $10,000. Joaquin" (68). Elsewhere, however, Murieta is paradoxically handicapped by his linguistic facility. In certain passages his sentiments are ceremoniously expressed and his speeches seem studied. Here Murieta resembles the romantic stereotype of the "eloquent Indian."[28] A backwoods Shakespearean, who refers at one point to the man "whom you wot of" (55), Murieta wrestles with stilted language that the author has given him and commits literary offenses that would make Mark Twain cringe.

Created by an author who was half-white and half-Cherokee, Murieta sounds like a white man's idea of a stereotypical Indian and, at the same time, like an Indian's idea of an unconventional Mexican. Alternately, the character speaks as if he were merely the author's instrument, a puppet who mouths language woodenly, and as if he were an actor who controls his own destiny, a Mexican Indian whose forked tongue gives him the power to function subversively. Murieta chooses his words with authority, to the extent that his command of the English language and his ability to use it to accomplish his purposes make it possible for Murieta to assume authorship, at least metaphorically. At one point, after describing an episode of particular violence and horror, the narrator claims that "all this mighty and seemingly chaotic scene had its birth in the dramatic brain of Joaquín—an author who acted out his own tragedies!" (109). Because it suggests that Murieta acts out his *own* tragedies, killing others in the same way that Captain Love will one day kill him, this sentence problematizes the way in which one interprets him. As the "author" of events and as the central character in his own self-made narrative, Murieta determines what happens to others yet can't control his own fate; as the instigator and as the ultimate victim of punishment, he creates the need for his extermination by sparing almost no one who crosses his path. He is the embodiment of stereotypical Mexican savagery and, at the same time, the surrogate for the doomed noble Indian, whose destined extinction is the subject of romance and tragedy.

It would be a one-sided simplification to argue either that Ridge, as a racial minority, sympathizes with his Mexican character, or that Ridge, as an acculturated citizen, sides with the dominant racial group on the western frontier. In the novel, two distinct points of view alternate.[29] Murieta is either a "noble man" (108) or a "wild beast" (153), depending on which view prevails at any given place in the narrative. To his pursuers Murieta is a demon, protected by "an invisible guardian fiend" (51, 58). But he is "an angel" to the white men whose lives he spares (79). Three-Fingered Jack, Murieta's second-in-command, shares his leader's duality. On his "raven-black horse," he reminds one of "old Satan himself" (84). But although he is "the very incarnation of cruelty," he is also "as brave a man as this world ever produced, and so died as those who killed him will testify" (154).

As a persecuted and dispossessed Indian, John Rollin Ridge may have identified with the character of the vengeful outlawed minority. But as an acculturated half-breed, educated by whites both at home and back East, Ridge could only imagine Joaquín Murieta in terms of stereotypes present in the dominant literary traditions of the late eighteenth and early-to-mid-nineteenth centuries. In *The Life and Adventures of Joaquín Murieta*, Ridge presents two competing versions of the

Mexican-as-Indian. In one of these versions, Murieta is the savage of Indian captivity narratives, who holds the entire state hostage during the course of his murder spree. In the other version, which alternates, the Mexican is an ennobled and romanticized Indian, who appears both sublime and benign due to his presumed imminent extinction.[30]

In one of the novel's most interesting passages, a gang member named Reis, racing through the countryside on horseback one evening, sees a beautiful young woman in the window of a house that he passes. Seduced by her fair skin and golden hair, and by a bosom that seemed "as if it would burst its gauzy covering and strike the gazer blind with its unspeakable loveliness" (98), Reis acts on impulse and kidnaps the maiden. On the way back to his cave, however, he loses his nerve and decides not to rape but to ransom her. Yet after three days of guarding and ogling her, Reis still can't bring himself to release the girl from his lair. Murieta pays a visit one evening and discovers the girl with her kidnapper. After he asks if Reis has deflowered her, and after Reis replies in the negative, Murieta declares, "I have higher purposes in view than to torture innocent females. I would have no woman's person without her consent" (105). Returning to civilization with the man who has rescued her, Rosalie thanks Murieta and tells her angry fiancé: "I care not if he were a robber a thousand times, he is a noble man—shake hands with him" (108).

Here the Mexican plays the role of the Indian in a narrative depicting the horrors of frontier captivity. The move from "civilization" to "savagery," symbolized by the retreat from a well-lit home to a dark cave that tunnels 300 feet underground; the prospect of miscegenation, more terrible perhaps for a nineteenth-century reader to contemplate than any other form of social profanity—these fears inform the scenes in which Reis abducts Rosalie. Mitigating these fears are the noble words and deeds of the novel's main character. For it is Reis, not Murieta, who offends the reader's sense of propriety. And because Murieta, on this occasion, uses his authority to make pretty speeches and exercises his discretion to act like a gentleman, one might forget for the moment that it is Murieta who, by practicing a particularly widespread form of bloodthirsty savagery, holds not just one woman but a whole frontier hostage.

Like the Indian, who can be embraced and idealized only when he no longer poses a danger to frontier society, Joaquín Murieta can be romanticized only now that the United States has won the war and seized California from Mexico.[31] At the same time, Murieta must be represented as savage in order to retrospectively justify the government's and the nation's right to expand further westward. (Arriving in 1850, the same year in which California enters the Union, Murieta offers an early challenge to white statehood and sovereignty. Although thousands of Mexicans were born and raised in California prior to the time in which the novel takes place,[32] Ridge emphasizes that Murieta is a foreigner who comes north from Mexico. He is an "outsider" whom the new state of California has the right to eliminate.) In one sense, *The Life and Adventures of Joaquín Murieta* is a western regional narrative that participates in an imperialistic national enterprise.

The removal and extermination of Indians corresponded with the increasing appearance of Indians in literature by the mid–nineteenth century, suggesting that Indians, although they had no place in society, had roles to play as conquered subjects in a national literature advertising frontier progress and enterprise.[33] As the United States defeated Mexico and acquired California in order to satisfy the dictates of Manifest Destiny, so Ridge sacrifices Joaquín Murieta in order to create a regional mythology that complements a larger national narrative. However, Ridge can't decide whether to willingly sacrifice the Mexican-as–Indian for the sake of Manifest Destiny or whether to side with local minorities who resist white oppression. The Frontier Myth, as Richard Slotkin has argued, presents American history as a "heroic–scale Indian war, pitting race against race."[34] But like some nineteenth–century writers, who Slotkin claims revised the Frontier Myth, Ridge depicts an alternative race war in which the sympathetic party isn't cowboys but Indians—or, in this case, Mexicans masquerading as Indians. In *The Life and Adventures of Joaquín Murieta*, Ridge works against himself, unsure which side he's fighting for.

His competing agendas in the text help create ambiguity. Nowhere is this clearer than in the poem that interrupts the novel's main narrative. Originally published by "Yellow Bird" in 1852, "Mount Shasta, Seen From a Distance" modeled itself after Shelley's "Mont Blanc."[35] As a novelty—as an imitative example of Romantic poetry—"Mount Shasta" initially demonstrated the ability of an "Indian" to master English language and literature. However, as the poem reappeared two years later, inserted in *The Life and Adventures of Joaquín Murieta*, it seemed to memorialize a Mexican bandit who opposed white society. The poem offers two views of Mount Shasta, each of them arguably positive. The first thirty-two lines depict the Faust-like Mount Shasta, its "tower of pride" aspiring to the heavens in a gesture of dreadful sublimity (23). Following a break in the poem, the last forty-four lines portray the mountain as protective and masterful.[36] The "monarch" peak (24) shelters loyal subjects who sit "at its feet" and who worship Mount Shasta as the representative of God in the "Golden State" (25).

As a gloss on the narrative, the poem provides readers with two views of Mount Shasta and hence with two perspectives on the book's central character. According to one perspective, Joaquín Murieta is an arrogant upstart who launches an assault on white frontier society. According to another perspective, the Mexican outlaw is a man who protects and defends the unrepresented, the oppressed, and the victimized. The poem attempts to locate Murieta within the landscape of western mythology. A tribute to one of the state's highest summits as well as a celebration of one of California's first legends, "Mount Shasta" is an exercise in cultural geography. Murieta's role as a resistance figure is suggested by the fact that various California Indian tribes claimed the base of Mount Shasta as their homeland until the mid-nineteenth century.[37] As a resistance figure, however, Murieta's failure and tragedy are foreshadowed by the fact that Indian chieftains, during this same period in literature, were often associated in defeat with rocky mounts, high bluffs, or cliffs: tomblike memorials or projected eminences, symbolizing heights from which they must fall.[38] Hence the problematic characterization of Murieta as a sublime but doomed figure in frontier iconography.

III

The Life and Adventures of Joaquín Murieta is a snapshot taken of California during the transitional stages of nation-formation. Having been claimed by Spain, by Mexico, and by the United States, respectively, within the space of less than a century; having been "civilized" by the Catholic Church and then gradually secularized; and having been forced to change pace, as the region shifted from the pastoral tempos of mission life to the manic rhythms of California's preindustrial Gold Rush economy, the province-turned-territory-turned-state was in a state of confusion, as rendered by John Rollin Ridge.

Homi K. Bhabha has referred to the "Janus-faced discourse" of particular texts; to the "constitutive contradictions" inherent in narratives dealing with the ongoing and confusing process of forming a nation's identity. Like the subject of a blurred photograph, "the image of cultural authority" in these works may seem "ambivalent because it is caught, uncertainly, in the act of 'composing' its . . . image."[39] Coming to California in the mid–nineteenth century, Ridge was well qualified to image the state's dynamics in literature. As a writer with a mixed racial heritage, he could view Murieta from different, sometimes conflicting perspectives. As a citizen living in a politically contested, recently secularized, and multicultural frontier society, he could also portray California's ambivalence toward the Mexican outlaw as due to the breakdown of monolithic structures of legal, moral, and cultural authority.

The Life and Adventures of Joaquín Murieta encapsulates and narrates the state's early history. As Ridge states in the novel's first paragraph, he examines the general "social and moral" conditions that make the hero's rise possible (7). Divided societies, separated by distinct cultural boundary lines, polarized by racial and ethnic hostilities, and segregated by laws that prevent political and economic equality, typically give birth to hatred and to scourges who seek revenge on their enemies. However, the same conditions that foster injustice and institutionalized bigotry also create confusion and chaos, enabling subversives such as Murieta to act with impunity.

At one point in the novel, in order to provide his gang with fresh mounts, Murieta steals horses from a wealthy California ranchero. Accompanied by a group of white men (35), the Mexican chases the bandits onto land owned by Indians. Once they cross tribal boundary lines the hunters meet with Chief Sappatarra, who has jurisdiction over the outlaws–in–hiding. Choosing not to extradict the criminals, although he has the authority, Chief Sappatarra turns for advice to "The Great Captain," the white county judge of Los Angeles. The judge, not knowing that one of the horse thieves is the famed Murieta, and supposing that the dispute is a routine quarrel between "greasers" and Indians, advises Chief Sappatarra to set the gang free (39). But before releasing them, the Chief decides to inflict on the men his own brand of punishment. After stripping and binding them, the Chief orders the men whipped with willow rods. Instead of retaliating, Murieta walks away, while at the same time laughing mysteriously (40).

The "social and moral" conditions of the region shape and determine key events in the narrative. Here, the partitioning of California has led to the creation of various cultural zones, each with its own system of government. The problem of communication and the lack of consensus among different racial and ethnic groups, a sign of complete social breakdown, means that outlaws such as Murieta answer to no single authority. Mexicans, white men, and Indians argue over who has legal jurisdiction and the right to set penalties, allowing Murieta to escape with a relatively light form of punishment.

In times of transition, confusion, and upheaval, criminals exploit the instability of policing institutions such as the church and the government. Hence Murieta defies moral as well as legal authorities. In order to appropriate the wealth of the Catholic Church, the Mexican government began secularizing Spanish missions in the 1830s and 1840s, redistributing church property in the form of land grants to citizens. During this period of transition, from Spanish to Mexican ownership, California—although still nominally Catholic—became more concerned with exploiting its natural resources and commercializing its rural economy.[40] Like Mexico, Ridge's Mexican character has the same difficulty reconciling his need for spiritual salvation with his quest for earthly supremacy. At first, real moral outrage provokes Murieta to take revenge on his enemies. But gradually, righteous indignation turns into unbridled hatred and noble ideals give way to greed. After evening the score with his rivals, Murieta continues to kill out of habit. In addition, he steals horses by moonlight, takes gold dust off corpses, and stockpiles weapons to arm his guerilla troops, transforming himself into a megalomaniacal border lord. Ridge sees the secularization of the church as the partial cause of Murieta's moral corruption and as a symptom of California's degeneracy. For instead of condemning Murieta's actions, the church joins the bandit in an unholy conspiracy. Padre Jurata, "the robber-priest" (72), provides alibis and forges pardons to prevent members of Murieta's gang from being convicted and hanged (96). When they need to hide from authorities, the men escape to dens of iniquity such as Mission San Gabriel (44).

Only occasionally does Ridge frown on the actions of his immoral characters in a halfhearted effort to redeem parts of his narrative. Although some critics have identified religious themes in his literature,[41] readers will notice that the moralizing that occurs in *The Life and Adventures of Joaquín Murieta* is vague and not always Christian. Ridge refers to "Fate" (12), to "evil fate" (29), and to "inexorable Fate" (153) as if it were an inscrutable pagan force that decided things randomly. The book's final lesson, that everyone might have been happy "had man never learned to wrong his fellow-man" (159), seems like a wishy-washy cliché, an almost meaningless sentiment. Perhaps the author, a half–breed who had been instructed by missionaries, had never been thoroughly converted and Christianized. Perhaps his instructors, who were Protestants, had prejudiced Ridge against the institution of the Catholic Church. Or perhaps Ridge—understanding that the real mission of his white "saviors" had been to subdue, indoctrinate, and acculturate the "savages"—recognized that the Catholic Church in California had treated Indians there according to the same crafty policy. In any case, Ridge refused to privilege religious preaching exclusively. Like Murieta, whose war with society is initially motivated by the need to alter the conditions in California that make injustice possible, but later fueled by the desire to achieve his own self–aggrandizement, Ridge's narrative is characterized by the tendency, on one hand, to moralize and by the inclination, on the other hand, to narrate an action–filled, fast–paced adventure that is potentially more commercially lucrative.

The alternation between forms of narration suggests that Ridge was torn between writing a sentimental political treatise that might move the reader and hence effect social change, along the lines of *Ramona* (1884) or *Uncle Tom's Cabin* (1851); and constructing a potboiler that would be sure to make money. The death of a Mexican gang member provides one of many opportunities in the novel to shift from one literary genre and form of narration to the other and back again. Commiserating with Rosita, who mourns the loss of her lover, the outlaw Reyes Feliz, the narrator interrupts the action and comments consolingly: "It is well that woman should, like a weeping angel, sanctify our dark and suffering world with her tears." Then, announcing the "return to a simple narration of facts" (53), the speaker resumes cataloging the crimes committed by both whites and Mexicans, in an unsentimental, straightforward style.

The first edition of *The Life and Adventures of Joaquín Murieta* sold fewer than ten thousand copies. Ridge blamed his publishers. Saying that they had fled the state after filing for bankruptcy, the author claimed that his publishers had misrepresented their ability to market and distribute his literature.[42] The anonymously authored 1859 version—which was plagiarized, although substantially altered, and printed in the California *Police Gazette*—enjoyed more noteriety, in part because the magazine was more widely distributed.[43] But the commercial prospects of the 1854 version may have been sabotaged by the author as much as they were by his publishers.

Ramona, for example, featured a half–breed and a full–blooded Indian, long–suffering lovers who endured discrimination within and exile from California society. The novel, published thirty years after *The Life and Adventures of Joaquín Murieta*, became one of the bestselling books of the late nineteenth century. Even in 1884, the events in the novel seemed romantically distanced and therefore nonthreatening. For without feeling implicated by the novel's charges of racism, a white audience might condemn the unfair treatment of Indians, knowing that the action takes place near the end of the Spanish mission era, during the period preceding extensive white settlement. In addition, readers could safely shed tears over victims who had earned the right to redress their grievances but who had chosen instead to trade their vengeance for martyrdom.

By contrast, *The Life and Adventures of Joaquín Murieta* has never experienced great popularity. The story, which once appeared too topical and realistic for comfort, still seems confrontational. Murieta isn't peace loving, passive, or likable. He challenges the middle–class white status quo,

Joaquín Murieta (Warner Baxter) encounters white lawmen in MGM's 1936 film, *The Robin Hood of El Dorado*. (The Museum of Modern Art, Film Stills Archive.)

attacking the members of mainstream society with whom many readers would most likely identify. Some critics have wished to romantically soften the text, comparing Ridge's hero to Robin Hood.[44] But Murieta doesn't steal from the rich and redistribute their wealth to the poor. He robs the rich and poor alike, and often tortures and murders them. Because he persecutes minorities as well as the mainstream establishment, the hero of Ridge's work hasn't been adopted as a resistance figure by cultural underdogs.[45] Since he doesn't defend or empower the peasantry, Murieta the folk hero hasn't been granted much credibility.

Ridge's work hasn't been canonized, unlike other important works in nineteenth-century literature, in part because the hero rejects the traditional role of the noble savage or martyred minority. More of an avenger than Ramona and less of a protector than Zorro (California's first Robin Hood),[46] Joaquín Murieta lacks a sentimental political cause as well as a sense of romantic chivalry. However, *The Life and Adventures of Joaquín Murieta* shouldn't be dismissed on the basis of its unpopularity. The qualities that make the book inaccessible—its vacillations, its ambivalence, and its sheer inconsistencies—are the same traits that make Ridge's "borderland" work representative. As a "frontier" text, the novel's internal divisions reflect the chaos that affected California during a period in the state's early history. At the same time, the novel's disunity suggests the problems of union or nationhood, as they existed on the country's borders in the mid-nineteenth century.

THREE
Wife #19, Etc.

T he association between slavery and Mormon polygamy first arose in
the mid–nineteenth century. In 1852, the publication of *Uncle Tom's
Cabin* coincided with Brigham Young's first public decree that Mormons could take plural wives.[1] Four years later, in their first party platform, Republicans denounced these "twin" forms of slavery.[2] In the
interval, between the formal announcement and the nationwide con-
demnation of Mormon polygamy, a new kind of literature began to
appear in the marketplace. Autobiographies, novels, and travelogues
featured personal, fictitious, and alleged eyewitness accounts of women
who had been captured, married, and in some cases tortured by Mormon men.[3] Harriet Beecher Stowe penned the preface to one of these
shrill exposés, lending credibility and seriousness to a genre that horri-
fied and entertained readers throughout the mid- and late nineteenth
century. In the introduction to Fanny Stenhouse's 1874 autobiography,
Stowe compared the "slave-pens of the South" to the homes of Mormons out West. "Shall we not then hope that the hour is come to loose
the bonds of a cruel slavery whose chains have cut into the very hearts
of thousands of our sisters—a slavery which debases and degrades
womanhood, motherhood and the family?" the famous abolitionist
pleaded.[4] One of Brigham Young's wives, in *Wife No. 19* (1876), referred
to the Mormon custom of marriage as "a system more cruel than
African slavery."[5] After divorcing her husband and publishing a lurid

account of her married years, the author, like Frederick Douglass, embarked on a lecture tour, reenacting her flight from bondage to freedom for thousands of thrill-seeking spectators.[6]

In some ways, polygamy was considered both more offensive and more difficult to abolish than slavery. Although the enslavement of blacks was an issue that divided the nation, the enslavement of middle-class white women was a notion that outraged all U.S. citizens. While millions of Americans supported black slavery in the mid-nineteenth century, virtually no one outside Utah territory defended Mormon polygamy. Whites opposed an institution that debased their own race; men revolted against a system that devalued the fairer sex; and gentiles—regardless of religious affiliation, ethnic background, or region—were inclined to distrust a society that was geographically isolated from the rest of the nation, unique and extremist in some of its views, and clannish by temperament. The U.S. government—in its effort to abolish polygamy, if not all of Mormondom, by equating the effects of plural marriage with the evils of slavery—found itself hampered by political precedent. If the government managed the Mormon crisis in the same way that it settled the western debate over slavery, it would be forced to treat Utah like Kansas and let the territory exercise its right to popular sovereignty. Since Mormons outnumbered gentiles by an overwhelming majority, a territorial election probably wouldn't have outlawed recently mandated practices.[7]

To stem the pernicious influence of the Mormon religion, it was therefore necessary to submit Utah to outside control. Because the equation between polygamy and slavery was a rhetorically powerful but politically useless analogy, President James Buchanan, in 1857, cited sound legal arguments as well as less noble motives for sending U.S. troops to fight in the Mormon War. Buchanan claimed that Brigham Young had violated the separation of church and state by serving as head of the Mormon Church as well as territorial governor. In addition, Buchanan manipulated racial fears by suggesting that the Mormon people had incited the Indians, encouraging them to join forces in resisting U.S. authority.[8] The fact that Mormons had a lengthy and well-documented history of dealing with Indians—combined with the fact that the popular media caricatured both groups as polygamous, bloodthirsty savages—made these new accusations of guilt by association seem even more plausible. In the anti-Mormon literature that appeared throughout the second half of the century, writers exploited these fears by equating Mormons with Indians, suggesting that the treatment of wives in polygamous marriages resembled the treatment of female hostages in early Indian captivity narratives. Deriving inspiration from one of the earliest genres in American literature, writers compared polygamous marriages to race crimes that predated black slavery. Turning away from the South, they looked to the West and an older frontier tradition as a source for material.

I

The Book of Mormon identified North American Indians as one of the scattered, lost tribes of Israel. It charged Mormons with the task of redeeming the "Lamanites," a rebellious and savage race that had been stigmatized with dark skin as a sign of God's disapproval. Through conversion and, in some cases, intermarriage with Indians, missionaries hoped to salvage and lighten the race. "The scales of darkness shall

Joseph Smith Preaching to the Indians (1890), by William Armitage. The work may commemorate a meeting between the Mormon leader and members of the Sac and Fox tribes, held in August 1841 in Nauvoo, Illinois. The artist has added a Utah mountain range in the background and has posed Smith with the Book of Mormon in hand. (© The Church of Jesus Christ of Latter-Day Saints. Used by permission.)

begin to fall from [the Lamanites'] eyes," it says in 2 Nephi, chapter 30, verse six; "and many generations shall not pass among them, save they shall be a white and delightsome people," it prophesies.[9]

From the beginning, the association between Mormons and Indians made gentiles uneasy. In 1830, federal agents, calling them "disturbers of the peace," ordered Joseph Smith and his followers out of western New York for consorting with Indians.[10] In the mid- and late 1830s, persecuted Mormons were expelled from Missouri, in part because gentiles feared that Mormons were instilling Indians with a false sense of power, preaching that Indians, as members of God's chosen people, should inherit the land.[11]

The fears of gentiles intensified in the late 1840s, when Brigham Young moved the Mormons to Utah, the home of approximately twelve thousand Indians. Utes lived in the center of the region, surrounded by Gosiutes, Paiutes, Shoshonis, and Navajo.[12] Almost immediately, Mormons established links with Utah's five native tribes. Of the various methods they used, four in particular enabled Mormons to appease, convert, and/or assimilate Indians. By establishing the Indian Relief Society to administer charity and by offering stores of food from its tithing house, they staved off enemy predators; by teaching them new farming methods, agricultural missionaries hoped to domesticate and stabilize tribes; by adopting and marrying Indians, they sought to increase the Mormon flock; and by practicing more traditional methods, such as preaching and baptism, they tried to save fallen Lamanites.[13]

To a certain extent, Indians felt a reciprocal kinship with their new Mormon neighbors. They identified with the fact that Mormons, unlike many gentiles, managed their "property interests collectively, practiced cooperative herding, and shared with the poor."[14] Wallace Stegner, writing about early enclosed Mormon villages, described them as self-contained social, economic, religious, and educational units, not unlike pueblos or cliff-dwellings.[15] Indians, observing that Mormons were hounded by U.S. authorities, sympathized with the dispossessed religious minority.[16] In fact, although Mormons exploited Christian typology—comparing their persecution, expulsion from the Midwest, and trek through the desert to Moses's forty-year search for the promised land[17]—the expedition, which cost many lives, seemed more like a Trail of Tears than an exodus.

But instead of retreating like cowardly victims of prejudice, Mormons earned a reputation for retaliating with violence by acting like

Indians. The Danites, a group of vigilantes dedicated to preserving the Mormon Church's authority, terrorized gentiles as well as Mormons who risked disobedience, meting out punishment while costumed in native disguise.[18] In 1857, an emigrant caravan, passing west through the territory on its way to the coast, was attacked by what appeared to be Indians. However, subsequent investigations revealed that the depredations were committed by Mormons in camouflage, who acted without Brigham Young's knowledge. In the Mountain Meadows Massacre, which lasted five days, many of the 137 emigrants, including most of the children, were killed.[19]

It was widely suspected, though never proven, that actual Indians also took part in the massacre. Rumors of a conspiracy were partly responsible for persuading President Buchanan that Mormons and Indians were preparing for war. In the same year as the massacre, Buchanan appointed Alfred Cumming to replace Brigham Young and be the territory's first non-Mormon governor. Fearing Mormon resistance, Buchanan ordered the 5th and 10th Infantries, soldiers on horseback, and men armed with artillery to protect Cumming from harm. Believing that Brigham Young would enlist Indian allies to combat a U.S. invasion,[20] Buchanan chose Cumming, who had previously served as head of Indian affairs in Missouri. Cumming's experience in dealing with Indians—in a state where the Mormons had lived before being expelled—made him the logical choice for resolving this new civil unrest.[21]

In addition to fearing an uprising led by Mormons and Indians, the nation dreaded the growth of polygamy. Although rumors had been spreading since the mid-1830s, it wasn't until 1843 that Joseph Smith announced to his followers that Mormons could take plural wives. Brigham Young made matters worse by waiting another nine years before acknowledging Smith's "revelation" from God. Mormon theologians justified the church's new outlook on marriage. Contending that there were millions of spirits in heaven waiting to take human shape, they reasoned that men who married more than one wife could father more children, thus making it possible to save more souls for the church by providing bodies for unhoused spirits to claim.[22] As the nineteenth-century church elder Orson Pratt reminded his congregation: "The Lord has not kept [souls] in store for five or six thousand years past, and kept them waiting for their bodies all this time to send them among the Hottentots, the African negroes, the idolatrous Hindoos, or any other of the fallen nations that dwell upon the face of the earth."[23]

Mormons envisioned polygamy as a method for rescuing souls. Gentiles, however, imagined it as a form of earthly captivity. From the time of Brigham Young's public announcement until the end of the century, when the Church banned the controversial practice, works that were often a blend of fiction and nonfiction attacked plural marriage. The novel was the most popular form that anti–Mormon literature took, with only five of the fifty such novels published in the nineteenth century supporting polygamy.[24] The typical plot featured a New England heroine. After being mesmerized by a charismatic stranger, who married her and then revealed his membership in the bizarre secret cult, or after learning that her husband of many years had suddenly become one of Joseph Smith's followers, the heroine was taken by her husband out West and forced to live in captivity. Separated from civilization, the heroine suffered the loss of her husband's affection, watched indignantly as her husband married more wives, subsequently lost her status as head of the household, and ended up living in poverty, shame, and neglect. Before managing to break free from imprisonment, the heroine usually had to fend off the advances of Mormon bishops and elders, who represented additional threats to her safety and purity.

Anti–Mormon novels, and other forms of literature that followed this formula, modeled themselves after "the first coherent myth–literature" in

Ann Eliza Young, Brigham Young's nineteenth wife and No. 289 in a series of stereoscopic images entitled "Mormon Celebrities." The doubling effect reminds viewers that Mormons took plural wives. (Denver Public Library. Western History Department.)

early America.[25] The works resembled Indian captivity narratives in their dramatization of a heroine's capture, suffering and torture, and final escape. The typical heroine in captivity narratives found herself surrounded by "Indian–devils"; according to Richard Slotkin, her incarceration constituted a frontier version of "hell."[26] Although anti-Mormon literature substituted Mormons for Indians and replaced the Puritan New England wilderness with the nineteenth–century western frontier, it differed most importantly in the way that it reworked Indian captivity narratives. Roy Harvey Pearce notes that while early captivity narratives addressed genuine Puritan fears (hopes and anxieties concerning the Indians, doubts about the ability to found a new world in the wilderness), subsequent narratives chronicled sensational, made–up adventures rather than featuring psychological explorations of personal religious experience. Like "penny dreadfuls," as Pearce labels these narratives,[27] anti–Mormon works were aimed at a growing popular audience. While spreading propaganda against polygamous Mormons and Indians, these works also succeeded in dispensing cheap thrills.

The literature not only suggested that Mormons mesmerized their wives by entrancing them into a symbolic state of captivity[28] but also maintained that men kidnapped and imprisoned their victims as well. In the preface to *The Husband in Utah; or, Sights and Scenes among the Mormons* (1857), by the pseudonymous Austin N. Ward, the author's "aunt," Maria, claimed that some Mormons kidnapped their wives. "Nor is it always the case that efforts to secure fresh victims are confined to the use of persuasion and advice, but physical assistance can be rendered when necessary to abduct and carry off, in some emigrant train or caravan, such youth . . . as circumstances throw in [men's] way."[29] This treatment was consistent with the reported behavior of Indians. In his travelogue, *The City of the Saints, and Across the Rocky Mountains to California* (1862), Richard F. Burton said that native polygamists acquired their "squaws" through abduction and trade.[30] J. H. Beadle repeated these assertions in his account of strange frontier practices, *Life in Utah; or, the Mysteries and Crimes of Mormonism. Being an Exposé of the Secret Rites and Ceremonies of the Latter-Day Saints* (1870).[31] Mrs. B. G. Ferris, in her personal history, in part based on anecdotes, alleged that Mormons and Indians often swapped wives. In *The Mormons at Home; with Some Incidents of Travel from Missouri to California, 1852–3* (1856), she told the story of a Mormon who attempted to sell one of his wives to an Indian. The man offered his wife in exchange for ten horses. But when the Indian saw that the white woman's cheeks were "sunken and pallid," that "her countenance exhibited . . . deep-drawn lines of unmistakable agony," and that her eyes were "red and swollen with weeping, [he] turned his back with disgust, saying, '*me no want old white squaw.'*"[32]

Writers often suggested that polygamous marriages were crimes of premeditation; that Mormons, in order to ensure that their wives remained in captivity, settled in Utah's Great Basin Valley. In *The Women of Mormonism; or, the Story of Polygamy as Told by the Victims Themselves* (1882), editor Jennie Anderson Froiseth quoted one Mormon woman who noted that settlers were separated from the Missouri River, a key source of transportation, by almost 1,000 miles. Hemmed in on the east by the Rocky Mountains and on the west by the Sierra Nevadas, they were effectively shielded from civilization.[33] Another "victim" told Froiseth that she used to gaze on the valley, and then over the mountains, and think that "God could not make a lovelier spot. . . . But I lived to see the day when I cursed those mountains for being my prison walls, and almost cursed God for allowing them to exist."[34]

Women used western geography as a metaphor for gothic imprisonment and exploited rituals of the Mormon religion as symbols for being buried alive. In her autobiography, *Wife No. 19, or the Story of a Life in Bondage, Being a Complete Exposé of Mormonism, and Revealing the Sorrows, Sacrifices and Sufferings of Women in Polygamy*, Ann Eliza Young described baptism by immersion as a "watery burial."[35] In the first of two exposés, Fanny Stenhouse explained the mysterious purpose of "sealing" partners in marriage. Stenhouse punned on the term, which indicated that partners were wed for eternity, by suggesting that women who contracted with Mormons were "sealing" their doom.[36]

In addition to exploiting the conventions of gothic romance—including mesmerism, sexual ravishment, and underground burial—writers drew parallels between Indian domestic life and Mormon captivity. Mark Twain, the severest of critics, acknowledged that Mormon communities had well-designed streets and clear gutters, tidy yards and clean homes.[37] But the authors of exposés and muckraking literature compared Mormon families to savages. Mrs. B. G. Ferris, in *The Mormons at Home*, characterized the dwellings she visited as filthy, anarachic slums. One place—which housed a Mormon, two wives, and their children—had the appearance of "shiftlessness"; in another "small hut," because of cramped quarters, the quality of life was extremely "unfavorable"; in a third home, unsupervised children exhibited an "extreme want of neatness"; and elsewhere, one of three wives looked "poorly dressed, poorly fed."[38] The slovenly households, filled with overworked women and unruly children, had some writers searching for the basest analogies. Jennie Anderson Froiseth recalled "a miserable adobe hut, I could not conscientiously call it a house, where lived a [Mormon] saint with three wives. . . . I had seen nothing equal to it among the Digger Indians," she testified, claiming that the heathen tribe was refined by comparison.[39] One novel from the period sarcastically echoed these sentiments. In *Elder Northfield's Home; or, Sacrificed on the Mormon Altar* (1882), novelist A. Jennie Bartlett mocked Mormon housewives who successfully adapted to circumstance. These women were "natives" who embraced the uncivilized wilderness, not captives, she noted disdainfully.[40]

Among anti–Mormon novels, the biggest bestseller was the one that most romanticized the relationship between Mormons and Indians. In 1855, a writer, probably Mrs. B. G. Ferris,[41] using "Maria Ward" as a pseudonym, published a work of pulp fiction masquerading as autobiography. *Female Life among the Mormons: A Narrative of Many Years' Personal Experience* sold 40,000 copies in its first few weeks of release, was translated into several foreign languages, and was reprinted under various titles as late as 1913.[42] Next to its original title, the work was probably best known as *The Mormon Wife: A Life Story of the Sacrifices, Sorrows and Sufferings of Woman* (1873). Ostensibly, the book recounted the author's experience, first as a woman who falls under the spell of a Mormon, then as a wife held in western captivity, and finally as a victim who breaks free from marriage. The novel's main story line reenacted the traditional plot of anti–polygamy literature, presenting the heroine's seduction and capture, bondage and rescue, in sequential stages. Two subplots, however, recasting the same basic story with Mormons and Indians, distinguished the novel from its less outrageous competitors.

One of these subplots involves Emily, a member of the Mormon migration, and Harmer, a scout for the caravan. The delicate orphan girl, having been raised in society, falls in love with the scout but wonders whether she could adapt to life on the plains. As she debates Harmer's proposal of marriage, Emily imagines herself choosing between freedom and a state of captivity. "Could she be contented in a hunter's lodge, living in Indian style, with none of the luxuries and very few of the comforts of civilization. Sleeping on skins, dressed in the rudest manner, feeding on roots and roasted buffalo–meat, a companion for female savages...?"[43] Emily conquers her fears, marries Harmer and, instead of submitting to the call of the wilderness, begins taming Harmer's instincts to roam. But shortly after the honeymoon, Indians kidnap Emily (351) and take her to meet Brigham Young. When the patriarch melodramatically announces that he is her father, Emily, disgusted to discover her parentage, risks death by escaping from Mormon captivity. After returning to her husband, she and Harmer flee to the West Coast but are ambushed en route by Mormons and Indians (440).

A variation on this story line involves an Arapahoe maiden, Ethleen, whom the Snake tribe holds prisoner (227). The Mormon caravan rescues Ethleen, and a gentile who works for the caravan then falls in love with her. Charley Moore, like Natty Bumppo, embodies an unlikely combination of qualities. A dandy is who expert at "twirling a cane, or curling a moustache" (235), and at the same time a "western ranger" who handles a rifle with grace, the "hero" is admired by white men and women and "beloved by the Indians" (236). The marriage of Moore and Ethleen symbolizes the union of unrefined "civilization" and modified "savagery." The white man, who is respected by natives, and the Indian maiden, who is adopted by Mormons, are complementary romantic opposites, brought together and then pulled apart by Mormons and Indians. After Moore is killed in the Mountain Meadows Massacre, along with the rest of the caravan, his widow returns to her tribe, spending the rest of her life in seclusion, if not in captivity (400–402).

Female Life among the Mormons depicts courtships and marriages, murders and kidnappings, and rescues from slavery. It features Mormons and Indians, Mormons who commit crimes while disguised as Indians, and Indians who live among Mormons before reverting to "savagery." The novel suggests the way in which the nation's dominant culture equated the two groups of outcasts in the mid- and late nineteenth century, refashioning early captivity narratives in order to demonize contemporary religious and racial minorities. It offers the best proof that readers imagined Mormons and Indians as members of a hostile conspiracy, while at the same time slandering both groups by providing a paranoid, fictitious, worst-case scenario.

II

A smaller, lesser known body of literature viewed Mormons favorably. Mormon women, such as Eliza R. Snow, who was married to Joseph Smith and then Brigham Young, published their poetry. Other women wrote personal testaments to the Mormon religion and diaries that were later deposited in the archives of the Latter-Day Saints.[44] A few gentile observers who toured Utah kept open minds. In *Twelve Mormon Homes, Visited in Succession on a Journey through Utah to Arizona* (1874), Elizabeth Wood Kane, after inspecting the aforementioned domiciles, pronounced them "clean and well-aired." Although she found "the Mormons disposed to justify and examine the Indians more than . . . the hideous creatures deserved," she lauded their efforts to redeem heathen tribes.[45]

Scholars acknowledge, however, that Mormons didn't produce enough writing to counterbalance "the predominant unfavorable image" of Mormons in literature, theorizing that settlers were too busy establishing their kingdom to contemplate and create works of art; adding that most Mormons considered it frivolous, if not actually sinful, to fashion art anyway. Anti-Mormon literature was more influential in molding public opinion, in part because opponents of polygamy, inspired by moral outrage or profit, published prolifically, and in part because the sensational stories they told naturally appealed to a much larger audience.[46]

While these works tapped into interest in the frontier and fear of the "other" by sensationalizing a well-known tradition in American literature, the works also revised that tradition in significant and interesting ways. Unlike early captivity narratives, nineteenth-century examples of the genre stressed assertive and confident attitudes. Doubts about the original Puritan mission to settle the wilderness were dispelled by enthusiasts who promoted nineteenth-century expansion, conquest, and settlement. Mormon captivity/anti-polygamy literature, stimulated by the muse of Manifest Destiny, argued that the nation should never capitulate to the forces of savagery. Just as the federal government challenged the rights of Mormons and Indians, using public opposition to western religious and racial minorities to justify U.S. intervention in frontier affairs, so anti-polygamists envisioned their heroines escaping from and defeating their foes.

Maria Ward, the author and heroine, escapes from the Mormons at the end of her "autobiography," but Mrs. Bradish, a supporting player, is the most vivid character. Although Joseph Smith recruits Mrs. Bradish because of her fortune, the wealthy widow would rather be a soldier than one of the patriarch's wives. Dressed as an Indian and armed with pistols and knives, she fights gentile troops in Missouri. "There was something sublime in her appearance, as she stood grasping [a] weapon, her head

uncovered, her dark hair streaming in the night wind, and her brow un-
blenched, though surrounded by . . . foes" (117). Later, in the novel's most
outrageous and unintentionally hilarious scene, Mrs. Bradish, disguised
as a man, is captured by Indians who test her bravery by taking turns
shooting arrows at "a small piece of board on her head" (188). Eventually,
however, Mrs. Bradish identifies Mormon men as the enemy. When she
learns that the church has failed to reward her for valor and excluded her
from the innermost circles of power, and when she realizes that Mormon
men are in league with the Indians, she renounces her allegiance to the
embattled religious sect (416–17), leads an expedition of discontented
settlers from Utah (446), and thus ends her self-imposed bondage to
Mormondom.

Leslie Fiedler has argued that the frontier was a place in which white
men, escaping from the femininizing influence of civilization, found
themselves attracted to "heathen" society; where women, "in their inexorable advance from coast to coast," followed and sought through the
spreading reforms of civilization to tame white men and "savages."[47] To
some extent, anti–Mormon works confirm this hypothesis. In most of
the literature, patriarchs of the Mormon religion relocate the church on
the frontier and join with natives in covert alliances. Rather than escaping from women, however, men capture and marry them, settling their
spouses out West. In a variation on the traditional formula, the wives
then seek to escape from their husbands, instead of vice versa. Advocating female purity, Christian self-righteousness, and Victorian stan-
dards of decency, the escapees, who represent Protestant New England
society, then use their influence as moral arbiters to outlaw polygamy.
(Mrs. Bradish, a variation on the heroine, is more unconventional. She
resists Mormon marriage, assumes male drag, and from the outset
demonstrates militant tendencies.)

Complementing Leslie Fiedler's hypothesis, Jane Tompkins contends
that men embraced the outdoors in order to seek liberation from
women, who ruled churches and homes in early New England communities. The western, developed in response to sentimental novels written for women, featured male instead of female characters, action and
violence versus domestic dramas and stories of piety, and rugged outdoor locations rather than scenes from the private sphere.[48] Anti-
polygamy literature, however, is a combination of western and New
England influences. Like the western, it dramatizes the conflict between
"civilization" and "savagery." But unlike the western it situates the conflict in the church and the home. Whereas in the sentimental novel

these sites preserve the authority of "civilization," in anti-polygamy literature they constitute the "savage" domain.

In these works Mormon husbands, who are spiritual tyrants, control the church and the home. The patriarchal Mormon religion relegates women to secondary and relatively powerless roles. Polygamy, a divisive church practice that makes itself felt in the home, allows two or more wives to coexist in one family, thus undermining female domestic authority. Mormon captivity/anti-polygamy literature, most of it written by women,[49] demonizes the church and the home (what the Republican Party in 1856 called the "twin" institutions of slavery), insinuating that Mormons, like Indians, were capable of treating women like subhuman hostages. Like Harriet Beecher Stowe, in her preface to one of these narratives, women preached to a passionate female readership, one that believed that there was "a power in combined enlightened sentiment and sympathy before which every form of injustice and cruelty *must* finally go down."[50]

However, the women who protested against female slavery found the pulpits of genteel persuasion already occupied by Mormon divines. In order to compete with male church leaders, who announced "revelations," issued sacred prouncements, read sermons, and wrote doctrines and covenants, all in support of polygamy, women adopted unconventional rhetorical strategies. While the male-run church ensured the obedience of its members by emphasizing the importance of religious faith and social conformity, anti-Mormon writers, led by a female majority, stirred opposition by appealing to the baser instincts of readers. Exaggerating the bizarre nature of the western religious sect, distorting the relationship between Mormons and Indians, and shrilly proclaiming the evils of frontier polygamy, abolitionists dispensed with decorum, publishing works that exploited the most gaudy attributes of sentimental melodramas, pulp propaganda, and western dime novels. This unique brand of popular literature emancipated women writers, enabling them to call attention to the plight of other women in servitude. It also freed writers from the shackles of artistic restraint and good taste. The subject matter—including kidnap and torture, and rape and enslavement in marriage—necessitated dealing graphically with violence and sex in a manner that was unusual for women artists in the mid- and late nineteenth century.

Because these writers addressed the same issues and often followed the same provocative formula, their novels, alleged autobiographies, and prurient histories constitute a little-known but distinctive subgenre of western American literature. While drawing inspiration from a variety of sources, most of these works imitate, revise, or sensationalize early captivity narratives, substituting Mormons for Indians, but otherwise reproducing some version of the traditional story line, involving imprisonment, domestic or sexual slavery, and movement toward liberty. Today these works are neglected because they involve a religious sect that has never received much attention in mainstream society, because they oppose a practice that no longer exists, and because, in addition to seeming irrelevant, they have little aesthetic value as literature. But if Richard Slotkin is right in believing, as he argues in his three-volume study, that the nation has always imagined itself in a race war with Indians,[51] stretching from the Puritan colonies into Vietnam and beyond, then Mormon captivity/anti-polygamy narratives comprise a chapter in the intellectual history of American literature. By defining Mormons as Indians, and polygamy as a refined form of savagery, the nation fashioned a political rhetoric that attempted to justify its intervention in Utah's affairs. The military campaign to establish U.S. control of the colony, which led to the Mormon War, and the literary and legislative efforts to abolish polygamy[52] rationalized national conquest by superimposing the face of the racial "other" on a white religious minority.

While these works dealt cavalierly with issues regarding race and religion, they examined matters concerning gender and region with more thoughtful scrutiny. Perhaps because most of these works were written by women, they featured strong heroines. Coming from New England, where they exercised spiritual and cultural influence, female authors and characters claimed to have been abducted from home, subjugated by the Mormon Church, and stripped of authority. Polygamy reinscribed traditional modes of female oppression while at the same time providing women with new opportunities. Addressing sexual abuse, female degradation, and spiritual tyranny, women writers drew inspiration from nineteenth-century Mormon polygamy, composing works that were topical, scandalous, and culturally powerful, while at the same time revising one of the earliest genres in frontier American literature.

FOUR

Mother Lode

The death certificate of Louise A.K.S. Clappe serves as an ignoble epitaph. When she died in 1906, the physician, who worked at the "old ladies' home" where Clappe had lived for the past nineteen years, recorded that his once famous patient had succumbed to the effects of chronic diarrhea combined with senility. Adding insult to injury, the writer, once known by her pen name "Dame Shirley," had died in a nursing home run by nieces of the well-known writer Bret Harte.[1]

Harte had made his reputation in the 1860s and 1870s, publishing newspaper pieces, novels, plays, poems, and short stories. Among his most popular and memorable writings were stories about gold miners who lived on the California frontier. "The Luck of Roaring Camp," first printed in the August 1868 issue of the *Overland Monthly*, took the country by storm. The sketch was marked by melodramatic incidents, pious sentimentality, comic touches, and dashes of quaint local color. It told the story of bachelors who raise an orphaned boy in a mining camp, slowly and self-consciously reforming themselves while tending their charge in the absence of women, on the outpost of western civilization.

Harte spent little time visiting and researching mining camps. In addition, he exaggerated the few facts at his disposal for the sake of comic effect. However, his story accurately reflects the historical fact that men, in certain homosocial frontier communities, compensated for the absence of women by enacting domestic roles.[2] "The Luck of Roaring Camp" argues, at least metaphorically, that miners who functioned as nursemaids also acted as midwives in relation to the gold–bearing earth. The men in Harte's story mine for gold in the Mother Lode, an area located in the foothills of the Sierra Nevada. Just as Stumpy, the miner turned amateur midwife, performs an act of humanity, helping the baby's dying mother give birth to Luck, the prospectors in Roaring Camp, according to Harte, compassionately take from the Mother Lode only what the earth wants to yield. "The Luck of Roaring Camp" represents and revises the relationship between early miners and the frontier environment. Instead of depicting mining as a selfish, destructive act, inspired by greed, the story reconceives it as a selfless, nurturing process, motivated by the miners' displaced maternal desire to aid Mother Nature in delivering her hidden wealth to the world.

"The Luck of Roaring Camp" not only imagines the relationship between miners and the landscape in the most precious terms; it also completely disguises the relationship between Harte and "Dame Shirley," who was his artistic inspiration and the source of his commercial success. Just as men sought to profit by mining, while at the same time denying that mining occurred at the expense of the environment, Harte plagiarized passages from the work of "Dame Shirley," reaping financial success by recycling her less well–known stories while at the same time altering particular incidents so that "The Luck of Roaring Camp" would seem wholly original. Harte never acknowledged his muse, who died forgotten and practically penniless. Like his own characters, Harte exploited his Mother Lode yet appeared as her caretaker, due to the fact that his nieces supported and sheltered "Dame Shirley" in the last years of her life.

I

Traveling to California in order to witness the Gold Rush, a visitor to one of the mining camps unexpectedly encountered a friend from back East. The man, a former dandy, appeared almost unrecognizable. Dispensing with padded clothing, hair dye, makeup, and a "dental device" that he had worn to fill out his checks, the man had let his hair go gray, acquired a suntan, and toned his body in the process of working outdoors. "Thanks to California, " he said, "I have broken my chains. I am fifty–two this year and I don't care who knows it!"[3]

This anecdote illustrates a belief that was commonly held in the mid-nineteenth century: That men who went West to prospect for gold were breaking free from the feminizing influence of eastern society, choosing instead to become bold, self-reliant, toughened adventurers.[4] But rather than escaping from civilization, men who went West recreated it, assuming both "masculine" and "feminine" roles in homosocial frontier communities. Shortly after the rush to California began, the 1850 U.S. census proclaimed that men comprised 92 percent of the state's population.[5] In mining camps, partners or friends of the same sex often shared residence, living together in tents, hillside dugouts, brush lean-tos, and cabins. Such labor-saving arrangements allowed men to mine in pairs or in groups and to divide household chores.[6]

The distinction between the male workplace and the female domestic sphere, which was evolving in the mid- and late nineteenth century, had little relevance on the mining frontier. In addition to working together outdoors, men jointly participated in domestic and leisure activities. They cooked, sewed, laundered their clothes, and nursed each other through illnesses. Songs such as "The Mountain Cottage" and "The Shady Old Camp" painted pictures of pastoral harmony. (The refrain of "My Log Cabin Home" claimed: "The wild flowers blossom round the log cabin door, / Where we sit after mining all day."[7]) Theodore H. Hittell, the famous California historian, noted that miners held dances in which some men "acted" as women. "The absence of female dancers was a difficulty which was overcome by a general understanding that every gentleman, who wore a large white patch on his pantaloons, should be considered a lady. Such being the understanding, these patches became rather fashionable than otherwise and consisted usually of large squares of canvas, cut from old flour bags, showing brightly on a dark ground, so that the 'ladies' of the parties were as conspicuous as if they had been surrounded by the ordinary quantities of muslin and gauze."[8] One recent critic has argued that the absence of women confounded men's notions of "what constituted 'good' and 'congenial' society."[9] More than one hundred years ago, Charles Howard Shinn, in the first piece of scholarship written on mining camps, described the unorthodox unions of miners even more forcibly. "Two men who lived together, slept together, took turns cooking, and washing their clothes," in addition to working "side by side" in the diggings, he theorized, "were rightly felt to have entered into relationships" that resembled the "marriage bond."[10]

A SUNDAYS AMUSEMENTS.

OCCUPATION FOR RAINY DAYS.

"Sundry Amusements in the Mines," a series of comic lithographs featuring four same-sex couples performing domestic chores and past time activities.

A DAILY PLEASURE.

A PLEASANT SURPRISE.

(Reproduced by permission of The Huntington Library, San Marino, California.)

Because of the inseparablity of men—at work, at play, and at home—the actions of domestic and leisure life at times mimicked the labor of mining for ore. In California, during the first phase of mining—which lasted from 1848, when gold was discovered, until 1851–52—prospectors looked for gold dust and nuggets in rich surface soil. Rain and snow, eroding hard–rock deposits called "lodes," often washed valuable residue into creeks, streams, and rivers. Miners were able to separate gold from less precious minerals using standard domestic utensils and sometimes playful, homemade materials.[11] For example, men used the same pans to prospect for gold that they used to prepare and serve food. A miner recalled that one forty–niner waded through streams armed with only his "frying–pan."[12] Another man wrote in his journal that his "gold–washer" also doubled as a pan to bake bread.[13] If a miner mentioned doing his "washing," he might be referring to cleaning his clothes or to letting water sift through the sediment as he operated his pan, long tom, or sluice.[14] "Dry–washing" took place when miners threw dirt on a bedsheet, tossed the sheet in the air, and sought

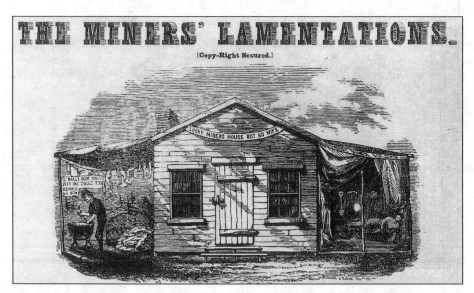

"The Miners' Lamentations." A banner draped over the door of the shack reads: "Lucky Miners House But No Wife." While a miner lies asleep (right), his partner (left) does the laundry and says: "O Sally How You'd Pity Me Could You Behold Me Now." (Reproduced by permission of The Huntington Library, San Marino, California.)

by means of a crude "dusty winnowing method" to catch the gold as it fell.[15] An Englishman, visiting the mining region in the early 1850s, witnessed a parade in a town called Columbia on the Fourth of July. As they marched down the street, hundreds of miners pushed wheelbarrows in front of them loaded with axes and shovels, and waved frying pans, tin cups, and coffee pots. The tools "were emblems of the miners' trade, while the old pots and pans were intended to signify the very rough style of their domestic life," the writer explained for the sake of his audience.[16] This interpretation, however, would appear too schematic. The performance of multiple (and sometimes conflated) labor, domestic, and leisure routines reinforced the fact that miners' hybrid identities were made up of inter-related rather than independent components. On Independence Day, the equal attention accorded these "emblems" of mining and signs of "domestic life" signified the union in mining camps of normally unattached spheres.

The metaphorical language used to describe the process of mining suggested that miners performed pseudo-maternal as well as domestic roles. By a process of analogy, miners compared themselves to midwives whose job it was to remove ore from the Mother Lode, the alleged source from which all gold derived.[17] Miners extracted nuggets from "pregnant" veins and looked for gold dust in river "beds." (If they were "dry-washing," they "delivered" gold on bedsheets instead.) Miners sometimes operated an instrument called a "rocker" or "cradle"—a small oblong box that washed water over dirt and gravel as it tipped back and forth. The process of sifting for gold resembled the action of soothing a small newborn child.[18] Tending a "pregnant" vein in a "mother lode"; producing gold from a rich "bed" of dirt; washing this precious commodity, swaddling it in bedsheets, and rocking it: in each of these instances, miners acted as though they were merely assisting with the process of birthing and nurturing, rather than conceiving and waging a campaign to rape and plunder the soil.

The concept of male midwifery has no place in the model that critics most frequently use to explain the relationship between men and landscape on the western frontier. Annette Kolodny, who invented this model, has theorized that nineteenth-century males related to the landscape in one of two ways: Either they presented nature with a set of "passive and even filial responses" in exchange for gratification, or they actively conquered the land, figuratively raping or impregnating and literally possessing the soil.[19] The second phase of mining, which intensified after 1851–52, demonstrated the validity of Kolodny's second hypothesis. During the period of subsurface mining, men dug horizontally into hillsides and mountains; plunged vertically into the earth, making shafts or "coyote holes"; and blasted rocks with hydraulic hoses and dynamite, thrusting aggressively into the earth in order to pillage its resources.[20]

Although it involved a disturbance of the earth's surface, the first phase of mining seemed benign by comparison. The word *placer*—indicating a spot where gold could be gotten merely by washing—means "content," "satisfied," or "placid" in Spanish.[21] Indeed, men who washed for gold at placer sites were engaged in small-scale, pretechnological, relatively peaceful activity. Their labor, and the ways they envisioned it, force one to rethink the relationship between men and landscape out West. Kolodny's scholarship, now more than twenty years old, should therefore be modified. Miners in California in the late 1840s and 1850s wouldn't have identified with either characterization of male behavior that her model provides. These men represented themselves as active, quasi–maternal beings, not as passive or filial. Rather than conquering the land, they existed with mother nature, metaphorically, in a domestic copartnership; rather than impregnating the soil, they helped pregnant nature give birth; rather than possessing the earth, they tended and nurtured its progeny.

Offering fictional evidence supporting this premise, "The Luck of Roaring Camp" depicts miners as nursemaids and chaperones. The action takes place in 1850–51, during the gentler first phase of mining. When Cherokee Sal, the camp prostitute, dies after giving birth to a child, the miners, realizing that any one of them might be the father, agree to raise the baby together. In order to create the proper setting and atmosphere, the men decorate their camp quarters and furnish the baby's room with a cradle, start washing and shaving more frequently, stop shouting and swearing so the infant can sleep, and put on clean clothes before holding and rocking him.

Their delicate treatment of Luck parallels the sensitive quest of the miners for gold. The camp is located in Mother Lode country,[22] "in a triangular valley between two hills and a river."[23] Miners deliver gold from this vaginal region, just as Stumpy, "the extempore surgeon and midwife" (8), helps a pregnant woman bring forth her child. The other men treat the baby as though it were valuable ore. "Mighty small specimen," one of them claims; "hasn't more'n got the color," another one testifies (9).

(When prospectors searched for gold in their pans, amid the gravel and mud, they were said to be looking for "color."[24] In this case, the miners may also be checking to see if the baby looks more like his presumably white father or more like his mother, who was Native American.) The men rock the boy in their arms, as they wash gold in its cradle. One of the miners, a former sailor, sings Luck a lullaby. As the man sways back and forth like a "ship" (14), he recreates the movement of water. This act foreshadows the flood at the end of the story. When the snow melts, enlarging the river and threatening to sweep Roaring Camp away with the tide, it reminds men of nature's duality. "'Water put the gold into them gulches,' said Stumpy. 'It's been here once and will be here again!'" (16). In the past it has brought gold, but this time it takes Luck away.

Harte expressed differing opinions about miners depending on whether he was speaking in public or private. In private he was once reported as saying that the real West was "crude and barbaric," that miners were brutal and oafish, and that stories which represented miners as sentimental or civilized were just "shoddy legend[s]."[25] However, Harte helped spread those legends by telling his audience, while conducting a lecture tour, that miners "were, above all, faithful to their partners and loved them with a love passing women."[26] In "The Luck of Roaring Camp" he also suggests that miners, like women, could experience maternal desire. Although Harte personifies Nature as motherly—writing that Nature took Luck to her "breast" (12) and that Nature was Luck's "nurse and playfellow" (15)—he makes it clear that the miners play a similar surrogate role. Just as Nature imitates the actions and expresses the emotions of men (9), through Harte's well-known use of pathetic fallacy, so men carry out the will and convey the feelings of Nature. The men are honorary women, so to speak, in that they function as midwives and domestic companions. Their "regeneration" (a term that is used more than once) is a form of reproduction, made symbolically rather than biologically possible. In the absence of Cherokee Sal, the homosocial frontier community can't reproduce; but it can remake itself in the image of civilization, transforming Roaring Camp into a town that is sweetly genteel.

II

The Shirley Letters, written by Louise A.K.S. Clappe, differ so drastically in subject matter, perspective, and tone that it is hard, at first glance, to see what Harte could have plagiarized. Sometime in 1848–49, the author married a doctor named Fayette Clappe and moved with him from New England to San Francisco, where his new practice failed. The couple started over in Plumas, near Marysville, and in 1851 moved to Rich Bar, a mining camp on the north fork of the Feather River, where Clappe divided his time between practicing medicine and mining for gold. The Clappes lived here and in Indian Bar, a camp further up river, until 1852, when—for reasons that may never be clear—they left camp and their marriage dissolved.[27] Several years later, in 1854–55, a San Francisco newspaper, *The Pioneer*, published twenty-three letters that "Dame Shirley" had written to her sister back East regarding life in the mining camps.

Although she claims in the twelfth letter that miners "possess many truly admirable characteristics,"[28] more often than not she suggests that men are rough and uncivilized. In the second letter, "Dame Shirley" states that Rich Bar lacks "the softening amenities of female society, and the sweet restraining influences of pure womanhood" (20). Here men use profanity, which would be considered *"vulgar"* for gentlemen (42). After a night of dancing together, they wake up and find themselves lying in drunken heaps on the barroom floor, reduced to their "animal- ized selves" (93–94). As a doctor's wife, "Dame Shirley" notices how inef- fectually men nurse each other in the absence of women. One man, who has injured his leg in a rockslide, "languishe[s] away his existence in a miserable cabin, his only nurses men—some of them, it is true, kind and good—others neglectful and careless.... My heart aches as I look upon his young face, and think of 'his gentle, dark-eyed mother, weeping lonely at the North,' for her far away and suffering son" (32). The only thing men seem able to care for is an orphaned grizzly cub, which one miner teaches to climb a wood pole (164).

Unlike Bret Harte, who emphasized his miners' nurturing qualities, "Dame Shirley" believed that men who went West risked becoming less civilized. Furthermore, women who joined men, with the intention of improving frontier society, ended up experiencing the same degrada- tion. Eliza Farnham, the author of *California, In-Doors and Out* (1856), painted a grim picture of life in the mining camps. Outside one home she saw "a few cabbages, laden with dust, plead silently for water, and half a dozen rows of choked potatoes remonstrate against their hard lot. At the door of this shanty, you, perhaps, see a child, which looks much like the plants; for its mother cannot keep it clean, and she, per- haps, sits within, or may be by her husband's rocker in the bared bed of the river, working it while he shovels the earth."[29] "Dame Shirley," like Farnham, thinks that mining takes its toll on the "gentler" sex. She begins the tenth letter by proclaiming sarcastically that she has become an amateur "*mineress.*" "I wet my feet, tore my dress, spoilt a pair of new gloves, nearly froze my fingers, got an awful headache, took cold and lost a valuable breastpin, in this my labor of love" (74). In the fifteenth letter, she alleges that she not only ruined her clothes and her health but also risked her life in order to experience mining firsthand. Writing in 1852, as subsurface mining was becoming more prevalent, "Dame Shirley" describes having visited a shallow new mining shaft. "Did I not martyrize myself into a human mule, by descending to the bottom of a dreadful pit, (suffering mortal terror all the time, least it should cave in upon me,) actuated by a virtuous desire to see with my own two eyes the process of underground mining. . . . Did I not ruin a pair of silk vel- vet slippers, lame my ankles for a week, and draw a 'browner horror' over my already sun-burnt face, in a wearisome walk miles away," she wonders self-mockingly (116–17).

When she writes about the danger that mining life poses to children, however, "Dame Shirley" turns serious. Children, she notes, are aban- doned by parents who work very long hours. While the men mine, the women earn extra money by cooking, waiting tables, and taking in laundry. One woman, leaving her eight-month-old child with "two other children" in order to go hunt for gold, ends up in Rich Bar, where she crosses paths with "Dame Shirley." By now the absentee mother has a new two-week-old child, which she lets scream in its crib while she serves miners day and night in a run-down hotel. When she and her overworked husband get sick, a well-meaning miner takes clumsy care of her son (22). "Dame Shirley" shows that children are not only neglected but exposed to the worst kind of behavior in mining camps. Although Harte's Roaring Camp gets its name because of the loud and indecent noise made by men who like roughing it, after a baby is born the most notable sound one hears is the singing of nursery-rhyme lul- labies. "Dame Shirley," on the other hand, reports hearing a "lullaby of oaths" in her angry sixth letter: "It is not the swearing alone which dis- turbs my slumber," she says. A "dreadful flume, the machinery of which keeps up the most dismal moaning and shrieking," reminds her of a sick "suffering child" (43). The tender care that adults lavish on Luck is consistent with the fact that Harte's male characters operate during the comparatively peaceful first phase of mining. But the men in *The Shirley*

Letters are beginning to embrace new mining methods and forms of technology. Their noisy, invasive, and rapacious activities threaten the well-being of others and disturb the surrounding environment. Thus, "Dame Shirley" metaphorically blames the actions of subsurface mining for the injuries sustained by an innocent, vulnerable child.

Part of the inspiration for "The Luck of Roaring Camp" seems to come from "Dame Shirley's" fifth letter.[30] Here, the author describes the circumstances surrounding the death of "poor Mrs. B." When "Dame Shirley" goes to visit Mrs. B.'s family and offer them sympathy, she finds the body of the deceased, laid out for mourners, on a "board" supported by "butter-tubs," concealed from view by a sheet in the rude one-room cabin (37). While the grieving husband and a sickly ten-month-old child cry in a corner, the family's other child, a six-year-old girl, runs around happily, apparently not comprehending that her mother is dead even though she occasionally peeps "laughingly under the handkerchief" (38). Adding poignancy to the situation is the fact that the child has been uncared for since her mother's death. Her untucked and loose-fitting calico dress sweeps the floor as she plays, and later, when she wanders outside, no one stops her from walking up to the edge of an uncovered mining hole. "This is an awful place for children" (41), "Dame Shirley" warns in her letter.

Harte may have been inspired by "Dame Shirley's" account of Mrs. B.'s crude makeshift funeral. In "The Luck of Roaring Camp," the miners pay their last respects to Cherokee Sal as they file by her corpse, which lies on a "low bunk or shelf" (9). More importantly, Harte may have been struck by the fifth letter's conclusion—that men in mining camps were incapable of supervising and tending to children—and thus prompted to imagine a hypothetical situation in which men disproved this assumption. The other part of her text that seems to have captured Harte's fancy is "Dame Shirley's" seventeenth letter. This letter narrates the story of a young "Indian" boy who wears "a large, red shirt" that trails to "his little bronzed feet" (134). The boy accompanies the men in his tribe who go fishing, and the men make "such a petted darling of him" that it is "impossible to tell which [is] his father" (135). Harte seems to have focused not only on the idea that any one of these men might be the boy's father but also on the minor detail of what the boy wears, for when the reader is first introduced to Luck, the illegitimate half-breed is wrapped in "staring red flannel" (9).

These two separate excerpts from *The Shirley Letters* seem unrelated, but they complement each other in terms of the way that the text "genders" race. If the husband of Mrs. B., the white miner in "Dame Shirley's" fifth letter, seems unable to function as a substitute mother, the Indian men in the seventeenth letter successfully play similar surrogate roles. "Dame Shirley" witnesses the reversal of gender roles in the unidentified tribe. The women are described as ugly "squaws" who "do all the drudgery" (133), while the men are depicted as kindhearted creatures who spend their time tending children. The men's physical beauty is almost unnatural, as "Dame Shirley" suggests in a subsequent paragraph. One morning, shortly after having encountered the Indians, the author sees a young brave in camp wearing a flowing white sheet. "We at first thought him a woman," she says, and her mistake made him giggle in "ecstasy" (135).

Harte appropriated and altered portions of the fifth and seventeenth letters, making his male characters white rather than Native American and comically reinforcing their stereotypical resemblance to women. Moving the dates of the action backward, from 1851–52, when *The Shirley Letters* were written, to just a year earlier, Harte freed Roaring Camp from the stigma of subsurface mining, taking the machine out of the garden and making it seem as though "pastoral happiness pervaded the camp" (14). With the same intention in mind, Harte made his characters more sympathetic to a largely white audience. In part, "The Luck of Roaring Camp" became popular because it justified Manifest Destiny: It reassured readers that white men weren't mistreating the land and that they were spreading civilization as they went further West.

Just as real-life miners justified their acquisition of wealth by defining it as a rescue of gold from the Mother Lode, as a professional midwife's kind but disinterested act, so scholars who write about Harte's theft from "Dame Shirley" often resort to the same kind of subterfuge. One critic has written that Harte's short story was "a flash in the pan"; that in order to produce this nugget the author depleted a "rich vein of Western material."[31] Another has stated more bluntly that Harte wrote mainly for money, "strip–mining" his subjects for all they were worth.[32] In a subtle but troublesome manner, the comparisons between plagiarism and mining, although dramatically vivid, deny moral agency. While describing Harte's theft in a series of colorful metaphors, they diminish Harte's culpability by removing his actions from the realm of the real. If Harte was a plagiarist, "Dame Shirley" was his inspiration or source—the woman whose Mother Lode literature he plundered, refined, and then sold. "The Luck of Roaring Camp" not only supports the notion that miners took gold with nature's consent but also defends Harte's own success by disguising its artistic origins.

FIVE

Anastasia of Oregon

For many years, white men such as Lewis and Clark, Parkman and Dana, Turner and Roosevelt, and Wister and Remington represented what many Americans considered the "true" western frontier. Recently, however, people have started to realize that the "western frontier" is a geographically vague, ideologically loaded, and often undefined term. Furthermore, wherever and whatever it is, the western frontier is a place about which many stories, not just one, have been told. The history, literature, folklore, and artifacts of under-represented groups are more frequently studied now, with the intention (and sometimes with the unintended effect) of questioning, complicating, and even confusing an understanding of what the West really means, and to whom.

Of all these groups, children are perhaps least represented in western history and literature and, as a consequence, most neglected by today's western scholarship. The lack of attention to children can be attributed to a problem that is partly conceptual. Scholars rightly tend not to perceive children as cohering into one well-defined group since they are dispersed throughout all other groups in society. Children are members of both sexes, all classes, each racial and ethnic group, and most cultures and communities that have existed out West. It would therefore be wrong to assume that they share a monolithic identity. But the difficulty in examining the lives and works of children is partly concrete as well. Children neither write nor publish extensively. They seldom produce documents or materials that scholars might examine for clues.

Childhood, one of the most intellectually imaginative and psychologically impressionable periods in life, is also one of the least understood, due to the fact children seldom record their own thoughts and impressions, their own dreams and fantasies. This observation certainly applies to children who lived in the West in the middle and late nineteenth century, when children seldom had leisure time to enjoy forms of self-expression, contemplation, and play. The difficult business of subsisting on the early frontier often made it necessary for parents to enlist their children in the full-time performance of farm and ranch work and household domestic tasks. Conceiving the family group as a unit of industry, men and women sometimes reproduced for the sole purpose of providing themselves with an independent and cheap source of labor.

Because they were involved in the day-to-day struggle to survive on the early frontier, or because they were simply too reticent, parents seldom discussed personal subjects such as children, even in their own private writings. Letters and journals reveal the relatively impersonal concerns of white western settlers and immigrants: the best geographical route to take on one's expedition or travels, the effect of weather and climate on crops, the threat of Indians to white western settlements. Historians speculate that if children were dealt with at all, it was in conversations that wives and mothers held privately. Secretly, among themselves, women may have discussed such topics as menstruation and pregnancy, abortions and miscarriages, and home remedies for treating childhood illnesses.[1] Children were typically represented in frontier culture in one of two ways. Either they were the subjects of a shared oral discourse in which wives and mothers addressed reproduction, childrearing, and other practical and sometimes unpleasant realities; or they were the authors, years later, of a literary tradition that depicted frontier childhood nostalgically. Childhood autobiographies about life on the western frontier were written by adults who looked back on their early years. More often than not, these memoirs retrospectively romanticized the harsh dreary lives that many children of white settlers led.[2] Perhaps unwittingly, they also contributed to the propaganda that portrayed the process of frontier conquest and settlement as a satisfactory and beneficial experience, even for those who may have participated in the process reluctantly.

If one statement about the difference between children and adults can be made with some certainty, it is the generalization that children and adults observed the West, as they view the world, very differently. Thus, *The Story of Opal: The Journal of an Understanding Heart* (1920) seems to contrast sharply with books that were written by adults about their lives on the early frontier. *The Story of Opal* was allegedly written by Opal Whiteley when she was six and seven years old. The childish document, now all but forgotten, initially created a tremendous sensation among readers who believed that its author was not only a literary prodigy but also a long lost daughter of the French aristocracy. Opal claimed to have been mysteriously whisked away from Europe once her parents had died, to have been transported by unknown means to the Pacific Northwest, and to have been secretly swapped for the daughter of a lumberjack's family that resided in Oregon. This frontier Anastasia spent her whole life insisting that her bestselling book about a child's adventures in the enchanted forests of Oregon was not a fairy tale but a factual account of her history. In the years since its publication, believers and skeptics have debated whether the book narrates Opal's actual experiences and impressions or whether it illustrates her childish confusion of real life with fantasy. In either case, writing from a child's point of view enabled Opal to produce a work of imaginative power, unlike any other children's literature at the turn of the century.

I

On September 19, 1919, a waifish young woman arrived in Boston, hoping to interest the *Atlantic Monthly* in a rather amateurish manuscript. She showed *The Fairyland Around Us* to the editor, Ellery Sedgwick, who glanced through the work and politely rejected it. The magical nature book read in part like a treatise on the flora and fauna of the Pacific Northwest and in part like a concoction of childish gibberish and fantasy. The proper technical names of flowers and animals—and useful information regarding their habits—had been inserted into a fanciful, sentimental, and awkwardly written narration about wood nymphs and sprites. The author had apparently cut out illustrations of nature from magazines, pasting them onto blank pages that she had randomly dispersed through her narrative. Intrigued by the manuscript's odd combination of sophistication and artlessness, Sedgwick asked Opal Whiteley, its author, about her early childhood in Oregon. When she told him that her father had worked as a lumberjack and that she remembered living with her migrant family in nineteen different logging camps, Sedgwick, who saw possibilities in the story of such a seemingly picturesque life, asked Opal if she had kept track of her early impressions by writing a diary. At this point Opal, overwhelmed by grief, suddenly burst into tears.[3]

Eventually Opal confided to Sedgwick that she had kept a record between the ages of six and thirteen, scribbling in colored pencils and crayons on envelopes, odd scraps of paper, and grocery bags. Traumat-

Boston, 1919. The author pieces together her diary, surrounded by thousands of tiny torn fragments. (Courtesy Massachusetts Historical Society.)

ically, Opal recounted that, at the age of thirteen, she had stopped writing in her diary after a younger sister had found it and torn its pages to shreds. But Opal told Sedgwick that she had saved the fragments and that she had stored them in a box in Los Angeles, where she had lived while writing the manuscript that she had brought Sedgwick to read. The editor, excited by this discovery, had Opal's secret box shipped from Los Angeles. He persuaded his mother-in-law, Mrs. Walter Cabot of Boston, to lodge Opal in her home for nine months, during which time Opal painstakingly reassembled the thousands of pieces of pages into one single manuscript.[4]

The effort resulted in the reproduction of an ingenuous narrative. The journal told the story of a girl whose family lived in the woods in the Willamette Valley in Oregon, surrounded by lumber mills for which the girl's father worked. One of six children, Opal went to school and in her spare time helped her mother with housework and yard chores. But whenever she could Opal escaped to the forest, where she lived in a fantasy land populated by friendly beasts, wild flowers, and fairies. This magical kingdom became the real world for Opal, who seemed in her diary to be scarcely aware of the timber mill, the town, and its citizens. In a childlike language that was dreamily precocious yet strangely insistent in emphasis, Opal wrote as if to attest to the actuality of the imaginary world she inhabited. In one passage, for instance, she described riding on her horse past a group of children who waved to her. Ignoring them, she headed into the forest to play with the trees, who were her own special friends. As she trotted into the wilderness, she claimed that the fir trees stretched out "their great arms to welcome to [me].... I have thinks I was once a tree growing in the forest; now all trees are my brothers," she reasoned illogically.[5]

Sedgwick resolved that, because of its length, the Atlantic Monthly Press would publish only the first two years of the diary. In 1920 it launched *The Story of Opal*, chronicling the impressions of Opal when she was six and seven years old. The book created a splash in the marketplace, cresting through three editions and 15,000 copies in less than one year. The onslaught of its success was due in no small part to its marketing. The public appeared eager to purchase a book that was advertised by its publisher as having been written by a newly discovered literary prodigy. And the public was further intrigued by additional, unsubstantiated, seemingly outrageous claims that its author made. First, in the "Introduction by the Author," published along with the "Preface" by

Sedgwick, and later in comments she made, Opal identified herself as a long–lost member of the French aristocracy. She insisted that she was really Francoise, the daughter of the famous French naturalist Henri, Duc d'Orléans. In fact, historical records showed that the real Henri d'Orléans had died in 1901, at the end of a botanical expedition in Indochina and India. Although Henri hadn't married, Opal stated that he had had a love child with his cousin, Princess Marie. (Later, at one point, Opal changed her mind and suggested that Henri had impregnated an archduchess in Austria.[6]) In addition to vague, contradictory accounts of her parentage, Opal offered only dim recollections of her mother's death and of Opal's subsequent voyage to America. In the "Introduction by the Author," which she wrote in adulthood, Opal claimed that she remembered traveling somewhere with her mother by boat, accidentally falling into the water with her mother and watching her drown, and being rescued and cared for by a shadowy governess figure who promised to return the orphaned Opal to her father's parents in France. Instead, however, Opal mysteriously found herself living on the forested frontiers of Oregon. There Mrs. Whiteley either bought or adopted her, naming her Opal and accepting her in place of her own daughter, Opal, whom Mrs. Whiteley had "lost" (2–3).

The real Opal Whiteley was born in Colton, Washington, on December 11, 1897. This Opal moved with her family to Wendling, Oregon, shortly before her fifth birthday in 1902. A year later the family moved to Walden, Oregon, a logging community near the mill town of Cottage Grove. The replacement of the "real" Opal with the daughter of Henri d'Orléans allegedly occurred some place between Wendling and Walden, sometime between 1902 and 1903. (Opal's claim to have been brought to America during this time fit in with the 1901 death of her alleged father, Henri d'Orleans.) The "new" Opal lived in Walden while writing the first few years of her diary. Later she and her family relocated in Star, a logging town just east of Cottage Grove. Opal lived here, in the southern end of the Willamette Valley, and later in Springfield and Eugene, where she finished high school in 1916. After completing her first year of college at the University of Oregon, where she studied science and botany, Opal left Eugene in 1918 and went to Los Angeles. Having run out of money to pay for her studies, Opal hoped to finance her college education by acting in Hollywood. She circulated photographs of herself to the studios. But when the studios didn't offer her work, Opal decided to support herself by giving paid tutorials and

OUT OF DOORS

Do you want to know more of the life of the woods and fields?
Would you like to find joy in the everyday things around you?
Hear this Nature Lecture by Miss Opal Whiteley.

Topic _____

Date_____ Time_____

Place _____

Admission 10 Cents

A handbill advertising one of the lectures that Opal gave in Los Angeles (circa 1918–19). Butterflies flutter around her and perch on her hands and her hair, while a transfixed Opal maintains an ethereal gaze. (Image #CN83, Opal Whiteley Collection PH204, Special Collections, University of Oregon Library.)

lectures on nature, following in the steps of her alleged father, the famous French naturalist. Writing *The Fairyland Around Us* while she lived in Los Angeles, Opal recorded the sum of her nature lore, which she had acquired both at home and in college in Oregon. It was this book that she brought to Boston to publish in 1919.[7]

Shortly after the Atlantic Monthly Press published *The Story of Opal*, Opal's father, siblings, and friends created a scandal by fervently denying that Opal was a member of the French aristocracy. (Opal's mother, who had died of cancer several years earlier, hadn't lived to refute Opal's claims.) Wounded by the accusations, which they felt slandered the family's good name, and hounded by the press, which gave the family much unwanted publicity, Opal's siblings moved, changed their names, and begged relations not to reveal their whereabouts and assumed new identities.[8] But the accusation that Opal had perpetrated a hoax quickly spread through America.

As members of a developing nation that had begun to outgrow its innocence, Americans wanted to cling to the notion that a frontier like Opal's still existed beyond the corrupt reaches of an expanding industrial society. Opal seemed to represent the inner child that still existed in the hearts of many Americans, and her fairyland beckoned, like Shangri-la, to dreamers who lived on the opposite side of the continent. But like Huck Finn, whose own loss of innocence enabled him to realize that the Duke of Bridgewater and the Dauphin weren't really members of the English and French aristocracy, the young nation grew to suspect that Opal had played a confidence trick on her audience. Within months of the publication of her diary, three inter-related questions about Opal were posed: Had she lied about her birth and her ancestry? If she had lied about who she was, had she also lied about when she had written her diary? (Had she written it when she was six and seven years old; had she forged it as an adult, writing to impersonate a child's point of view; or had she written a draft as a child and polished the manuscript as an adult in order to make it seem more precocious and salable?) And if she wasn't a liar, was she a schizophrenic who believed one moment that she was a young woman from Oregon and then insisted the next that she was the orphaned daughter of French aristocrats?[9]

Those who knew her and sought to discredit her insisted that they had never known Opal to speak either in French or in fractured, accented English, as she must have, at first, if she had come from France to America. Certain French words appeared in her diary. But a woman who claimed to have rented a room to Opal when Opal lived in Los Angeles said that Opal had taught herself French by reading language instruction manuals that she had borrowed from libraries. This accusation supported the contentions of those who believed that the grown-up Opal had forged the young child's diary. Those who challenged the journal's veracity noted that several passages in the text, referring to people who had allegedly lived in her neighborhood and to events that had theoretically happened there, could be proved by local eyewitnesses to be based not on facts but on Opal's lies, distorted memories, or fantasies.[10]

Those who looked for evidence to substantiate Opal's alleged European ancestral heritage seemed to find clues in her narrative. Opal's childlike use of the French language appeared to testify to her understanding of French family history and local geography. At one point in the narrative, for example, Opal writes about a trip that she took with her horse through the wilderness. "When we were come to the bridge, we made a stop and I did sing to the rivière a song. I sang it *Le chant de Seine, de Havre, et Essonne et Nonette et Roullon et Iton et Darnetal et Ourcq et Rille et Loing et Eure et Audelle et Nonette et Sarc*" (108). In addition to listing the names of French rivers and employing foreign grammatical constructions ("I did sing"/"J'ai chanté"), the passage contains a French family anagram. If one adds together the first letter in the name of each river, the list spells out "HENRI D'ORLEANS." The fact that there are errors (including the name of the first river, the Seine) and substitutions (the Nonette is named twice) instead of detracting from seems to contribute to the song's authenticity. Only a child, believers argued, would fail to notice and correct such mistakes. Opal's supporters reminded critics that the d'Orléans family was known to have enjoyed making anagrams. They suggested that Henri and his wife had used this particular anagram as a nursery rhyme to teach their child French geography.

As for the landlady who claimed to have seen Opal studying French in Los Angeles, supporters pointed to the fact that the pieced-together pages of her manuscript had been examined by experts, who had determined that Opal's work had been written on various papers that had been manufactured only before World War I. These experts had apparently verified that the pages of Opal's diary had at some point been exposed to damp weather, consistent with Opal's account of having hidden her diary in a hollow log in the forest in an effort to prevent her sister from finding it. Supporters believed it was highly unlikely that the adult Opal would forge the diary, then rip it into thousands of pieces, and spend months reconstructing it, as part of a crazy scheme to gain noteriety. They also found it difficult to imagine that Opal had premeditated a forgery by laboriously inserting French words and anagrams into the diary. As for Opal herself, she said only that she remembered having written in a mixture of English and French, never knowing at the time that she was combining two separate languages.[11]

With Opal's credibility in question and with the authenticity of her work cast in doubt, the Atlantic Monthly Press decided to pull Opal's book from the marketplace. In 1921, after the scandal had died down, Opal returned to obscurity. Believing now that her "real" father had secretly married and impregnated a princess in India, Opal traveled to France in order to meet the mother of Henri d'Orléans. (Opal's swarthy complexion apparently led her to believe that she was part French and part Indian. However, her father in Oregon claimed that Opal owed her dark skin to his side of the family, which was part Native American.) Unsure whether to acknowledge Opal's connection to the d'Orléans family, but curious to learn more about her late son's last years, Henri's mother funded Opal's expedition to India. In 1924 Opal traveled to India by train, camel, horse, ox cart, and elephant, and for ten months she lived in the palace of the Maharana of Udaipur, the ranking prince of Rajputana. Whether she persuaded the prince and his family to acknowledge a relationship with them is unclear. But she was welcomed into the palace and taken into the intimate family circle, where she was known as Francoise d'Orlé. At one point she sent photographs of herself to Sedgwick, her editor. In one of them Sedgwick identified Opal, sitting poised on a howdah on the back of an elephant, marching with the royal family into the jungle on what looked like a tiger hunt.[12]

Leaving India, Opal traveled around Europe for the next several years. Regrettably, she never gained acceptance in France. The mother of Henri d'Orléans died while Opal was living in India, and her children thereafter denied any blood ties to their "sister" Francoise. Beginning in 1926, Opal spent two years residing in a convent in Austria, but the nuns eventually asked her to leave, telling her politely but firmly that her place was "out in the world."[13] Finally she went to London where, unable to maintain employment, she became a ward of the city, starving herself in order to buy books so that she could continue researching her history. During World War II she was often seen in London scavenging for books among the rubble of buildings. And in 1948 she was discovered living in poverty in the suburb of Hampstead, with no possessions other than 10,000 books. She was taken to Napsbury Hospital, a public institution outside London, where she was rumored to live in a state of partial senility, staring at the turned-off television set and complaining that the hospital staff was trying to poison her food. She died in 1993, when she was close to one hundred years old, shortly before a musical about her life opened off-Broadway.[14]

II

Opal may or may not have invented her alter ego, Francoise. Unless conclusive evidence comes to light, we may never resolve a debate that has waged for almost one hundred years. Yet in spite of this, critics persist in attempting to determine who Opal was rather than seeking to assess the significance of what Opal wrote in her diary. Interestingly, when it is subjected to scrutiny, *The Story of Opal* demonstrates a quaint-seeming artistry and a uniquely inventive expressiveness. It narrates two years in the imaginative life of a child, or alleged child, whose adventures in the forests of Oregon form one of the most distinctively original and yet, at the same time, one of the most oddly typical stories in the history of western American literature.

In *The Story of Opal* the author spends most of her time either working in the house or frolicking in her playground outdoors. Referring to Mrs. Whiteley not as her mother but as "the mamma" who is her real mother's surrogate, Opal appears to chafe under Mrs. Whiteley's domestic supervision and seeks to escape from household routines so that she can play in the enchanted forests that beckon her. Each time the wind calls, "Come, petite Francoise, come go explores" (63), Opal abandons her chores and embarks on a nature trip.[15] She moves from the civilized realm of the domestic space into the forests of Oregon. But once she arrives there she imaginatively recreates the civilization that she has just left behind. In the forest she creates a community comprised of flowers and trees, birds and insects, and animals. Each member of the community is assigned a birthday and, thenceforth, a history; a name and, therefore, an identity based on a figure in mythology, politics, religion, or literature. (Opal names a calf Mathilde Plantagenet, a tall tree Charlemagne, a squirrel Geoffroi Chaucer, a red rooster Napoleon, a pig Aphrodite, a bat Aristotle, and a horse William Shakespeare. The source upon which Opal drew

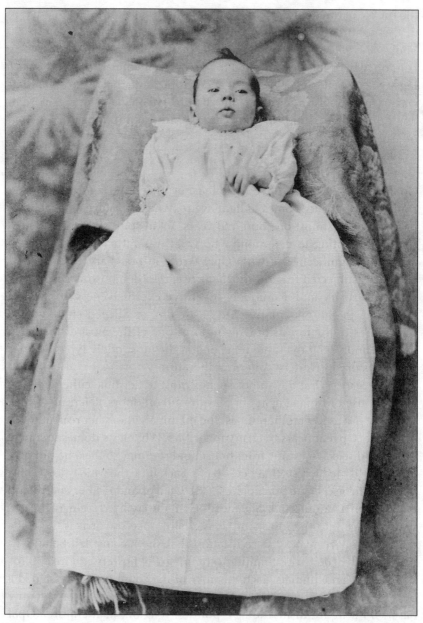

The "real" Opal Whiteley, photographed shortly after her birth in late 1897 or early 1898. (Image #CN2, Opal Whiteley Collection PH204, Special Collections, University of Oregon Library.)

The "real" Opal (left) sits for a picture with her sister, Pearl. (Courtesy Massachusetts Historical Society.)

for these names has not yet been conclusively determined by scholarship.) In the woods Opal constructs a microcosmic society in which she acculturates the wilderness. She christens reborn members of nature, naming them after bearers of culture; she educates them by teaching them in her own forest school; she tends wounded plants and birds in her "hospital" nursery (68); and she buries them with funeral rites when they die or get killed (251).

Richard White has argued that immigrants who went West in the nineteenth and early twentieth centuries weren't concerned with tranforming the frontier into a new civilization but with re-creating an older civilization that they had left behind while, at the same time, improving their place in it on the newly transformed frontier.[16] Opal's diary confirms the process of replication as a frontier phenomenon. In the course of her "explores," Opal moves from the house of "the mamma" to the forest, from civilization to wilderness, imaginatively transforming the forest into her version of a familiar society. Whether

The "imposter" Opal (left) with the same sister, Pearl. (Image #CN82, Opal Whiteley Collection PH204, Special Collections, University of Oregon Library.)

she has actually journeyed from France to America, or whether she has spent all her early life simply living in Oregon, around which she claims to have moved nineteen times, Opal compensates in her diary for her dislocation and disorientation on the western frontier by recreating, stabilizing, and shrinking into miniature an imaginary society—one that, at least theoretically, a young child can control. Even her short daily excursions from Mrs. Whiteley's house to the woods—one small segment of her travels, if we are to believe Opal's narrative—represents not a rejection of the domestic world but a rejection of Opal's subservient place *in* the domestic world. Opal runs into the woods to escape from maternal authority, only to appropriate for herself that authority. She becomes the mother–figure she herself has rebelled against: as teacher, surrogate mother, and nurse of nature, she assigns to herself all the powerful roles that were then available to women in frontier society.

The setting in Opal's diary—so strange and so magical—is at the same time traditional. Representative of works about nature in American literature, Opal's writings depict the "middle ground" of the pastoral, the landscape in which Leo Marx says "the sophisticated order of art and the simple spontaneity of nature" seek and find compromise.[17] A survey of the historical situation in the Pacific Northwest would reveal that lumberjacks at the turn of the century were working methodically to lay bare the wilderness.[18] But in *The Story of Opal*, the landscape of the imagination seems unconflicted, timeless, and tame. The sounds of civilization—noisy saw mills and axes—never interrupt Opal's peacefulness; a fear of the silent primeval forest never erupts into consciousness. Only the most charming and least frightening elements of civilization and wilderness exist in the "Jardin des Tuileries" (43)—in the pastoral "garden" of a French orphan's fantasy.

Annette Kolodny has maintained that western women imagined the frontier landscape as an exterior domestic space—as a garden that they could enclose and then cultivate.[19] To some extent one could argue that the little girl, Opal, does this as well. But her forest is more than just a garden. It is a Garden of Eden in which Opal functions like the new American Adam. R.W.B. Lewis describes the archetypal hero in nineteenth–century American literature as "an individual emancipated from history, happily bereft of ancestry, untouched and undefiled by the usual inheritances of family and race." Opal, who represents herself as an orphan and alien immigrant, shares with the American Adam a lack of family and ancestry. An individual who lives in her fantasies, Opal exists outside history. Like the prelapsarian Adam, whose "moral position [is] prior to experience,"[20] Opal's childlike perspective is due to her innocence. And like Adam, whose moral superiority and innocence justifies his reign over God's lesser creatures, Opal's spiritual purity justifies her rule over unredeemed nature. In addition to writing and speaking French in her diary, Opal demonstrates a quaint understanding of the Roman Catholic liturgy. She fits squirming caterpillars into tiny handmade robes before she baptizes and christens them (238). After planting potatoes in rows, she sings with them as if they were members of her own forest choir: "Sanctus, sanctus, sanctus, Dominus Deus" (38). Like Adam, who names the other elements in the Garden of Eden, Opal baptizes and christens her subjects in the forests of Oregon. She tends the ferns in her outdoor "cathedral" (24); plants trees and then prays (83); and lectures on God to birds, wood–rodents, and animals (26). In *The Story of Opal*, she functions as the self-ordained child priest of the Pacific Northwest frontier.

Opal uses language to civilize God's natural world. Ritually naming the subjects in her kingdom enables Opal to systematically identify, experience, acculturate, and organize an otherwise unfamiliar and untamed environment. Writing her diary further permits her to use language rationally to construct and order her fantasies, as reassembling the pages of her diary in 1919 would later allow her to reconstruct her fantastic lost world. Her language, like the half-wild and half-civilized world that she writes about, seems simultaneously crude and refined. Like Natty Bumppo—the archetypal western Adam in early American literature, schooled in the ways of nature and in the customs of nineteenth-century society, and thus able to converse with equal ease in the languages of white men and Indians, Opal speaks in a democratic—and thus uniquely American—mixture of languages. She communicates with animate and inanimate nature, with other human beings, and with God—all on the same level of discourse—in a sophisticated mongrel language that is part English, part French. In spite of primitive mistakes in spelling, syntax, and grammar, the childlike gibberish reads on the page almost lyrically. On the frontier, where immigrant Americans and foreigners have come to found new societies, Opal invents a new language to describe the unique western world of her fantasy.

The Journal of an Understanding Heart is the subtitle that either Opal or her publisher assigned to her narrative. But the generic classification is misleading, if not inappropriate. When early explorers and settlers went West they often kept journals and diaries. Disoriented by their unfamiliar surroundings, they wrote routinely each day, structuring and stabilizing personal narratives in order to maintain semblances of order and normalcy.[21] Most nineteenth–century journals and diaries therefore usually acknowledged only progress, events, and ideas that were public, prosaic, incremental, and practical—not emotional desires, psychological fears, and spiritual anxieties that might have revealed unexplored private states of feeling and consciousness. Opal's journal is different, however, in that it records her imagination triumphing over exterior, objective reality. Chronological time—the passage of days and years—doesn't structure her diary. In spite of its fantastic strangeness, the world in her narrative has a magical logic of its own, an unchanging sameness that seems to exist outside time. One day is much like another and, in spite of the odd language and events that make up the diary, the child's imaginative speech and actions seem to be guided by rules that have their own private rationale and internal consistency.

The constant mobility that may have led early frontier explorers and settlers to write journals and diaries as a way of maintaining imagined stability, at the same time may have caused Opal to retreat into fantasy. Robert Coles has observed in migrant children the tendency to seek refuge from their uprooted lives by creating within their imaginations a constant and welcome world, one that distances and secures them from an inconstant, unpleasant outside reality.[22] Whether Opal arrived from France in America or whether she lived her entire early childhood in migrant logging camps, moving nineteen times throughout Oregon, Opal may have compensated for whatever disruption she experienced in life by creating a fantasy world in which she could function successfully. Whether her physical mobility in childhood resulted in her mental instability as a child or later in life, it is worth noting, as Lillian Schlissel has written, that madness was as frequent an affliction on the frontier as it was in society. By the middle of the nineteenth century, three mental institutions had already been established in the Pacific Northwest alone—one in northern California and two more in Oregon.[23]

Because so few people wrote from the point of view of children who lived on the early western frontier, it is difficult to decide by comparison whether Opal's diary expresses a "normal" child's typical daydreams and fantasies or whether it instead reveals signs of the author's insanity. Sarah Bixby–Smith, who wrote as an adult about her years as a child spent living near the California mission town of San Juan Bautista, claimed in *Adobe Days* (1925) that she believed as a child that "angels and fairies were normal parts of [her] universe."[24] But although Bixby-Smith, as an adult, stopped trusting in make-believe, Opal, when she grew up, continued to cling to her fantasies. For instance, as she had in her diary, Opal in later life referred to her "real" deceased parents as her Angel Mother and Father. She spent her adult life in England and Europe attempting to research and track down their origins.

If Opal wrote the diary in adulthood, then it is even more striking that she failed in the narrative to distinguish between the real world and fantasy. The best-known works written by adults about children living on the western frontier either deny the child's world of fantasy or, while acknowledging it, contrast it with the adult writer's view of reality. In the *Little House* books, for instance, Laura Ingalls Wilder, the character, spends little time indulging in fantasy. She devotes her energy and attention to learning how her parents adapt and survive in a changing series of frontier environments. Through Laura we learn, for example, how Pa builds a log cabin and how Ma bakes a pie. The *Little House* books don't create a make-believe world in which young readers can escape from experiencing life as it was actually lived on the western frontier; they invite readers into the practical "real" world of adults and make it seem interesting. Conversely, in *The Wonderful Wizard of Oz* (1900), Frank L. Baum initially makes Dorothy's colorful world of fantasy seem more inviting than the black-and-white reality of the stark Kansas plains. But by the end of the novel Dorothy prefers to leave Oz and return to the real adult world, where Uncle Henry and Aunt Em live in pre–Dust Bowl hardship and poverty.

Unlike the *Little House* books, which acknowledge a serious (albeit an optimistically envisioned and charmingly rendered) reality—and unlike *The Wonderful Wizard of Oz*, which posits an imaginary parallel universe existing next to, not in place of, reality—*The Story of Opal* creates an imaginary world that exists *instead of* reality. Rather than documenting the lumber economy, the lower-middle-class working conditions, and the history of the Pacific Northwest at the turn of the century, the diary depicts an imaginary world that can be found only in folklore, literature, and religious mythology. Opal's version of Oregon isn't one distinct world or even two separate worlds. It is a combination of at least three different worlds (the paradisical, the pastoral, and the magical), none of which exists in reality. The woods of Oregon resemble not only the gardens of Christian paradise and the pastoral landscapes of literature but also the enchanted forests of fairy tales.

In Opal's forests, all animate and inanimate objects and beings have both souls and intelligence. Opal rules over all these subjects in her kingdom of fantasy. When she isn't outside reigning triumphantly, she is inside toiling submissively, waiting to be released from her bondage by being discovered and acknowledged as royalty. Whether Opal knew the story of Cinderella and reworked it as part her alleged autobiography, or whether she simply narrated a tale that was strikingly similar, illustrating in the process of doing so that the story of Cinderella unconsciously expresses every little girl's fantasy,[25] Opal represents herself in portions of her diary as an unredeemed heroine. Like Cinderella, she performs menial household chores for her wicked stepmother ("the mamma"), who constantly spanks Opal for attempting to escape from her servitude (11, 62, 154, 268); like Cinderella, she suffers indignities at the hands of her evil stepsisters, one of whom eventually tears up her diary; and like Cinderella, in a manner of speaking, she waits for her prince to come, believing that she is a royal member of the French aristocracy. If Opal was not who she claimed she was, then her diary, like the story of Cinderella, may have been her way of articulating her fantasy—her wish to deny her real mother, who represented maternal authority, and her desire to rise above her sisters, with whom she was engaged in intense sibling rivalries. Attributing souls and assigning baptismal names to the animals may have been a ritualistic way of expressing her wish to transcend her own lowly origins.

Like her namesake, the opal, the author reflects a rainbow of ideas in her narrative. *The Story of Opal*, written in English and French, plays with Christian theology, pagan folklore, and Greek and Roman mythology. In addition, it suggests strains of eighteenth-century European romantic and nineteenth-century American transcendental philosophy. An innocent child who lives and studies in nature, Opal is the progeny of the Jean-Jacques Rousseau; an artist and religious divine who transforms nature into a poetic and spiritual universe, she is also the ideological offspring of Ralph Waldo Emerson. In his essay on "Nature" (1836), Emerson claims that the "sun illuminates only the eye of the man, but shines into the eye and the heart of the child." The imagination, which Emerson compares to "the spirit of infancy," imbues brute nature with divine spirit and poetry. "It is this [spirit of infancy] which distinguishes the stick of timber of the wood-cutter from the tree of the poet," he postulates.[26] *The Journal of an Understanding Heart* reveals both the heart of the child and the Emersonian spirit of infancy. The forest exhibits an Over-Soul: Opal projects onto nature her own thoughts and sympathies, attributing to herself and to nature the same felt experience and the same spiritual intelligence. She imagines that she and the willows share the same "feels of gladness" (6), that she and the rocks have quaint conversations (126), and that she and the flowers communicate their thoughts telepathically (225). In addition, she literally projects onto nature her soul and her poetry, writing messages for fairies on plant leaves (34) and seeing her deceased friends and neighbors spiritually reincarnated in the physical growth of new trees (80, 203). Opal views the forest as grist for her imagination, not as timber for lumber mills. She transforms the material economic landscape in Oregon into a transcendental dreamscape that is part spiritual revelation and part pagan poetry.

In *Summer on the Lakes, in 1843*, Margaret Fuller, the American transcendental philosopher, describes her travels through the region of the midwestern Great Lakes. Visiting an island whose trees have recently been cut down by lumberjacks, Fuller appeals to her creative intellect to recreate the forests that men have destroyed. "I trust by reverent faith to woo the mighty meaning of the scene, perhaps to foresee the law by which a new order, a new poetry is to be evoked from this chaos, and with a curiosity as ardent, but not so selfish as that of Macbeth, to call up the apparitions of future kings from the strange ingredients of the witch's caldron," she testifies. In the physical absence of trees, Fuller imagines reproducing forests in the form of new mental "growths."[27]

Although they write in different times and locations, Margaret Fuller and Opal Whiteley nevertheless respond to various western landscapes in ways that are similar. The Great Lakes region in the mid-nineteenth century and the Pacific Northwest at the turn of the century were both frontiers of industry. Fuller recoils from outward signs of civilization, seeking comfort in the wilderness of her mind's creativity. Opal sets herself apart from lumber camps that comprise her society, seeking refuge in the enchanted forests of her own childish fantasies. Fuller, one of the intellectual giants of the mid-nineteenth-century, and Opal, an unsophisticated woman (or girl) by comparison, for all of their alleged differences in age, education, and background, receive inspiration from the same muses of religion, witchcraft, and literature. Fuller stokes the "caldron" of her imagination with the kindling of her own Christian "faith," with the three weird sisters' prophecies, and with dreams of a "new order" of poetry. Opal inhabits edenic gardens, enchanted forests, and pastoral scenes within the fantastic realms of her diary. Like Fuller and many other Americans who have written about various western frontiers, Opal tries to synthesize different conflicted responses to the land in her literature, seeking to integrate a variety of impressions into an imaginative work that creatively reorganizes experience and subjectively interprets reality.

III

Roderick Nash has written that human beings traditionally have imagined forests as the oldest of all forms of wilderness. In the Teutonic languages, the word "wilderness" originally referred to uncultivated land, which in most parts of northern Europe tended to be heavily forested. In Old English the word "weald" or "woeld," a term meaning "forest," also signified wilderness.[28] In the early seventeenth century, when the first Puritans voyaged to the New World, they encountered forests that ran up and down the northeastern shores of the continent.[29] For these early Puritans, and for many later Americans, forests represented not only the spaces of wilderness but also the lines of frontiers.

For much of seventeenth- and eighteenth-century America, the forests of New England symbolized an unredeemed moral wilderness. Witches and Indians, and other outcasts who lived there, embodied the worst fears of Puritans. As long as forests and their inhabitants existed, so would threats to emerging New England communities. American civilization sought to convert and conquer the wilderness, cleansing the landscape of Indians and felling the trees of the forest in order to make way for society. Lumbermen, having depleted many of the forests in New England by the mid-nineteenth century, moved next to the area surrounding the midwestern Great Lakes.[30] By this time, historically, America had already removed from or contained within the wilderness most signs of "savagery." By this time, also, the figure of Paul Bunyan had begun to appear in frontier tall tales.[31] The Indians, who had inhabited the psychological forests of the terrified Puritan mind, once were an obstacle in the path of progress to an expanding but still insecure nation. Paul Bunyan, however, symbolized how much progress into the forested wilderness white Americans had made by the mid-nineteenth century. Americans now conceived the forest not as a savage moral wilderness but as a frontier of industry. Accordingly, the giant white lumberjack grew out of an effort by early industrial America to create a new frontier mythology. In its alter ego, Paul Bunyan, America identified its own strength and power, its epic size and accomplishments, and its optimism and sense of self-confidence.

In terms of forested landscapes, the Pacific Northwest in the late nineteenth century represented the last real frontier. *The Story of Opal*, however, illustrates the failure of that frontier to produce anything more than a personal and now obscure narrative. The forests of New England inspired religious tracts, sermons, captivity narratives, and other great works of literature. In the allegorical wilderness, Puritans contended with forces of evil and savagery. In *The Scarlet Letter* (1850), for instance, the forest welcomes illegitimate children and outcasts like Pearl, who chooses the wilderness as the site in which to imagine a war with society. "The pine trees, aged, black and solemn, and flinging groans and other melancholy utterances on the breeze, needed little transformation to figure as Puritan elders; the ugliest weeds of the garden were their children, whom Pearl smote down and uprooted, most unmercifully."[32] Opal—allegedly deprived of her legitimate place in the French aristocracy—also imaginatively reconstructs a society while she lives on the Pacific Northwest frontier. But while Pearl is invested with symbolic significance, the little girl Opal is not. Pearl's imaginary confrontation with New England society represents the psychological moral struggle that many nineteenth-century Americans waged with their puritanical heritage. Opal's magical illusion constitutes nothing more than her individual attempt to escape from reality. While Pearl's dilemma is representative, Opal's is personal. Hawthorne's novel criticizes early New England society. But Opal's diary nurtures only her own private fantasies.

Even the forests surrounding the midwestern Great Lakes generated narratives that could be considered more potent and meaningful. The stories of Paul Bunyan, although originating in regional folklore, grew to articulate a developing country's sense of its destiny. Stories about Paul Bunyan circulated publicly and nationally; Opal's little-known diary was originally read privately. Stories about Paul Bunyan portrayed the forested frontier as gigantic and epic; *The Story of Opal* shrinks the great outdoors into miniature.

But in spite of the fact that it examines matters that are personal and seemingly trivial, Opal's diary has literary importance and symbolic national significance. It expresses what D. H. Lawrence has called "the myth of America." In *Studies in Classic American Literature* (1923), published three years after Opal's diary, Lawrence noted that the Leatherstocking Tales, when read in the order in which Cooper wrote them, depict Natty Bumppo becoming younger and younger as he retreats into history. He "starts old, old, wrinkled and writhing in an old skin. And there is a gradual sloughing of the old skin, towards a new youth. It is the myth of America."[33] In the national imagination, America conceives itself as a mythic New World. And in American literature, writers cast heroes who experience a mythic rebirth when they venture into the New World's uncharted frontiers.

If young heroes best represent the frontier experience, then it is appropriate that a child should represent the New World's youngest frontier—the far West, which the nineteenth-century French observer, Tocqueville, described as still in its "infancy."[34] Whether Opal wrote as a child or whether she wrote as an adult, from the point of view of a child—stripping away the years, as Cooper, in a series of novels featuring Natty Bumppo, gradually decreased the age of his character—Opal in either case intended to narrate the experience of a child who had lived on the western frontier in the early twentieth century. In *The Story of Opal* she projects a childlike imagination onto the forest, transforming the frontier into a New World that is as imaginatively young as her character. As the character of Opal reinvents herself when she comes to America, assuming an American name and identity, so the reborn young heroine creatively reconstructs her America. She relocates the primal scene of the wilderness, imaginarily resituating it within the mental boundaries of consciousness. Opal asks: What does it mean to be an American, and what does it mean to explore and inhabit America? She answers those questions in literature, creating an alter ego who, by virtue of her youth and unknown origins, exists outside time and history. She positions her alter ego in a timeless New World—part Garden of Eden, part pastoral landscape, part fairy tale. Opal, the child, explores and inhabits the forest, the oldest of all forms of wilderness—America's paradigmatic frontier. Filtering her experience of the external environment through her imagination, she distills into literature the kinds of dreams, myths, and fantasies that the western frontier always inspires.

PART TWO

REDISCOVERY

SIX

Toga! Toga!

In 1983, a hiker, walking among the dunes of central California, tripped over the head of a sphinx, which the windswept sands had uncovered. The artifact was something that Cecil B. DeMille—not an Egyptian ruler—had conceived long ago. Before filming his first version of *The Ten Commandments*, sixty years earlier, DeMille had constructed a series of sets in the desert. One of these sets recreated the city of Ramses the Magnificent. Twenty-four sphinxes, weighing five tons apiece, and four thirty-five-foot-tall statues of Pharaoh, made of concrete and plaster, had been erected and photographed, then dismantled and buried. Although film historians had subsequently searched the region for years, it took decades before the sands revealed where the lost city lay. In 1993, ten years after the hiker had rediscovered the head of one sphinx, a team of experts was still slowly digging to see what else was there. "Ground radar readings confirm that materials lie below the shifting dunes," claimed one cautious reporter.[1] But whether they indicated the presence of vast secret treasures, no one would speculate.

The U.S. frontier has provided the inspiration and setting for many great epics, some of which ostensibly take place in exotic foreign locales. *Ben-Hur* (1880), one of the bestselling novels of the late nineteenth century, tells the story of one man, a Jew, who escapes Roman bondage, finding personal salvation at the foot of Christ's cross. The author, Lew Wallace, governed the New Mexico territory in the late 1870s while he was writing *Ben-Hur*. In addition to using the southwestern landscape as a substitute for the deserts of Palestine, Wallace based the action in his novel on contemporary local historical incidents. While he was working to make the recently acquired U.S. territory "safe" for white settlement, placing Indians on reservations and arbitrating range wars between bandits and cattlemen, Wallace was simultaneously narrating "civilization's" rise over "savagery." *Ben-Hur* demonstrated the hero's conversion and triumph over pagan, decadent Rome. The novel glorified the decline of a barbaric culture and the dawning of a new Christian age at the same time that U.S. imperialist policies were attempting to justify white expansion on the western frontier. However, a decided ambivalence—an identification first with the agents of "civilization" then with the forces of "savagery"—plagued Wallace throughout his life and careers. *Ben-Hur* was the best-known but not the only example of Wallace's mixed views on the subject of empire, both at home and abroad.

|

Lewis (Lew) Wallace was born in 1827 in Brookville, a small town on Indiana's frontier. His father, David, after training and teaching at West Point, had given up the military, returned to his home state, and gone into politics. In the early 1830s, before his father became governor and moved to the capital, Wallace's family lived in the small town of Covington. Here, near the Indiana–Illinois border, Indians had begun to wage war. The Illinois state militia, fighting on behalf of white settlers, had tried to remove native peoples from land near the border. The warrior Black Hawk, however, having rallied five tribes of Indians, had declared war on intruders. In the spring of that year, tribes had killed two settlers not far from Covington. Because of his military experience, the townspeople elected Wallace's father (whom they nicknamed "the Colonel") to train a defensive militia. Although the militiamen never faced war, they prepared for encounters with Indians in a field next to town. In his autobiography, published in 1906, Wallace recalled watching the troops and then going home, inspired by this dress rehearsal to sketch "real" battle scenes in chalk on his slate. (Wallace would later use the same materials to compose the first draft of *Ben-Hur*.) "Alexander, Caesar, Napoleon, Genghis Khan, and Tamerlane the limp-legged, were heroes in reserve," he wrote, compared to the subjects of his early battlefield drawings; "none of them—no, not all of them together—slew half the number of men I wiped from my fields of carnage in [the] course of a week."[2]

Wallace enjoyed watching and reproducing scenes of men armed for combat. The reproduced scenes, in fact, realized the bloody encounters in which Covington's men never fought. However, reared on the literature of Irving and Cooper, Wallace could sympathize not only with the victors but with the vanquished as well. When he read about the death of Uncas, for example, it caused him "the keenest anguish," he claimed.[3] For the Indians, once they were wiped from his slate, could be remembered as noble heroes of a now–extinct race.

As a child, Wallace sympathized with both sides in battle. As an adult, he demonstrated the same conflicting loyalties, both in life and in literature. In 1846, he served as a second lieutenant in Company H of the First Indiana Infantry during the Mexican War. Although he never saw action, he nevertheless supported the cause of Manifest Destiny, which claimed divine title to northern Mexico's land. But after returning to the private sector and practicing law, and after serving in the Civil War as a low–ranking general, Wallace went back to Mexico in 1865, this time joining forces with Benito Juárez. Having earlier defended the right of the United States to annex part of Mexico's land, Wallace now worked with a rebel Mexican army to prevent another invasion and colonization by foreigners. By ousting Archduke Maximilian of Austria, the puppet dictator whom Napoleon III had installed, Wallace hoped to prevent the expansion of the French ruler's empire.[4]

His first novel, *The Fair God*, demonstrated that Wallace could side first with the conquerors and then with the conquered in what was now Mexico. Wallace finished the first draft of the novel in 1853, after serving in the Mexican War, and published the final draft in 1873, after working with Benito Juárez. Set in the past, the epic narrates the conquest of the Aztecs by Spain. Rallied by the hero, Guatamozin, Aztec warriors attempt to fight off invading Spanish troops led by Cortés. At times, Wallace seems to sympathize with the Aztec leader, whose courage and cunning in war help the Aztecs win several battles. But at other times, Wallace seems to identify with the Spaniards, whose triumph is destined by history.

The author, sometimes referred to on the title pages of his books as "General Lew Wallace," was a military man who had fought on the winning side in two recent wars. His family, along with the rest of the nation, had also been waging an undeclared war on American Indians who refused to give up their land. While he was governor, Wallace's father had ordered hundreds of Indians sent west to Kansas; traveling by a route called "The Trail of Death," 150 captives had died on the way. And while Wallace was writing *The Fair God*, the United States was continuing to displace and eliminate its own native peoples. Spain's victory over the Aztecs, in Wallace's novel, if not intentionally justifying U.S. acts of aggression against indigenous people, at least inaugurated a history of imperialistic conquest and settlement, one that dated from the arrival of the Spanish in Mexico to the nineteenth-century U.S. government's invasion and colonization of various western domains.[5]

The political imprint of one culture on that of another was sometimes accomplished using the stamp of religion. In 1878, President Rutherford B. Hayes appointed Wallace, a well-known war hero and loyal Republican, to govern New Mexico. Until then, the Catholic Church, led by Franciscan friars, had enjoyed only partial success in their efforts to convert Pueblo Indians. In *The Land of the Pueblos* (1888), Wallace's wife, Susan, depicted the Pueblos as a passive race, yearning for Anglo-European missionaries to rescue their souls. Perhaps because her husband was writing *Ben-Hur* at the time, she compared the Pueblos to the Jews who had been converted by Christ. Although they were as different from the white settlers as "the Jews are from the other races in Christendom," the Pueblos were one day bound to adopt the "one model" of Christ and to succumb to "the influence of the same inspiration," she prophesied.[6]

Wallace himself, however, entertained conflicting opinions about the "civilizing" role that religion should play. In a lecture entitled "Mexico and the Mexicans," delivered in 1867, Wallace blamed the Catholic Church for making the people complacent, arguing instead that the Mexican peasantry should protest against members of the land-owning elite who exploited them.[7] In *The Fair God*, published just six years later, Wallace seemed almost to prefer the Aztec religion, which included disturbing elements of superstition and sacrifice, but which appeared no worse than the enslaving Christian religion that was introduced by Cortés.

While the Catholic Church was trying to convert the Pueblos, the U.S. government was attempting to confine the Apaches and Navajo.[8] During Wallace's years in New Mexico, the government made a series of efforts to contain warring tribes. In 1877, the year before Wallace arrived, 453 Apaches and Navajo were transferred to Arizona from their home reservation in Warm Springs, New Mexico. In transit, approximately 300 Indians escaped from captivity. Although some of them eventually turned themselves in, the rest of them, led by the Apache warrior, Victorio, remained at large for four years, running south into Mexico and returning periodically to attack U.S. cavalry. In 1881 Joaquin Terrazas, the cousin of the governor of Chihuahua, in league with the U.S. government, led a posse that tracked down the fugitive warrior in Mexico, killing Victorio and seventy-six fellow conspirators.[9] Wallace, who had asked the U.S. government for more money and troops to help capture the Indians, was satisfied when the warring escapees were killed, believing, as his wife claimed, that the natives were "what they were when the Spaniards found them—cunning, blood-thirsty, untamable." But during the feud, Wallace had also grudgingly admitted that he admired the chief for resisting white rule. "In some respects," he said of Victorio, "he is a wonderful man, and, commencing with a band of seventy-five warriors, he succeeded in uniting tribes always hostile to one another before, and in a few weeks he had three hundred well-armed followers. He has held his own against us from that day to this."[10]

Wallace had well-deserved reasons for respecting his foes. By comparison, some of the white invaders who appropriated Indian land were themselves less than admirable. The recent acquisition of the southwest by the United States had made it possible for white bankers, lawyers, cattlemen, gamblers, and bandits to move into the area. Establishing their own rings of influence, these vigilantes and entrepreneurs had murdered men, rustled cattle, and conspired in their efforts to wipe out competitors. In Lincoln County, in southeast New Mexico, during Wallace's tenure as governor two factions held sway; and in 1878, shortly after Wallace took office, violence between the two factions broke out. Wallace declared a state of insurrection and then offered amnesty, but neither his threats of force nor his promises of forgiveness stopped outlaws who would continue their depradations for the next several years. Finally, Wallace attempted to prosecute some of the worst offenders in court. As part of a program to make witnesses testify, Wallace struck a bargain with Billy the Kid, a hired gun who had worked at different times for various gangs. In exchange for his testimony, Wallace allegedly promised not to punish Billy for his own role in the war. (Billy had killed one man in Lincoln and was thought to be implicated in the deaths of at least several more victims.) But after appearing in court in 1879, Billy escaped from jail and went on a killing spree, violating the terms of his amnesty. After being captured and jailed several more times, Billy was eventually tracked down and killed in 1881 by sheriff Pat Garrett.[11]

History reveals Billy to be not a noble hero who fought selflessly for a worthwhile cause but a ruthlessly violent and pragmatic man. The facts, few though they are, cast a harsh light on Wallace as well. Some

Lew Wallace's letter to W. H. Bonney, alias Billy the Kid. (Indiana Historical Society Library, Negative No. C5741.)

critics have argued that Wallace tricked Billy into testifying in court by promising to give Billy amnesty, and that Wallace then revoked or conveniently forgot the promise once the case was resolved. Others have contended that Wallace made the promise in earnest but that Billy's later crimes violated the terms of his amnesty. Letters exchanged between the two men suggest that both of them, being in difficult straits, tried to strike the best deal that they could. Billy, a troublemaking loner who had no stake in the feud and fought for both sides, gave his testimony not because he cared whether justice prevailed but because he wanted to save his own neck. Wallace, a former military leader who had no experience governing disorderly citizens and a political novice who had little initial understanding of the complex inter-rivalries of New Mexico's gangs, also seemed desperate to find a solution that worked. Negotiating with an unsavory criminal was a means to this end. The man who, when he first came to New Mexico, declared a state of insurrection and then proclaimed amnesty, switched back and forth, threatening and conciliating Billy in letters that he wrote to the outlaw-in-hiding. In a letter dated March 15, 1879, Wallace told Billy that he had arranged for them to meet on neutral ground so that the two men could talk. "The object of the meeting at Squire Wilson's is to arrange the matter in a way to make your life safe. To do that the utmost secresy [sic] is to be used. *So come alone*"[12] (Wallace's emphasis). If history were as dramatically satisfying as westerns, in which heroes and villains play well-defined roles, this meeting between Billy the Kid, the West's most famous outlaw, and Lew Wallace, the territorial governor of New Mexico and the author of the epic *Ben-Hur*, would have been a momentous showdown. Instead, two men, who desperately needed each other for their own distinct purposes, came together under the cover of darkness to transact their shady business in a small frontier town. The clear-cut victories and defeats in western legend and literature gave way to a historical reality that was problematic and much more mundane.

Wallace's career as a soldier-politician was shaped by some of the most important events of the mid- and late nineteenth century: by the Black Hawk War, the Mexican War, the Civil War, various local Indian skirmishes, and the famous range wars in Lincoln County, New Mexico. Wallace's novels, however, were set in the long distant past. Writing at a time when literary realism was beginning to come into prominence, Wallace clung to romances that he had read as a boy, writing adventure tales that were situated on foreign frontiers. Having fought, Wallace could realistically describe the grisly horrors of war in his autobiography. Having governed in peacetime as well, he could chronicle the historical process of conquest and rule with the calm detachment of one who knows which side is destined to win. But in his historical fiction, looking back on the past, he tended to idealize and romanticize those who were doomed to defeat. Wallace made various careers for himself, first as a soldier, then as a politician, and finally as the author of one of the most popular historical epics in American literature. But sympathy for the losing side sometimes caused him to criticize institutions that had contributed to Wallace's success in real life. The army, the government, and even the church could appear as instruments of oppression, used by the conquerors to impose their will on the conquered. Wallace's identification with one side, then the other, continued throughout his life and his literature. But nowhere did it play itself out more dramatically than in his famous novel, *Ben-Hur*.

II

Because Wallace wrote parts of *Ben-Hur* while living in the West; because he based it on a conflict between "civilization" and "savagery," the novel in certain respects resembles the formula western, which was then in development. No western, no matter how representative, fulfills every requirement, and *Ben-Hur*, because it isn't a member of the genre but merely a relative, lacks certain signs of affinity. But in addition to its resemblance to the historical epic and religious conversion tale, the novel manifests three traits that John G. Cawelti claims all westerns share. According to Cawelti, one of the most influential critics to posit a formula, the typical western is characterized, first, by an action that "takes place on or near a frontier."[13] This action, occurring at "the epic moment" when "civilization" and "savagery" clash (66), loosely resembles the plot of Wallace's own epic narrative. Ben-Hur's defeat of the Romans in battle, his victory in the chariot race over his former friend and rival, Messala, and his conversion to Christianity at the end of the novel, which redeems the Jewish hero as well as his followers, mark successive stages in the dismantling of Rome's evil empire and the founding of a new holy society.

Cawelti's ideal western is also populated by three types of characters: law-abiding "townspeople," who make up society; "savages," who inhabit the unredeemed wilderness; and a "hero," who remains poised between these two opposed spheres (46). In Wallace's novel, these three types of characters are represented by the Jews, the Romans, and Ben–Hur, respectively. The hero lives among Jews, who are destined to be converted to the new Christian faith, and among Romans, who are heathens and blasphemers. Born as a Jew in Jerusalem, Ben–Hur is later adopted by a tribune from Rome. Subscribing first to the Old Testament law of an eye for an eye, he wreaks revenge on Messala and schemes to attack Rome with his troops; accommodating himself later to the New Testament teachings of Christ, he scuttles his plans for further destruction and dedicates himself instead to constructive good works. Just as the western hero performs acts that are alternately ruthless and civilized, so he finds himself attracted to women who are both morally dangerous and honorable. Simultaneously drawn to the heroine (a schoolmarm, for instance) and to the villainess (a saloon girl or prostitute), the hero identifies equally with characters who exist both inside and outside society. Moving back and forth between "civilization" and "savagery," Wallace's hero also finds himself drawn to two different women: Esther, a Jewess, who is modest and loyal, and Iras, a Roman spy who betrays Ben–Hur while seducing him at a desert oasis.

Finally, Cawelti insists that the western be staged against the backdrop of nature (39–40). The desert or high plains, a sweeping prairie or mountain range, dramatizes the fact that pioneers could easily become stranded, dwarfed, or engulfed by the wilderness in the process of attempting to tame the frontier. In addition, the harsh extremes of the climate and the hostile "savages" who inhabit the unfriendly environment contribute to the impression that the chances for white survival are slim; that the struggles confronting a new civilization are great, even epic. Wallace modeled his Middle Eastern landscape on deserts in the southwest United States. While living in New Mexico, he observed that the Rio Grande Valley looked more like "the region of the Nile" than did any other place he had visited; his wife, Susan, noted that scenes of "low adobe houses" and herdsmen with their flocks, gathered to drink at a stream, reminded her of illustrations of biblical stories set in far distant lands.[14]

As Cawelti's work demonstrates, westerns share many of the same characteristics on film and in literature. Reading the novel, one can understand why *Ben-Hur* was filmed more than once. Because of its depiction of exploits, crowd scenes, and spectacles, many of which exist in the reader's imagination as indelible images, the novel anticipates the later techniques of cinema. At times, Wallace's audience seems to function less as a reader and more as a spectator, not so much processing narrative as simply witnessing scenes. (In the chariot-race scene, for example, the reader becomes one of the crowd in the Circus seats, watching and cheering Ben-Hur.) The unnamed narrator serves as an impersonal camera's eye, patiently guiding the reader-as-spectator through the excitement of the tumultuous throng. (In the race scene, again, the narrator says: "try to fancy it; . . . look down upon the arena, and see it glistening in its frame of dull-gray granite walls."[15])

Unlike Cawelti, the critic Will Wright, limiting himself to a discussion of films, argues that westerns follow one of four basic plots. In the "vengeance" plot, the hero is a member of civilization who temporarily leaves it in order to protect it from villains. But at some point during the struggle, a member of society asks the hero to give up his quest for revenge. Only after defeating the villains, however, does the hero return to society.[16] On film, as well as in literature, *Ben-Hur* narrates the archetypal "vengeance" plot. The hero first seeks revenge when Messala sends Ben-Hur into slavery. While in exile he fights, as an individual and as a representative of Jewish society, against bondage to Rome. The word *vengeance* appears more frequently than just about any other word in *Ben-Hur*. The hero swears "vengeance" when his mother and sister are cast into prison (105); he threatens "vengeance" when he thinks that his family is dead (163); he tells Sheik Ilderim that he is racing against Messala for "vengeance," not money (225); and he spends three years training troops to fight against Rome because he craves "vengeance" in war (445). Only at the end of the book, when he witnesses Christ's death on the cross, does the hero realize that he must accept God's will and lay down his arms.[17]

Cawelti and Wright agree that the western hero moves back and forth between the worlds of his friends and his enemies. Wright claims, for example, that the hero, in his effort to befriend civilization by engaging the villains in war, becomes like the villains, realizing his latent potential to kill or do harm (156). This seeming paradox explains one of Ben-Hur's early, crucial decisions. Even before he goes off in chains to serve as a galley slave, Ben-Hur indicates that he holds a grudge against Rome. In a conversation with his mother in the Palace of Hur, he says that he has decided to beat the Romans by joining them. If he wants to train an army to conquer Rome's troops, he must learn how to fight. And since Jerusalem doesn't have an army, he must therefore leave home. Infiltrating the ranks will enable Ben-Hur to spy on his enemies, thus allowing the hero to develop his own counter-strategy. "I will fight for her," Ben-Hur says of Rome—"if, in return, she will teach me how ... to fight against her," he promises (100).

Ben-Hur has a showdown with Rome—but not on the battlefield. On the racetrack at the Circus at Antioch, he finally conquers Messala. (Having been adopted by one of Rome's tribunes and having been given the chance to race horses enables Ben-Hur to master Rome's favorite sport. Thus, in the chariot race he beats the enemy at the enemy's game.) Wallace stages the race as a shoot-out between two western gunfighters,[18] stating that the contestants' horses burst forth from the gates at the start of the race "like missiles in a volley from so many great guns" (318). The fastest gun wins. The "quick report" of Ben-Hur's whip urges his horses on, causing them to pull the hero across the finish-line first (327). The 1925 and 1959 films simplify the encounter between Ben-Hur and Messala, representing it as a clear-cut triumph of

In the chariot-race scene, Messala (Stephen Boyd) and Ben-Hur (Charlton Heston) drive black and white horses, respectively. (© 1959 Turner Entertainment Co. All rights reserved.)

good over evil. But Wallace problematizes the race, suggesting that the adopted Ben-Hur, who over time has become more and more like the Romans, has also come to have few moral differences with his rival, Messala. In the 1959 film, Messala, seeking revenge, maneuvers his cart next to Ben-Hur's, using a protruding, rotating spike on one of his wheels to rip through the spokes of his competitor's wheel. In the novel, however, Ben-Hur attacks first, driving his chariot up to Messala's, running his "inner wheel" behind the other one's cart and causing his rival to crash (328). Ben-Hur's vengeful feelings match those of his enemy: They motivate the hero to commit an act of aggression and savagery. The film versions rid themselves of this disturbing complexity, reducing Ben-Hur and Messala to allegorical types. Here, the hero and villian drive white and black horses, respectively. In the novel, however, as these distinctions are blurred, so the colors of each man's horses are mixed (303).

Wallace's historical epic and religious conversion tale, set overseas in the biblical past, has something in common with westerns, which originated in the late nineteenth century.[19] Wallace spent much of his life manning outposts on distant U.S. frontiers. His experiences, which influenced Wallace while he was writing his masterpiece, explain why *Ben-Hur* has some of the qualities that all westerns share. But his ambivalent feelings about those experiences make *Ben-Hur* even more problematic than most western narratives.

III

Wallace wrote Books 6, 7, and 8—the last three books of *Ben-Hur*—while he lived in New Mexico.[20] Book 6, which Wallace wrote shortly after assuming office as governor, opens with the announcement that a "great change" has occurred: Pontius Pilate has replaced Valerius Gratus as governor. Wallace's doubts about the benefits of empire may explain why the appointment of a new governor in the novel is represented as no cause for joy. Wallace chose to use this transitional period in history, when the U.S. government was removing New Mexico's previous territorial governor and instituting Wallace instead, as the time to write about Rome's appointment of a new and even more evil tyrant. As Wallace noted, "the Jews knew the change of rulers was not for the better" (342), just as New Mexico's natives must have suspected that Wallace's tenure as governor would adversely affect their autonomy.

Wallace, the ruler, partially identified not with the Romans but with the subjugated Jews and their hero, Ben–Hur. In an essay entitled "How I Came to Write *Ben-Hur*," first published in *Youth's Companion* on February 2, 1893, Wallace alleged that a conversation with the famous agnostic Colonel Robert G. Ingersoll had inspired him to write a religious conversion tale. In a debate about the existence of God and the divinity of His Son, Jesus Christ, Wallace was forced to acknowledge his ignorance, confessing that he had spent his whole life dealing with worldly concerns and that he had previously "neither believed nor disbelieved" in the cornerstones of Christian theology.[21] Wallace converted to Christianity after resolving to study the question and make up his mind. The result was a novel, *Ben-Hur*, which tells the story of one man's religious awakening. Wallace, who stated years later that he had written the novel with a growing sense of reverence and awe, identified with the novel's protagonist, finding personal salvation while tracing Ben–Hur's road to enlightenment.

Wallace and his hero made the same holy pilgrimage. But Wallace and the Romans shared the same military and political goals: to invade, conquer, and govern their foes. Wallace's process of composing the novel was, to say the least, odd. After drafting the first version in chalk on a slate, Wallace then wrote the final version on paper in bold purple ink. Deliberately or not, Wallace linked himself with the enemy in the act of writing *Ben-Hur*: purple is the color adopted by imperial Rome. When they sweep through the streets of Jerusalem, the Romans barely touch the ground with the hems of their togas, which are trimmed in rich royal hues (97, 112). When they march on parade, they deck their horses in plush purple livery (101). When they attend sporting events, races, and games at the Circus, they sit under brightly colored canopies while the other spectators sweat (236).

Wallace's identification with both the Jews and the Romans explains why differences between the two groups sometimes seem blurred. In theory, *Ben-Hur*, like the formula western, dramatizes the conflict between "civilization" and "savagery." But the notion that Jews represent "civilization" and that Romans represent "savagery" is problematic at best. Can the Romans be said to represent "savagery" when their culture, even though it is now in decline, is at the same time responsible for bequeathing to western civilization numerous cultural legacies? And can the Jews, whose history reveals an equally impressive and extensive list of accomplishments, be viewed as exclusively "civilized" when Wallace characterizes them as unrefined natives who are destined to be subdued, either by Roman troops or by Christ? Like the Indians in westerns, the Jews are indigenous members of (Israelite) tribes. They are invaded by military forces representing an encroaching civilization that is looking for new land to inhabit and rule. If the Jews who defend their homeland aren't defeated by the Romans in war, they will be admonished and sweetly chastised by Christ, who will tame them by harnessing them to the yoke of religion. Like the Pueblos in the territory of New Mexico (whom Susan Wallace compared to unredeemed Jews) and, before them, the Mexicans in the New Viceroy of Spain, the Jews in *Ben-Hur* are refined only to the extent that they believe in one God; they will achieve total redemption when they come to accept that Christ is God's Son.

Ben-Hur resembles the formula western. Yet, at the same time, it doesn't. The chariot race between Ben–Hur and Messala, which concludes with Ben–Hur's triumph at the end of Book 5, represents, in the defeat of his rival, Ben–Hur's symbolic resolution of his conflict with Rome. After this, the conflict remains between Ben–Hur and Christ. By meekly suffering humankind's scorn and betrayal, the Savior teaches Ben–Hur that it is better to lay down his arms and spend his life performing good works than it is to fight against Rome. Slightly more than the first half of *Ben-Hur* is concerned with the Jewish hero's adherence to Old Testament law. The principle of an eye for an eye justifies Ben–Hur's righteous wrath against Rome; as an ideology it motivates the same kind of vigilante behavior that occurs in most westerns. But the remainder of Wallace's novel addresses the hero's need to accept and put into practice the teachings of New Testament law. This part of *Ben-Hur* reads not like a western but like a tale of religious conversion, emphasizing the virtues of self–sacrifice, love, and humility.[22]

Conforming alternately to one of two different kinds of behavior, Ben–Hur appears simultaneously passive and active, meek and recklessly bold. Thus, as a hero, Ben–Hur seems like a statue in motion, a static figure whose action seems more symbolic than real. In the novel's first epic set–piece, during the battle with pirates at sea, the galley slave is chained to his bench in the hull of the ship, forced to watch through the ship's porthole as the action plays out. Ben–Hur enters the chariot race, the second set–piece, and wins. But his triumph, although meaningful, is mainly symbolic: the race is a game and the win is merely a ceremonial victory over one of Rome's men. Christ's submission to his enemies not only motivates Ben–Hur's decision not to fight against Rome but also justifies his inconsequential actions (or his relative inaction) in the first part of *Ben-Hur*. For the hero learns, through witnessing the crucifixion of Christ, that submission on earth leads to triumph in heaven.

As a boy, Wallace had been disappointed that the Black Hawk War had ended before his father's militia could fight. As an adult, Wallace had felt frustrated that his infantry's company hadn't participated in any significant action in the Mexican War. During the Civil War, General Ulysses S. Grant had scapegoated and martyred Wallace's troops, blaming them for arriving at Shiloh too late to help the Union side win. Later, during the range wars and Indian wars in Lincoln County, New Mexico, Wallace had pleaded in vain for more assistance from the U.S. cavalry, believing that military action would have helped restore rule. Wallace's military career, in other words, had been marked by disappointment, postponement, and failure. But his excursion into literature yielded him an escape from the frustrations that he had encountered in life, for in his novel the hero is associated with the peripheral action or with a central action that never transpires. Nevertheless, Ben-Hur is justified by Christ in the end. His heroic status, as an advocate of peaceful resistance, is eclipsed only by Christ's shining martyrdom.

Wallace's religious experience, however, was less intense than Ben-Hur's. His admission, that he had become a believer in the process of writing his novel, piqued the interest of his readers to such an extent that Wallace eventually felt compelled to say more. At the outset of his autobiography, he attempted to satisfy his readers' profound curiosity. "In the very beginning, before distractions overtake me, I wish to say that I believe absolutely in the Christian conception of God. As far as it goes, this confession is broad and unqualified." Wallace didn't use the opening chapter of his autobiography to proselytize his readers or to proclaim his own ardent faith. He took the opportunity merely to issue a reticent statement ("As far as it goes") and to answer a seemingly tiresome question that fans of his novel, writing to him, had apparently asked more than once. Adding that "I am not a member of any church or denomination, nor have I ever been,"[23] Wallace made a profession of faith that consisted of bland generalities. In addition to his conversion, another event—of more worldly importance and of more immediate interest to Wallace, perhaps—occurred shortly after the author finished writing *Ben-Hur*. Reading the novel and being impressed by the author's religious devotion, which had led Wallace to write so movingly about the last days of Christ, President James A. Garfield offered Wallace the U.S. ambassadorship to the Ottoman Empire. Willing to forget his troubles in the New Mexico territory and take a new job abroad, Wallace was also no doubt pleased to accept a position that paid approximately four times his governor's salary.[24] It would be cynical to suggest that the career benefits were more important to Wallace than the spiritual rewards for writing *Ben-Hur*. Indeed, it seems unlikely that Wallace wrote with the idea of personal advancement in mind. But Wallace's military and political promotions, as they have been chronicled by Wallace and others, seem to have played a more obvious role in his life than his religious conversion did; in fact, his conversion, on the surface at least, seemed to help his career. For it was part of the President's plan that a devout Christian such as Wallace should be appointed to represent the United States in a heathen land overseas. Although Ben–Hur had been forced to choose between commanding troops on the battlefield and serving as a soldier for Christ, Wallace, professing his faith in the Gilded Age, when the gospel of wealth achieved dominance, didn't have to choose between earthly and heavenly glory. Conveniently, his well–known religious beliefs helped Wallace prosper that much more easily.

After reading *The Fair God*, an acquaintance remarked that Wallace wanted to be both a "conquistador" and a "Moses" in Mexico;[25] that Wallace fantasized about liberating the nation through both violent and nonviolent means. Again in *Ben-Hur*, Wallace identified with soldier–politicians and religious converts as well. His balanced affinity with "civilization" and "savagery" forces one to question whether those concepts represent polar extremes. Like *Ben-Hur*, the western defines "civilization" and "savagery" in relative rather than absolute terms. Through the actions of its hero, the western indicates the difficulties inherent in opposing these worlds. Moving back and forth between (moral) civilization and (spiritual) wilderness, the western hero—like Ben–Hur—exists in each sphere. Paradoxically, he defends civilization by resorting to uncivilized means, as Ben–Hur does when he wrecks havoc on Rome. In order to maintain social order he practices anarchy, claiming the vigilante's right to judge, punish, and kill, instead of leaving these decisions and actions to God. Although he fights for (Jewish) society, the individual hero has no social ties. Indeed, Ben–Hur doesn't seek revenge until he mistakenly thinks that his mother and sister are dead. (The supposed death of his family makes his rebirth as a war-hero possible.) The ambivalence that plagued Wallace throughout his life and careers resembles the dilemma that provides the tension in his novel, *Ben-Hur*. And the tension between "civilization" and "savagery" resembles the conflict that the western, through the actions of its hero, finally seeks to resolve.

Ben-Hur is a western in toga, in drag. Wallace used the conflict that motivated many formula westerns not only to work out issues that concerned the West as a region but also to explicate matters that affected the United States as a whole. The Mexican War and the Civil War—U.S. acts of aggression that dealt with issues of national priority, such as sovereignty, conquest, and race—were as influential for Wallace in the process of writing *Ben-Hur* as were matters of local priority: the Black Hawk War, the removal of the southwest Apaches and Navajo, and the resolution of range wars in Lincoln County, New Mexico. The novel, which relives the conflict between Romans and Jews, also reenacts major political and cultural struggles that were waged in the United States in the mid- and late nineteenth century. *Ben-Hur* contemplates imperialistic U.S. acts of aggression by narrating the historically and geographically distanced encounters between Rome and Jerusalem during the dawning of a new Christian age.

As a "spiritual" western, *Ben-Hur* functions as a transitional text in the history of American literature. The novel's enormous success was due to the fact that it combined characteristics of two popular genres, one of which predated and the other of which succeeded *Ben-Hur*. As a tale of Christian conversion, the novel modeled itself on the sentimental literature of the early and mid–nineteenth century. It endorsed the same brand of feeling and piety that had made *Uncle Tom's Cabin* (1852), the nineteenth century's other bestselling novel, such a triumphant success. Ministers who warned their congregations against the evils of reading fiction for pleasure made an exception and approved *Ben-Hur* because Wallace's novel was religious in emphasis. Clergymen testified to the phenomenal power that the novel exercised in converting their flocks. And some of those converts went so far as to write Wallace, claiming that *Ben-Hur* had inspired them to become missionaries and to preach overseas.[26]

As a tale of frontier adventure, *Ben-Hur* looked back to the works of Irving and Cooper, which Wallace had read as a child. It also looked forward to the genre of westerns, which would be developed in the decades to come. The theme of moral redemption, reverently explicated in the novel's contemplative passages, competes for the reader's attention with scenes of manly contests, heroic adventures, and war. And as the novel combines two different genres, so the novel's hero alternately plays two different roles. Ben-Hur is the sentimental hero(ine) whose spheres are the church and the home. In the course of the novel, he converts to Christianity, reunites with his mother and sister, and returns to his home/land, Jerusalem, where he is restored as the rightful Prince in the Palace of Hur. Wallace gives Ben-Hur soft womanly features that are intended to express extreme states of feeling: a "dimpled" mouth, "full eyes," and the rosy cheeks of a blushing young girl (71). When he asks Quintus Arrius for information about his mother and sister, Ben-Hur clasps "his hands in appeal" (126), using the same sentimental gesture that he later uses when he supplicates Christ. But passive humility gives way to anger when Ben-Hur believes that Messala has murdered his kin. The emotional change that comes over Ben-Hur is "instant," "extreme" (126). His womanly, expressive countenance becomes steely and stern. His muscles flex in rebellion, signifying Ben-Hur's intent to destroy his archnemesis. Immediately, Ben-Hur transforms himself into the avenger, into the vigilante hero whom fans of westerns admire.

Wallace's novel was one of the late nineteenth-century's bestselling books. It combined sentimental literature, one of the favorite genres of women, with literature of the strenuous life, for which there was a correspondingly large male readership. Like the novels of Harriet Beecher Stowe, Susan Warner, and others, *Ben-Hur* privileged the domestic and sacred spheres. (The hero's need for family and home/land is as great as his yearning for Christ.) But like the writings of Theodore Roosevelt, the works of Jack London, and early formula westerns, *Ben-Hur* glorified the adventures of men who lived on a distant mythic frontier. It became astoundingly popular, appealing to a diverse national audience by accomodating contradictory, multiple views on such subjects as race wars, religion, and Manifest Destiny, and by packaging such serious issues in an entertaining literary hybrid incorporating the historical epic, the sentimental conversion tale, and the early formula western.

SEVEN

X Marks the Spot

Treasure Island, the casino and family resort, is one of the new theme at-tractions dotting the Las Vegas Strip. A Disneyesque recreation of a quaint English harbor makes up the casino's facade. A wooden pier, extending over the water, leads from the street to the building's main entrance. Here, every evening, patrons and passersby watch Treasure Island put on a spectacle. While the *Hispanola* lays anchor and pirates prepare to unload their loot, the *HMS Britannia* sails around the corner and comes into view. After asking the pirates to surrender their ill–gotten gains, a British naval officer orders his men to take aim and fire. The pirates retaliate, launch-ing mock cannonballs that ignite the enemy's gunpowder storage room, setting off controlled explosions and cuing stunt men, who dive out of crow's nests into choppy waters below.

The defeat of the British and the success of the pirates in protecting their treasure pleases cheering spectators. The implication—teasingly and entertainingly offered, but at the same time hopefully seized upon by those who come to Las Vegas—is that Treasure Island gives gamblers the same opportunity: to win and keep money that isn't "rightfully" theirs. The casino extends this conceit in its game rooms, restaurants, and shops. Felt–covered tables represent the dangerous high seas. Like buccaneers sending their ships in search of doubloons, players cast their dice on green surfaces, hoping that their ventures will net them

Explosions occur during the sea battle outside Treasure Island, in downtown Las Vegas. (Photograph by R. Marsh Starks.)

blue plastic chips. Gentlemen and women of fortune can feast and celebrate in "The Black Spot," or join landlubbing tourists who dislike
gambling and prefer shopping for merchandise. ("Damsels in Dis' Dress"
sells women's sportwear and jewelry. "Captain Kids" features toys and
stuffed animals.)

As a fantasy theme park, Treasure Island succeeds in disguising the
fact that gamblers often lose more than they win. The resort and casino,
which promises fun for the family as well as adult speculation, resembles its namesake, the novel, which was written for children but at the
same time provides a mature meditation on the dangers of lusting for
riches. Robert Louis Stevenson wrote *Treasure Island* after touring the
western frontier and inspecting a ghost town and mining camp in the
late nineteenth century. Environmental devastation and human
decay—the consequences of a boom–bust economy and a resultant
migrant society—suggested to Stevenson that the pursuit of wealth was
a hollow and misguided enterprise. Although he was sobered by the
scene that confronted him, he was also seduced by the camp's haunting
atmosphere. Stevenson, a Scottish bohemian who was also the son of
stern Presbyterians, was a romantic moralist whose work exhibited
escapist as well as didactic tendencies. Thus *Treasure Island*, inspired by
Stevenson's western experience, captured the risk and excitement of
searching for treasure while demonstrating the effect that greed and
ambition had on its characters. Today, an entertainment mecca in the
desert reenacts *Treasure Island* near the source of its artistic origin. For if
gamblers go to Las Vegas now to prospect for gold, the California frontier, as Stevenson notes, is where the quest once began.

I

While visiting California, Stevenson married Fanny Van de Grift, an
American divorcée, in May 1880. Suffering from a respiratory illness,
the impoverished writer and invalid embarked with his wife on their
honeymoon, seeking fresh air. In the hills above Napa Valley, among
the rustic ruins of a mining camp, the Stevensons planned to relax and
live inexpensively. Before starting out, Stevenson imagined what his
new home would be like on the slopes of the famed Mount St. Helena.
But the site disappointed him. In *The Silverado Squatters* (1883), an account
of this period, Stevenson says that he was expecting "a clique of neigh-
borly houses ... swept and garnished," placed on a bright village green,
and populated by "great elms and chestnuts," a trout stream, songbirds,

and bees.[1] Instead he discovered a ramshackle mining camp, littered with technological refuse and human debris, and surrounded by scarred mountain scenery.

All that remained of the boomtown was a run-down hotel. Rather than stay there, Stevenson and his wife reclaimed a shack near the mine. Although the building stood near a precipice—overlooking a gorge filled with sedimentary extracts, trash, and rusty machinery—Stevenson, exercising poetic license, chose not to acknowledge the view. Although he admitted that the real Silverado didn't resemble his picturesque fantasy, he sought to transform dross into gold through the process of artistic alchemy.[2] In his sketchbook, he described the shack as a "sylvan" retreat (64). Tree sap, mountain flowers, and spices mingled their scents in the wilderness, so that standing near the edge of the dump the artist inhaled only lovely "perfumes" (98).

In fact, for the groom, Silverado proved a restful vacation site. For Fanny, however, it presented challenges not unlike those she had encountered in her failed first marriage. Fanny had followed her first husband, an unlucky prospector, through a series of mining camps. Working with limited resources in undomestic surroundings, she had learned how to cook beef fifteen different ways; how to wash clothes in a stream; how to dress herself while surveying her reflection in a battered tin pan; and how to shoot her husband's revolver when she was threatened by Indians.[3] Fanny refurbished the cabin and made it possible for Stevenson to enjoy an idyllic honeymoon: She draped calico sheets over the windows, swept out the litter, dusted for cobwebs, and packed the bunk beds with straw. In *The Silverado Squatters*, Stevenson suggests that he and his wife together "repaired the worst of the damages" (185); but Stevenson spent most of his time convalescing while Fanny massaged him with oil and brought him rum punch topped with whipped cream and cinnamon.[4] Once, when Fanny injured herself doing chores, the author tried roughing it. In a letter to a friend, written from camp, Stevenson admitted that he was having a "miserable time."[5] But in his published account of this episode, Stevenson waxed philosophical. The experience, he moralized, merely taught Fanny and him how much "labor it cost" to support their utopic endeavor (153).

In his excursions, as well as at camp, Stevenson found his initial impressions challenged by harsh western realities. Investigating the Silverado mine, for example, Stevenson discovered more grim statistics than frontier romance. During the Gold Rush, prospectors had searched there in vain. In the late 1850s, they had come back looking for silver, only to leave empty-handed. In the following decade, they had sold cinnabar until falling prices had turned it into a worthless commodity. After silver was discovered again in the mid-1870s, hundreds of people had settled there. When the vein of ore finally played out, most of them had left Silverado—this time for good.[6]

Mining in this region had been an environmental mistake and a costly human experiment. But in Stevenson's narrative, mining was also a colorful pastime imbued with romance. The author imagined that over the mining camp a "faint, diffused starshine" glistened like fairy dust, magically irradiating Silverado's near-distant past. Instead of emptiness and failure, he envisoned a quaint Sleepy Hollow in which the spirits of bygone miners were released from their "haunted ... obscurity" and allowed to resume their ancient activities (103). At the stamp mill, where miners once extracted ore by pounding rocks into gravel, Stevenson and wife peeked through the boards, deep into the building's interior. "Through a chink," wrote the author, "we could ... see sunbeams floating in the dust and striking on tier after tier of silent, rusty machinery." The deserted mill, like "the temple of a forgotten religion" (89), like a frontier Ozymandias, was a relic of its own grand ambitions. An abandoned shaft, filled with particles of dust that moved in and out of stray beams of light, suggested the desolation and chance nature of human experience. At the same time, a "faint, diffused starshine"—a romantic nostalgia—was evoked by the atmosphere. The trickling of water (69), which resonated deep down inside, recalled the "tide" of miners who had ebbed and flowed through the wilderness, "coming and going," now in small numbers, "now with a rush" (165). Like an enthusiastic yet skeptical tourist, peering over the edge of a precipice, Stevenson viewed the U.S. West with restrained curiosity. The uninhabited bowels of the stamp mill, like the desecrated ravine near his cabin, sparked his imagination while at the same time dampening his ardor, reminding the author that mining was a romantic adventure but also an unaesthetic and, in most cases, unsuccessful activity.

Robert Louis Stevenson and John Muir were both Scottish writers who came to California in the late nineteenth century. No two artists, however, could have been more dissimilar. While Muir settled here, falling in love with the state's scenic beauty, advocating the conservation of natural resources and the creation of national parks, Stevenson, like most tourists, was just passing through. In his literature, Muir worshiped the mountains as examples of the transcendental sublime; in his sketchbook, Stevenson described Mount St. Helena, preserving only the quaint picturesque. Whereas Muir sought to safeguard nature for the sake of posterity, Stevenson recycled it for personal use, transferring the scenery, as well as the quest for buried treasure, from the Pacific coastal frontier to the pages of his most famous novel.

II

Stevenson drafted *The Silverado Squatters* while he camped at the mine. In August 1880, he returned with his new wife to Scotland. He continued revising the manuscript during the next several years. In 1881–82, *Treasure Island* appeared as a serial in a boy's magazine. In 1883, after finishing *The Silverado Squatters*, Stevenson published the two volumes separately.

The first draft of *The Silverado Squatters*, composed before Stevenson wrote *Treasure Island*, suggests that the author was already beginning to compare his California vacation to an adventure at sea. Some of his original impressions survived in the published edition, which appeared three years later.[7] Standing on his "island" hilltop, observing the fog, which rose up like the "surf" and lapped at the mountain peaks, Stevenson exclaimed that the "Napa Valley was gone." The foothills and slopes were covered by opaque, gentle waves. In their place, "not a thousand feet below me, rolled a great level ocean. It was as though I had gone to bed the night before, safe in a nook of inland mountains, and had awakened in a bay [on] the coast" (128–29). Sometimes the cabin seemed like a ship set asail. Snuggled in their bunk beds, enveloped by candlelight, the Stevensons could imagine being transported on a romantic voyage (175).

Although Stevenson claimed that he conceived *Treasure Island* after returning to Scotland,[8] it seems clear that his trip to the frontier inspired him. While writing *The Silverado Squatters*, he began transforming his western experience into useful material. Entering the Napa Valley, he remembered having heard local reports citing travelers who had been terrorized by bandits and highwaymen: In that sense, the West was "like England [one] hundred years ago" (12). After touring the vineyards, he wrote that the "beginning of vine–planting is like the beginning of mining for the precious metals: the wine–grower also 'prospects'" he said (30). A few pages later, he indulged a fanciful whim, suggesting that an underground wine cellar resembled a bandit's cave (36). When he arrived at the mining camp, he nicknamed it "Juan Silverado" (70), creating a frontier antecedent for Long John Silver, the most famous pirate in literature.

Stevenson exported the oak trees, the dense forest undergrowth, and the snakes that he found atop Mount St. Helena, imaginarily reconstructing the scenery in a fictitious land.[9] Mapping the landscapes of Silverado and Treasure Island, which were strikingly similar, the artist created corresponding moral topographies, suggesting that the allegorical quest for mammon, which began as a reckless adventure, might end in catastrophe. At his hilltop retreat, Stevenson read nature for signs of human mortality. The decomposing leaves reminded the pensive romantic of "mummies" and "skeletons" (192). Spy-glass Hill, the novel's equivalent of Mount St. Helena, also projects an aura of romantic fatality. Here, Captain Flint murders his pirate crew, thus ensuring that no one leaves Treasure Island knowing where he has hidden his ill-gotten gains. Later, the novel's protagonists fight Long John Silver and his men at the same deadly site. The bleached bones of a skeleton, a haunting reminder of Captain Flint's crime, and the blood that the pirates spill during the novel's climactic episode,[10] resonate imagistically with a scene near the end of Stevenson's travelogue. Contemplating the damage to nature and the loss of life that occurred during mining, the author scanned the ground and saw that the "stones sparkled white in the sunshine with quartz; they were … stained red with cinnabar" (193).

Stevenson and his wife chose to go camping and to squat in a vacant shack because they were too poor to take a traditional honeymoon. Poverty may have made it easier for Stevenson to understand the desperate fortune-hunters who came West in search of success. But Silverado reminded him that the quest often went unfulfilled. *Treasure Island* serves as a parable, illustrating that some men lose their lives without finding Captain Flint's hoard, and that those who discover it don't necessarily have cause to celebrate. Marooned on the island, Ben Gunn locates the treasure but has no way of spending it. Cast out from society, like Robinson Crusoe, Gunn realizes that money has only symbolic value. When they return to England, Jim Hawkins, Dr. Livesey, and Squire Trelawney distribute the dividends. But Stevenson doesn't divulge what they do with their shares. Dismissing speculation, the author says merely that each of the men spends the money in his own way, either "wisely or foolishly" (193).

Stevenson was cheated out of a romantic ending, as were his characters. Although his previous literary efforts hadn't brought much success, the author hoped that this new work—his first novel—would turn things around. Even before he finished writing the novel, Stevenson felt convinced there was "coin in it." Later, when he learned that a magazine wanted to publish his work as a serial, he predicted that he would make this "book business pay."[11] *Treasure Island* fared modestly better than Stevenson's earlier literature. But the novel fell short of the public's as well as the author's own expectations. Boys found it "too slow, too deliberate, and lacking [enough] hectic action." Adult readers dismissed it as trivial.[12] For the book and the serial, Stevenson made less than 200 pounds.[13]

The Silverado Squatters proved even more disappointing. In revising the manuscript, Stevenson tried to instill more romance. For example, whereas the first draft compared the opening of a mine shaft to the "mouth of a tunnel," the final draft, written after Stevenson had composed *Treasure Island*, described the bleak excavation more vividly. Like a "treasure grotto in a fairy story," he insisted, it represented a place that no "boy could have left ... unexplored" (91). Stevenson imagined himself as a textual prospector, as "a miner" in a landslide, sifting through language, searching for the right words to use.[14] The "proper method of literature is by selection," he claimed. "Thus we extract the pure gold."[15] Stevenson mined his work thoroughly, "cutting, adding, rewriting"[16]—polishing the book's commercial prospects and artistic quality. However, like the men who mined Silverado, the author failed to realize his goal. Shortly after the book's publication, he confessed to a friend that the work was an "example of stuff worried and pawed about, God knows how often, in poor health, and you can see for yourself the result: good pages, an imperfect fusion, a certain langour of the whole. Not, in short, art."[17] The public shared the same view. *The Silverado Squatters* sold poorly and brought its author only 100 pounds.[18]

In 1881, one year after he left California, Stevenson published an essay on the vanity of human endeavor. Throughout the essay, Stevenson assumed a fatalistic romantic attitude, writing at one point that people would always pursue "El Dorado," even though their quests were doomed to come to "nothing ... below."[19] Alluring yet disappointing and perhaps even dangerous, Silverado, like El Dorado, was a fabled jeweled oasis, a barren frontier mirage. Like the cross on a pirate map, it suggested the existence of buried treasure and at the same time marked the site of unhallowed graves. Believing that Silverado offered a wealth of artistic material, Stevenson, like the miners before him, took risks and failed. Although his collected works eventually gained immortality, during his lifetime *The Silverado Squatters* and *Treasure Island* were no more commercially viable than the western mining enterprises on which the two works were based.

EIGHT

Little House on the Rice Paddy

I n April 1962, the White House hosted a dinner honoring American Nobel Prize–winners. Pearl Buck, the only woman among this select group of laureates, found herself seated next to First Lady Jacqueline Kennedy. Turning to Buck at one point during the evening's festivities, Mrs. Kennedy claimed that she had enjoyed reading Buck's novel *So Big*. Since Edna Ferber had won the Pulitzer Prize for this work almost forty years earlier, Buck was unsure how to respond to the First Lady's compliment. "Not wanting to embarrass her by telling her I had not written that book I merely smiled and thanked her," she confessed in a later biography.[1]

After dinner President Kennedy took Buck aside and asked her what policy she thought the United States should pursue in Korea. Buck, who was writing a novel set in that country, claimed that her work explained "the present situation in terms of the past." Buck promised to send the president a copy of the novel as soon as she finished it. But by then "he had gone to Texas," she wrote somewhat wistfully.[2]

By the early 1960s Buck was no longer considered one of the most important, or even, as the First Lady had unwittingly revealed, one of the most memorable writers in modern American literature. But she remained known as a goodwill ambassador whose novels had introduced the Far East to readers in the opposite hemisphere—whose work, as one critic has recently noted, helped bridge the "frontiers" between the United States and Asia.[3] It was therefore symbolically fitting that the president who had coined the phrase "New Frontier" should consult Buck on the subject of overseas intervention and foreign diplomacy. In accepting the Democratic National Convention's nomination for president, John F. Kennedy had challenged the Republican administration's previous isolationist policies, stating, as he stood in Los Angeles on the night of July 15, 1960, that he faced west on what was once the last U.S. frontier. After praising past pioneers who had overcome "hazards" and "hardships" to make the West "strong and free," Kennedy then told his audience that they now stood "on the edge of a New Frontier—the frontier of the 1960s ... a frontier of unfulfilled hopes and threats," represented by space exploration and new ventures into international politics.[4]

Buck was the first American writer to consistently focus the eyes of her readers on other parts of the globe. She made the Far East more visible by reminding Americans that places such as Korea, China, and India lay just beyond the horizon of the U.S. frontier. Her most famous novel, *The Good Earth* (1931), told the story of Chinese farmers weathering a plague of vicissitudes, not always triumphing over poverty, family hardships, and natural catastrophes. In its first year of publication *The Good Earth* won the Pulitzer Prize; in 1935 it received the Howells Medal of the American Academy of Arts and Letters (awarded once every five years); and in 1938 the novel was cited as one of the works responsible for earning Buck the Nobel Prize for Literature. Critics have accounted for the book's popularity—it was the nation's bestselling novel during its first two years in print[5]—by noting that the themes of "hard work, thrift, ceaseless enterprise, and the value of living close to the land" appealed during the Depression to audiences who were beginning to encounter, if not to experience, poverty, mass unemployment, and homelessness.[6]

For many U.S. readers, however, *The Good Earth* was even more historically significant and culturally relevant.[7] To live "close to the land" was not only something that the United States—an increasingly urban and economically unstable society—yearned for nostalgically, but also something that farmers in the 1930s were finding harder to do. Overzealous agricultural enterprise, commercial speculation, and intensive application of new farming technology, combined with poor weather conditions, had functioned as catalysts, precipitating dust storms that ravaged the Great Plains throughout most of the decade. The storms caused social, economic, and environmental upheaval, sweeping displaced tenants and bankrupted farmers from the regional landscape and national marketplace. *The Good Earth*, published in the same year that the dust storms began, offered solace while at the same time proposing a timely alternative. If the story of Wang Lung and O-lan inspired an audience begrimed by economic depression, the values that enabled the family of Chinese farmers to live "close to the land" were in some ways opposed to the agricultural habits and capitalistic philosophy that helped cause the Dust Bowl. *The Good Earth* critiqued the ideas and practices that eventually led in the United States to the devastation of the Great Plains frontier.

I

Until the mid–nineteenth century, the Great Plains (including portions of Oklahoma and Texas and parts of western Kansas, southeast Colorado, and northeast New Mexico) were perceived as "menacing" and "Asiatic" in character. The region, considered too dry for white farming and settlement, was populated by migratory Indian tribes that were considered "uncivilized." Comparisons between these tribes and the Bedouins of the Arabian desert or the Tartars of the Asiatic steppes were common, according to Henry Nash Smith.[8] Reinforcing this perception was the fact that the north China plains, like the U.S. Great Plains, had a harsh climate and barren topography. Deforestation, accomplished over a period of centuries, had made northern China increasingly more vulnerable to erosion and drought. Rainfall on this treeless expanse, which equaled the amount of precipitation on the western Great Plains, averaged twenty to twenty-five inches per year. Because it lacked moisture and ground cover, the north China plains produced dust storms in winter and spring, when dry winds traditionally swept through the area.[9]

In the mid– and late nineteenth century, widespread support for Manifest Destiny altered the public's perception of both the U.S. and Chinese frontiers. During this period, land promoters, railroad agents, and journalists, seeking to encourage U.S. migration and settlement, represented the Great Plains as a potential garden instead of a desert.[10] Correspondingly, missionaries, scholars, and tourists started envisioning northern China in a more favorable light. While still describing the region's landscape as hostile and the Chinese practice of farming as "primitive," writers now sensed the same possibility for change and improvement that they found on the western Great Plains. As a result of this gradual reassessment of China, the Far East was seen as a target for U.S. expansion. In 1894, having served as an overseas missionary for 22 years, Arthur H. Smith published *Chinese Characteristics*, one of the most popular works on China in the late nineteenth century. Claiming that Chinese farmers were industrious laborers, held back by lack of technology, stagnant social conditions, and a fundamental cultural resistance to change, Smith argued that peasants needed help moving from the dark ages into the dawning millennium.[11] The notion that northern China could be "improved" agriculturally gained ground throughout the early decades of the twentieth century. One U.S. critic compared Chinese farming to gardening, observing that the average Chinese family used old-fashioned tools to cultivate small plots of land. According to the writer, the "triumph of individual skill unaided by organized knowledge" constituted the barbaric art of a "pre-scientific age."[12]

The representation of the Great Plains as a garden instead of a desert, as well as other incentives—the passage of the Homestead Act of 1862, the ongoing removal and containment of Indians, the disappearance of huge herds of cattle from the Great Plains after the winter of 1885–86, and the introduction and refinement of the plow, along with other forms of technology—contributed in the United States to the general increase in farming by the late nineteenth century. During this period, having tentatively conquered and settled the Great Plains, the nation continued to expand economically, traveling westward until the Far East became the next U.S. frontier. By 1870 the nation was beginning to sell its surplus crops overseas,[13] whereas China, with 85 percent of its population living and working on farms, still couldn't feed itself without importing food from abroad.[14] Thus the United States identified China as a fresh market that it could exploit economically. Nine years after the "closing" of the frontier, as Frederick Jackson Turner had proclaimed with finality, came the formulation of America's "Open Door" policy, ushering the West into a world of new opportunities.[15]

Along with the effort to cultivate China's economic frontier went the U.S. attempt to tame the frontier's inhabitants. *The Oldest and the Newest Empire* (1870), Protestant missionary William Speer's cross-cultural comparison of the Far East and the American West, sought to substantiate the relationship between Chinese and Indians. Speer speculated that "aboriginal" races in the New World were of Asian descent. Working backward, he theorized that the continent's history of converting North

American Indians had effectively established a precedent, giving the United States the divine right to found overseas missions to convert "heathen Chinee."[16] Theodore Roosevelt also imagined the interaction between China and the United States as a "struggle between Red Men and White"— "between 'progressive' and 'savage' or 'regressive' races."[17] Between the late 1890s and the early 1900s, however, Roosevelt perfected a multipronged Progressive attack, one that would lead to the conquest of China and the creation of an informal empire, brought about not by military defeat but by cultural and social reform.[18]

The emigration of U.S. missionaries to China constituted one strategy of social control. Although Protestant missions had operated in China since around 1830, they expanded in number and purpose after the U.S. announcement in 1899 of its "Open Door" policy. The failure of the Chinese Boxer Rebellion in the following year encouraged those who had feared that the country was hostile to foreigners. Among the new arrivals were agricultural missionaries, who came to teach modern farming techniques as well as to save souls. By the 1920s and 1930s, Christian agronomists had begun administering government programs and infiltrating schools, preaching a curriculum of social science, agricultural technology, and Christian theology.[19]

One of these agricultural missionaries was John Lossing Buck. Born in 1890 on a farm near Poughkeepsie, New York, Buck graduated from Cornell, then a state agricultural college, in 1914. The following year he went overseas and was stationed at Nansuzhou, in the province of Anhui, on the north China plains. Three years later he married Pearl Sydenstricker, a missionary's daughter who had grown up in China. In 1921 Buck accepted a position at the University of Nanking, and eventually a professorship in the College of Agriculture, where he taught courses over the following years in economics, rural sociology, farm engineering, and management.[20]

The overthrow of the Manchu Dynasty in 1911, and the subsequent revolutions brought about by the Republican and Nationalist governments, made China more eager to modernize. Eventually Buck realized, however, that many U.S. farming techniques couldn't—or shouldn't— be applied on the north China plains. The tractor and combine had been introduced on the Great Plains by the late 1920s. But while flatland farming had lent itself to the implementation of automated technology, it had forced U.S. owners, who had discovered that they could farm more efficiently, to lay off workers and take out loans to pay for new expensive machinery. In order to recoup their losses, farmers had continued to plow even more land and to gamble on the market by planting single cash crops. The results had been the depletion of grass-land and the tilling of too much loose soil; the ebbing of small-time ranchers and farmers and the swelling of a new tenant underclass; increased debt, crop speculation, and a growing dependence on market trends.[21]

In order to teach Chinese students, Buck decided that he would have to learn Chinese ways. Sending his students to collect data from farms in the countryside, while at the same time going with his wife to visit dozens of villages, Buck slowly gathered enough information on sea-sonal planting and harvesting schedules, local seed varieties, and crop yields to form his conclusions. In 1930, after compiling and synthesiz-ing the data, Buck finally published his scholarship. *Chinese Farm Econ-omy*, a study of nearly 3,000 farms, advocated the increased use of chemical fertilizers, the practice of scientific seed selection, and the development of insect control. (It also recommended moral reforms concerning gambling, smoking opium, and "other unfortunate forms of self-indulgence," which were thought to decrease farm productivity.[22]) But Buck also noted that adapting to U.S. ways was not always practi-cal. Chinese peasants were too poor to purchase—and their farms were too small to accommodate—reapers, mowers, steam plows, seed drills, and harrows. While denouncing the need for U.S. technology, Buck praised the pre-industrial methods that had traditionally enabled the Chinese to farm so efficiently. Although they farmed less land per capita, the Chinese yielded more food per acre. In part this was due to northern China's longer growing season, which made it possible to grow two crops per year. But in large part it was due to intensive labor and sheer ingenuity. For example, Buck noted that Chinese workers cultivated fields without the aid of machinery and that they used urine and feces to fertilize crops that had never been treated with chemicals.

Scholars have rightly accused Buck of exercising a judgmental bias, comparing the United States and China without taking into account crucial differences.[23] Because he tended to focus on farming exclusively, Buck turned a blind eye to politics, failing to foresee that the growth and development of a militant peasantry, which was visibly present by the late 1920s in most Chinese villages, would one day lead to the collectivization of farms by the Communists. Buck also suffered from cultural and religious myopia. His western perspective and blind faith in Christian ideals caused him to criticize certain Chinese traditions, beliefs, and activities. Nevertheless, as one intellectual historian has testified, Buck was "perhaps the most important Western analyst of China's rural social conditions who worked in this century."[24] His textbook, which served as a manual for training several generations of Chinese agricultural economists, was among the first to acknowledge China's own real accomplishments.

In the years prior to the book's publication, Pearl Buck joined her husband on his fact–finding travels. Because she spoke fluent Chinese, she served during interviews with farmers and villagers as her husband's interpreter. When his eyesight diminished, as it did for a time in the late 1920s, Buck typed her husband's reports and (as one biographer has suggested) may have helped write his manuscript.[25] Observing local farm life firsthand, Pearl Buck came to realize that the Chinese were harder working and more economical than their American counterparts. If anything, she grasped this fact sooner than her expert companion did. As she wrote in her autobiography, years after their divorce, Buck grew disturbed as she followed her husband on his scientific excursions, gradually beginning to suspect that "he had more to learn than to teach." She wondered secretly what a young agricultural theorist could teach Chinese farmers who had been living for generations on the same plot of land and who "were still able to produce extraordinary yields ... without modern machinery. Whole families lived in simple comfort upon farms averaging less than five acres and certainly I had known of no Western agriculture that could compete with this."[26] *The Good Earth*, published the year after her husband's book, made this same point more famously. In what was to become one of the most widely read novels of the early twentieth century, Buck implicitly criticized U.S. methods of modernization by celebrating Chinese tradition, land conservation, and lack of technology.

II

In a review published in the *New York Times* shortly after the novel appeared, Will Rogers called *The Good Earth* "the best book of our generation," urging people to "get this and read it." (Later, Buck claimed that Rogers' endorsement had been the single most crucial factor in establishing the book's popularity.[27]) In the story of Wang Lung and O-lan—who live in a sod house on the plains of north China, enduring droughts, floods, wind storms, and locust plagues—Rogers, a son of the

Great Plains, may have identified a dramatic scenario that he thought other U.S. readers would recognize.

The novel represents the "good earth" as a Chinese farmer's most precious commodity. When Wang Lung tells O-lan that they should purchase rice fields from the great House of Hwang, rather than hoard all their savings, he reasons: "Land is one's flesh and blood."[28] Later, when his family, suffering from starvation and poverty, fends off a mob that thinks that the farmer has food and money hidden inside his home, Wang Lung thinks triumphantly: "They cannot take the land from me. The labor of my body and the fruit of the fields I have put into that which cannot be taken away" (53). But after good fortune comes again, Wang Lung squanders his riches on a faithless young concubine. Enfeebled by the "sickness of love," he finds strength in "the good dark earth of his fields" (153). In old age and prosperity, he returns to the sod house where he lived as a young man and decides to be buried there, replanting his roots "in his own land forever" (257).

The family is an extension of Wang Lung's ambition as well as a symbol of rural prosperity. By successfully sowing his wife, Wang Lung reaps a daughter and three healthy sons. Buck portrays O-lan as an earth mother, emphasizing the character's sexual fertility and maternal excess. When she squats to give birth, her blood soaks the ground (26). Her breast milk flows uncontrollably when she nurses her children, who are "as brown as the soil" (29). O-lan's breasts symbolically encompass the source of all wealth: In a pouch that she hides here she keeps jewels that Wang Lung can use to buy property (104). Raising a family and sacrificing her possessions in order to leave her husband a legacy, O-lan finally yields up her life, claiming at the end: "I must die.... But the land is there after me" (185).

Initially, the relationship between the farmers and the landscape is intimate, like the early years in the marriage between Wang Lung and O-lan. Unlike their contemporary U.S. counterparts, who relied on technology, Wang Lung and O-lan make do with human labor, coarse tools, and animals, following in the footsteps of tradition and never sowing more than they can harvest through their own modest means. Wang Lung plows his fields with an ox, plants his crops with a hoe, and transports water and fertilizer in crude earthen buckets (33). O-lan uses a handmade rake to collect manure and dry grass for fuel (20). The couple cuts the wheat with short-handled scythes (25), beats it with flails, and winnows the grain in large bamboo baskets (29). Buck's idealization of peasant labor implies a critique of modern technology. In giving dignity to traditional Chinese methods of farming, Buck validates a "pure" way of life that is unadulterated by contemporary outside influences. *The Good Earth* lends truth to Richard White's observation that the sentimentalization of forms of "archaic work, most typically the farming of peasants," has been due in part to the demonization of machinery in twentieth-century literature.[29] Buck presents China to the rest of the world as an exotic alternative, as a quaint corner of the globe in which pre-industrial laborers still interact with their natural environment "authentically," in a holistic, unmediated, mutually sustaining relationship.

At the same time that she romanticizes North China's peasantry, Buck, like other writers during this period, realistically acknowledges that Chinese farmers were both more backward and more advanced than their U.S. competitors. Instead of growing one crop each year, farmers in north China planted wheat in the winter and sorghum, millet, or maize in the spring. On the Great Plains, where the seasons were shorter but the climate was similar, farmers who refused to diversify and who gambled on wheat as a single cash crop could go bankrupt if the weather or the marketplace performed unfavorably. Double-cropping, Buck's husband noted, utilized the land more effectively, distributed labor and income over a greater part of the year, and minimized the importance of crop failure.[30] In plotting the routines of her characters, Buck also graphs the economic benefits of Chinese farming and enterprise. In *The Good Earth*, by working continuously, Wang Lung and O-lan manage to cultivate every spare strip of land. After harvesting wheat in the spring, they flood their fields and plant rice (113). In addition, they raise barley and corn, garlic and onions (20), and gardens devoted to squash, beans, and celery (32, 43). A Depression-era novel depicting the hardships of rural life, *The Good Earth* features thrift, hard work, and grim self-sufficiency, as opposed to resource wastefulness, laissez-faire land practices, and cycles of poverty, which were contributing in the United States, at the time of the book's publication, to economic depression and environmental catastrophe.

In 1937 the Great Plains Committee, appointed by President Franklin D. Roosevelt, in singling out factors that had led to the Dust Bowl, reported to Congress that by the mid-1930s between 41 and 51 percent of farms in the Great Plains region were operated by tenants, not owners.[31] Donald Worster, the Great Plains historian, claims that tenancy

A photograph from Dodge City, Kansas, entitled "Sunday, April 14, 1935. Dust Clouds Rolling Over The Prairies." (The Denver Public Library, Western History Department.)

rates increased in the fifty years leading up to the Dust Bowl as the result of a spreading "frontier" mentality. An "environmental ethic of conquest" dictated that sod busters had the right to strip land, reap profits, and move again.[32] On the Great Plains, the rate of mobility, coupled with an inclination to view the land as disposable, meant that tenants and sharecroppers were more interested in realizing quick profits than they were in maintaining the soil for posterity. In China, however, there was little migration, due to the size of the nation's land mass, poor transportation, poverty, and the tendency of families to pass farms to sons through the rite of inheritance. Thus rural dwellers, such as Wang Lung and O-lan, were more apt to view the ancestral land-scape as "home."[33]

Buck sets her novel on the North China plains. Here, in a region that Buck and her husband knew had one of the world's lowest tenant rates,[34] preserving the farm—and returning to it—is the overwhelming obsession of the book's central character. Wang Lung refuses to sell his land when the famine comes, for example, even though his family faces death by starvation. "I will dig up the fields and feed the earth itself to the children," he threatens, "and when they die I will bury them" (61). After making his fortune, however, he loses touch with the soil. The more property Wang Lung acquires, the further removed he becomes from it. Renting out some of his land and hiring employees to work on the rest of it, Wang Lung retreats to his counting house, trusting others with the day-to-day supervision of his business affairs while he concentrates on finance and marketing. But in old age, as he lies on his deathbed, he repents and gains wisdom. "Out of the land we came and into it we must go—and if you will hold your land you can live—no one can rob you of land," he says (260).

The Good Earth has frequently been regarded as an anomaly in American literature. Buck's expert native knowledge of China—its people and language, its landscape and customs—enabled her to write a novel that seems authentically "foreign." *The Good Earth*, however, can best be contextualized by comparing it with *The Grapes of Wrath* (1939), John Steinbeck's critique of Dust-Bowl America. In their shared distaste for tenancy, land abuse, and modern technology; in their parallel stories of poor, uneducated, uprooted farmers trying to get back to the land; in their representations of earth-mothers (O-lan/Ma Joad) who hold their respective families together; and even in their use of sentimental conventions and vaguely biblical writing styles, *The Good Earth* and *The Grapes of Wrath*—appearing at the beginning and the end of the decade, respectively—strike one as remarkably similar.

Yet the works also reveal certain differences. For example, in telling the story of white farmers who migrated West, Steinbeck ignores Chinese, Filipino, and Mexican immigrants who also came to California during the Depression to work in orchards and fields. Buck rights this imbalance, universalizing and defamiliarizing her story by making her "typical" family Chinese. But the Joads, unlike Wang Lung, come to realize that they are pawns in the universe, not just farmers at the mercy of weather but workers in an economically unstable and politically unequal society. Although victimized by the old aristocracy, revolutionary warlords, and foreigners, Wang Lung never feels anything other than the slings and arrows of nature's outrageous fortune. "Ah, I have heard of a Revolution, but I have been too busy in my life to attend to it. There was always the land," he says (256). War is good, he propounds, because it creates scarcity and thus raises grain prices, not because it liberates the oppressed Chinese peasantry (232). Wang Lung's farm tools are ancient, his harvesting techniques are inefficient and outdated, and his paltry food stores are constantly raided by brigands. But no situation is so dire that it can't be rescued by the arrival of rain or sunshine from heaven (90).

The fate of Wang Lung's family is determined primarily by the natural environment, not by economic and political forces, heredity, or social conditioning.[35] Philosophically, *The Good Earth* mirrors Walter Prescott Webb's classic study, *The Great Plains* (1931), published in the same year as Buck's famous novel. Using Hayden White's terminology, one might say that the "mode of emplotment" in *The Great Plains* follows the dictates of tragedy.[36] Webb characterizes the Great Plains as a distinct western region defined by three tragic unities: flat land, lack of ground vegetation, and a dry or "sub-humid" climate. According to Webb, these "constant and eternal" forces of nature have had a flawed effect on farmers who settle there.[37] Webb's fatalistic assessment came as something of a shock to Americans who had believed for generations that they could conquer the Great Plains eventually. But in his dry-eyed analysis, Webb used geographic data, scientific statistics, and historical evidence to refute this myth, stating prophetically that "the prospects for agriculture in the Great Plains, taken as a whole, are not very encouraging."[38] Six years later, the Great Plains Committee, having studied the causes and effects of the Dust Bowl, added a tragic chorus that resonated with Webb's dire conclusion. Mortal endeavors, the committee wrote in its report to the president, aided by an unregulated marketplace and modern technology, had failed to transform the nation's desert into a garden, proving instead that "Nature is inflexible" and demands human conformity.[39]

The Good Earth sent the same message, phrased slightly more optimistically: people on the plains could persevere but not always triumph in the face of disasters caused by drought, insect infestation, and wind. The similarity between Webb's depiction of the Great Plains and Buck's view of rural Chinese society—the presentation of the same naturalistic landscape in which struggling farmers dramatized the human condition—meant that U.S. readers in the 1930s would have noticed something familiar in Buck's description of the stark, barren countryside, as opposed to the city, which in Buck's novel was represented as too "foreign" to recognize.

Although Buck has been hailed as the first novelist in the western hemisphere to write about China without resorting to bias, she has only half-earned the compliment. When *The Good Earth* was first published, the *New York Times Book Review* claimed that the novel offered no "mystery or exoticism," no racial stereotypes that the public might brand "Oriental."[40] The *Saturday Review of Literature* assured readers that "the China of fantasy so often exploited" in fiction was absent here.[41] Since then, most critics have agreed that Buck's greatest accomplishment was writing a novel in which she replaced "fantasy images of China and the Chinese held by most Americans with a somewhat more realistic picture of what China was like and a new, more intimate, and more appealing picture of the Chinese themselves."[42] But in fact, like a group of western writers whom Edward Said has identified, Buck characterizes Chinese cities as sites of "Oriental" splendor and decadence.[43] Pitting these lush urban centers against the austere Chinese countryside, Buck makes the rural setting of *The Good Earth* seem more "Occidental" and thus, in spite of its harshness and barrenness, more benign by comparison.

Although she was fluent in Chinese, Buck included only one Chinese word in her narrative. She used the word *li* in the text, on a single occasion, to emphasize the distance between Wang Lung's farm and the city: "it was far away, more than a *li* which is a third of a mile" (38). In *The Good Earth*, the farm is familiar turf, while the city is foreign, distant, and dangerous. The city is the site of the great House of Hwang. Here, the wicked Old Lord bestows oriental jade earrings on his nubile young concubines (48). The Old Mistress, his consort, "a very old lady, her small fine body clothed in lustrous, pearly grey satin," spends her days smoking opium (12). The great House in the south, in the city where Wang Lung takes his family to look for work when the famine comes, also displays symptoms of decadence. When a mob breaks in and ransacks the palace, the peasants discover finely carved furniture and lacquered walls hung with rare painted scrolls (97). In a secret bedchamber, they find an obese "yellow" man lounging wantonly (98). His skin, like that of the Old Mistress—a "gilt" (yellow) "idol" (12)—has an unhealthy hue. By contrast, the skin of the farmers is brown like the soil (14, 29)—not "colored" but neutral; not a marker of "otherness" but a symbol (like the good earth, another global common denominator) of standardized "normalcy."[44]

In *The Good Earth*, the fact that the city is interpreted as a "foreign" environment means that the Chinese countryside can be recognized by U.S. readers as a "local" terrain. Years after writing the novel, while traveling through Kansas, Buck noticed how closely the surrounding landscape resembled the North China plains.[45] Earlier, however, at least one other artist suggested the very same parallel. In 1935 Victor Fleming was chosen to direct the film version of *The Good Earth*, replacing George Hill, who had died. While in China to work out location shots, Fleming came down with malaria and was forced to resign from the project.[46] His experience with *The Good Earth*, however, influenced his work on a later film. In *The Good Earth*, an opening scene depicts Wang Lung standing nervously outside the open gates of the great House of Hwang. In the novel, the gatekeeper stands on the threshold and interrogates Wang Lung before letting him in (10). But in a restaging of the same scene on camera, the gatekeeper peers through a peephole and questions his visitor before opening the gates and escorting a meek and dazzled Wang Lung down a cavernous passageway. Fleming reinvented this scene two years later in his film adaptation of *The Wizard of Oz* (1939), in which Dorothy, seeking admittance to the renowned Emerald City, begs the gatekeeper for permission to enter and speak to the Wizard.[47] In the novel, Buck's distinction between the urban and rural spheres would have prejudiced U.S. readers to make the same choice as Dorothy, who prefers Kansas to Oz. Compared to the great House of Hwang, the great plains of China more closely resembled some place like "home."

III

The western historian Ray Allen Billington once proposed an intriguing hypothesis. What would have happened, he wondered, if China had settled the United States in the early eighth century? Initially, perhaps, the Chinese would have ventured across the North American continent in gorgeous silk robes, building Buddhist shrines and flooding fields to form rice paddies. But eventually, he suspected, the Chinese would have discovered that silk robes were less resistant to weather than clothes made of fur pelts and hides; that wheat and corn were more likely to grow in the wilderness; and that the "decrees of a distant emperor were easily ignored by a people whose unique problems demanded unique local solutions" on the new Chinese frontier.[48]

Like Walter Prescott Webb, Billington argued that explorers and settlers throughout U.S. history had—to some extent—always been forced to conform to their surrounding environment. Imagine the most extreme culture clash possible: If China were transplanted to the U.S. frontier, he suggested rhetorically, how could it possibly thrive? Although such a scenario was difficult for Billington to envision, it wasn't too hard for Hollywood. Preparing to film *The Good Earth* in the mid-1930s, MGM hired employees to travel to China; to purchase whole farms and villages, lock, stock, and barrel; and to ship these "sets" stateside, where they could be reassembled by studio engineers and designers. In re-creating and, for almost two years, cultivating and maintaining an "actual" Chinese landscape and rural society, Hollywood proved that it could, in fact, triumph over circumstances and the surrounding environment, ironically contradicting the main point of Buck's novel.

MGM sent expeditions to China in 1933–34, having ordered its employees to buy as many "props" as they could. Going from village to village, on the North China plains, scouts with cash in their hands would approach farmers and ask: "How much—for everything?" They purchased wooden plows, harrows, and flails; water buckets, baskets, and matting; stone grain–grinding mills, windmills, and water wheels. They assembled their own ark, filling it with water buffalo, pigs and ducks, donkeys, and pigeons. In addition to looting houses—taking gongs, ivory needles and toys, colored joss papers, China temple dogs, sundials, bronzes, earthenware water pots, and old teakwood furni-ture—the invading army from Hollywood sacked the houses them-selves. What they couldn't dismantle, pack, and export, they filmed on location—shooting the scenery and, in one case, even "renting" a funeral.[49]

The studio leased 500 acres in the Santa Clara Hills, located on semi-desert land twenty miles outside of Hollywood. Here art directors and carpenters reassembled the village and city sets. On a plain they con-structed a high walled enclosure, surrounding it with a moat and filling the moat with sampans and fish nets. They built a bridge leading to a gate in the stone wall surrounding the village, and connected the bridge to a main street featuring more than 200 shops selling roast pork, dried duck, and fresh "local" produce. A group of Chinese farmers, headed by Yee On, a transplanted native, terraced the hillsides on the sides of the canyon walls; planted onions, leeks, water chestnuts, Chi-nese cabbage, and radishes on the floor of the valley; sowed wheat by hand; and pumped water into a manmade river that irrigated (and sometimes flooded) the fields. Eight months of intensive farming were required to artificially reproduce or wither crops, which needed to appear to be growing or dying in each of the four different seasons. The studio erected a weather bureau on the set and operated it twenty-four

hours each day. If clouds beckoned rain, the crew filmed in rice paddies; if statisticians predicted light desert winds, the actors performed in
scenes that called for dust storms and drought.[50] Behind the scenes,
expert Chinese farmers and laborers, with the help of U.S. money, art,
and technology, transformed Buck's story of one family's war against
nature into a wide–fought, expensive, technologically sophisticated,
successful campaign.

In *The Day of the Locust* (1939), Nathanael West satirized the way in
which popular culture sapped the essence of 1930s society by comparing Hollywood's parasitic conversion of life and art into film with the
sweeping environmental devastation wrought by a locust plague.
Accounts of the attack that Hollywood launched overseas, in the
process of bringing *The Good Earth* to film, perhaps unintentionally
remind one of West's famous metaphor. One report claims that after an
encounter with one of the search–and–destroy missions run by the studio, a Chinese farmer would typically be left "with more money than he
had ever had in his life, standing before the bare walls of the house on
his denuded farm—and wondering what crazy sort of people these
'fan-quai' or Foreign Devils might be!"[51]

But the locust plague that it recreated for audiences was an even
better example of MGM's industry. The film version of *The Good Earth*
was dedicated to producer Irving Thalberg, who died before the project
was finished. Thalberg had a reputation for making sure that each of
his films featured at least one magnificent sequence or spectacle—in
this case, a locust plague. The scene, which occurred midway through
the novel, lasting only two pages, was expanded and moved to the end
of the script, where it climaxed the film.[52] But instead of symbolizing a
Nathanael West(ern) apocalypse, the locust plague finally celebrated
the advantages of U.S. science and enterprise.

Initially the studio decided to splice the film, using existing stock
footage of an African locust storm. Sidney Franklin, the film's third and
final director, wasn't happy with this sequence, however, and ordered
that a huge white screen be built in Los Angeles. Here tiny pieces of
burned cork were shot out of pressure guns. Wind machines blew the
airborne projectiles against the screen, cinematographers filmed the
strange spectacle, and editors mixed the footage with scenes of the
plague shot in Africa, which was then double–exposed against actors
performing on location outdoors. While *The Good Earth* was filming in
1936, a consultant on the production, one of the state's top entymolo-

gists, informed the studio that the grasshoppers moving through Utah at the time were the same insects (cicadas) that visited China once every seventeen years. After learning this, the project's assistant director flew to Utah, filmed scenes of the plague then in progress, and brought barrels of the live insects back to California, where he shot closeups of Chinese extras "lying on the ground, with thousands of grasshoppers crawling all over them." The final sequence—a "Chinese" locust plague, photographed in the United States and Africa, utilizing hundreds of stunt doubles, homemade special effects, and ingenious camera technology—caused a sensation and helped the film, on its initial release, gross the enormous sum of more than $3 million.[53]

If Buck's novel celebrated the dignity of poor, uneducated Chinese farmers, abiding by traditional ways, then the film, which was a product of Hollywood, advertised what advanced technology, creative

A hollywood replica of the Chinese village in MGM's *The Good Earth*. A dark cloud forms on the horizon as the locusts appear. (Courtesy Academy of Motion Picture Arts and Sciences. © 1937 Turner Entertainment Co. All rights reserved.)

enterprise, and U.S. money could buy. An army of moguls and studio headhunters, backed up by a corps of engineers, designers, and carpenters, and led by corporate decision makers investing more than $2.8 million,[54] combined their forces to seize, ship home, and rebuild a few Chinese farms and one tiny village. Some of the greatest visionaries and finest minds in the industry spent several years and huge sums of money transforming a portion of the U.S. West into an impoverished rural Chinese community, striving to simulate a world of simplicity by means of complex invention and artifice.

The locust plague, a disaster afflicting Wang Lung and his family, was turned into spectacle. In addition to entertaining a mass western audience, the big-screen finale, as well as the preproduction work and behind-the-scenes preparations, sent the same can-do message: that education, science, and enterprise were better than tradition, superstition, and ignorance; that new/U.S. methods were better than old/Chinese ways; and that these new methods would enable future generations to correct past mistakes that had been made in both the United States and China. In the novel, Wang Lung battles the plague, which he believes has been ordained by the heavens. He rallies the villagers, telling them to set several wheat fields on fire in order to drive off the locusts with smoke. He supervises the construction of fire breaks and digs moats for drowning the descending locusts in water (168–69). In the film, however, one of Wang Lung's sons conceives this plan of attack. According to the son, who attends university and who wears glasses to convey his "intelligence," the plague isn't heaven-sent. "It's a thing of nature," he claims. "We can fight it." He issues the same set of orders that his father gives in the novel to ward off the plague. (The son adds a few "extra" touches, starting the fire with kerosene and suggesting that the farmers beat pots and pans to scare off the predators. "It's nothing ... just something we learned from books," he claims modestly.) Whereas Buck's husband, teaching in a Chinese university, had discovered that traditional Chinese farming methods were sometimes superior, Wang Lung's son, who has cut his queue as a sign of his intention to adopt western ways, knows that the wisdom he has acquired at his new university will help save an older illiterate generation of conservative villagers. In a manner that is heavy-handed and sometimes unintentionally humorous, the film emphasizes the virtues of education, progress, and modernization, and concludes with the triumph of human beings over nature.[55]

Reportedly, when Thalberg told MGM that he wanted to film *The Good Earth*, Louis B. Mayer said, "Irving, the public won't buy pictures about American farmers. And you want to give them *Chinese* farmers?"[56] In fact, Pare Lorentz's landmark documentary, *The Plow That Broke the Plains* (1936), which detailed abusive farm practices that had led to the development of dust bowls in the early and mid–1930s, had opened to mixed reviews and lack of public enthusiasm a year before the release of MGM's film. Lorentz's work, which had been funded by the national government for the purpose of demonstrating the need for New Deal reforms, had been perceived by some viewers as overly propagandistic, depressing, and critical.[57] But *The Good Earth* was conceived and directed in Hollywood. Thalberg made sure that the film stressed the love story of Wang Lung and O-lan, that it entertained the audience with "Oriental" spectacles and thrilling effects, and that it made any messages, based on comparisons between the United States and China, uplifting and nonintellectual.

As a result, reviews and interpretations of *The Good Earth* were positive. The film premiered in the spring of 1937, just as a grasshopper plague was attacking the Great Plains, in the worst year of the Dust Bowl thus far.[58] The *Motion Picture Herald*, covering the film's opening in New York and Los Angeles, noted prophetically that a "certain special timeliness, a coincidence of fate, favors 'The Good Earth's' premiere, in that it is a story very much of man against nature—just as the United States, emerging from the scourge of drought from the 'dust bowl,' now suffers the devastation of flood. Understanding for the theme of this romantic tragedy from the plains of China may be had from the experiences of America."[59] The reporter concluded that the film was "wartime" propaganda disguised as Hollywood spectacle. In the United States in the late 1930s, the dark clouds of locusts, which swarmed on the Chinese horizon, could only be understood as the cinematic equivalent of dust bowls that audiences knew to exist in reality. The success of Wang Lung and his family in fighting the locust plague gave besieged U.S. citizens reason to hope that they could win their own war with nature.

The Good Earth, appearing at the beginning of the decade, merely intended to offer its readers a look at an honorable, old–fashioned, "quaint" way of life. It was timely coincidence that Buck published *The Good Earth* in the year that the dust bowls began. As the decade progressed, however, and the dust storms raged on, *The Good Earth* gathered rhetorical momentum, acquiring cultural and historical force. Hollywood now recognized parallels, rather than differences, between Wang Lung's misfortunes and the Great Plains catastrophe. As part of the entertainment industry's mission in the Depression era to revivify and rally its audience, MGM deliberately embellished these parallels. In the film adaptation, the strategies for fighting the locust plague (essentially the same ones as those described in the novel), although they still seem unchanged and "primitive," are now represented as educated alternatives based on advanced ways of thinking. The film edits out and replaces Buck's message, substituting the notion that progress improves on tradition, and gives the most "advanced" nation on earth reason to believe that it has nothing to learn from the good earth or history.

NINE

The Queer Frontier

In an essay on James Fenimore Cooper, published in *Studies in Classic American Literature* (1923), D. H. Lawrence recognized a special love between men. Lawrence claimed that the friendship between Natty Bumppo and Chingachgook constituted a "new human relationship"—one that was "deeper than fatherhood, deeper than marriage," "deeper than the deeps of sex," he enthused.[1] Beginning in the 1950s, Leslie A. Fiedler, who was indebted to Lawrence, wrote about the pervasiveness of male same-sex relationships in western American literature. However, while seeming to celebrate the homosocial and homoerotic, Fiedler inadvertently revealed his own homophobia. By defining frontier alliances between white men and Indians such as Natty Bumppo and Chingachgook—between "civilization" and "savagery"—as "sexless and holy" relationships, Fiedler stigmatized unions that weren't strictly celibate.[2] If platonic friendships were examples of "innocent homosexuality," as Fiedler maintained,[3] then sexually consummated relationships must be guilt-ridden, impure, and debased by comparison.

Fiedler claimed that the western glorified pure same-sex love.[4] But for Fiedler, "the West" was a loose term that signified any unsettled region existing outside society, and "the western" was broadly identified as any work dealing with white men who fled from society, establishing

interethnic frontier fraternities.[5] Hence, for Fiedler, the western included nontraditional and nonregional works, such as Huckleberry
Finn's adventures with Jim and Ernest Hemingway's short stories dealing with Indians, which were set in the South and in the northern Midwest, respectively.

Fiedler's definition of the western is idiosyncratic, somewhat un-
convincing, and vague, as definitions of the western historically tend to
be. Just as we argue today whether the West is a place or a process, a
state of mind, or simply a misleading and imprecise term, so we continue to debate whether westerns can be classified and judged according to one single formula. Films by John Ford; pulp fiction by Zane
Grey and Louis L'Amour; heterogeneous works by Walter Van Tilburg
Clark, E. L. Doctrow, and others ... How can we identify what these
westerns all have in common?

The presence of male same-sex relationships may not serve as a lit-
mus test. But these relationships occur more frequently, consistently,
and explicitly in westerns than they do elsewhere in literature. At the
heart of most westerns are male friendships and rivalries, complex
love-hate relationships. The association between a white man, who
represents "civilization," and a black man or Indian, who represents
"savagery," serves as the model for same-sex relationships. Occasional
variations only reinforce this basic unchanging paradigm. Sometimes,
for instance, a white man identifies with another white man who—by
virtue of his comparison with the racialized and socially ostracized
"other"—also represents "savagery." Together the white man and his
seducer, the outlaw, enjoy a same-sex relationship, a potentially dangerous transgressive love, outside the realms of society.

I

The Virginian, one of the early prototypes of the western and one of the
bestselling novels of 1902, features two white men who adopt transgressive identities in the process of enacting a same-sex relationship.
While one man becomes "black," at least metaphorically, the other one
imagines himself as a woman attracted to the racial "other" and consumed by forbidden desire. As the novel begins, the narrator arrives in
Wyoming to visit his old friend, Judge Henry, who owns a large cattle
ranch. Judge Henry has sent one of his ranch hands, the Virginian, to
meet the train at the station and to escort the narrator back to Sunk
Creek. Stepping onto the platform, the narrator observes the Virginian

teasing an elderly bachelor who has suddenly decided to marry. Mentally comparing the Virginian, a virile young man, with the bridegroom-to-be, the narrator comments, "Had I been the bride, I should have taken the giant."[6] In the cowboy's "face, in his step, in the whole man, there dominated a something potent to be felt, I should think, by man or woman," he reasons (6).

The bride in this scene becomes the unnamed narrator, whose anonymity throughout the text facilitates his shift in identity. Assuming the role of the cowboy's romantic companion, the narrator imagines himself in a hypothetical western marriage of males. Later, when the cowboy woos the schoolmarm and, on one occasion, shyly offers Molly a smile, the narrator claims that, "had I been a woman, [I would have let him] do what he pleased" (157). How could Molly resist such a seductive entreaty, he pleads with the audience? "I cannot tell you, having never (as I said before) been a woman myself" (160). Although he reminds the audience of his gender repeatedly, instead of soothing the reader's anxiety he disrupts the narrative—like Shakespeare's lady, by protesting too much, by inserting an unnecessarily obvious parenthetical clause: "as I said before."

By moving from civilized eastern to primitive frontier society, the narrator trangresses boundaries and breaches social decorum, entering into a symbolic interracial, homoerotic relationship with another ostracized male. The enigmatic Virginian—the archetypal cowboy, the outcast, the loner—like the narrator has no given birth name, no social identity, and only one physical attribute that the narrator comments on. His black hair (18) inspires a nickname that emphasizes the Virginian's uniqueness. "Who is that black man?" asks Molly, when the black-haired "stranger" appears at a dance sponsored by the local community (71). Even on the frontier, where men and women live in isolation from established society, the "black man" exists in his own separate sphere. Compared to other exiles, transplants, and emigrants, the Virginian seems different and his difference seems suggestively savage, transgressive, demonic. Like other men, the narrator respects and fears the Virginian, a dangerous opponent who guns down his enemies. Like women, however, the narrator finds himself attracted to the darkness that wards off his rivals. Acknowledging the Virginian's strange aura, which both alarms and seduces him, the narrator calls his "black" love the "devil" (21).

In Jack Schaefer's *Shane* (1949), the same-sex love-object is just as effectively demonized. The western hero, dressed in symbolic black, is an outcast like Cain, a roaming killer who strikes fear in the heart of western communities. When the Starretts ask Shane to help them fight a cattleman who wants to seize their small farm for grazing land, the outlaw comes to the poor family's aid. In the process of defending the Starretts, the gunfighter inspires the son's undying worship, the father's grudging affection, and the wife's secret love. While saving the family, Shane almost destroys it, initiating a romantic rivalry.

In order to preserve the family, Shane denies his feelings for Marion and displaces his feelings for Joe. Promising to love her platonically, as he does Joe and Bob, Shane says to Marion: "Could I separate you in my mind and [still] be a man?"[7] Paradoxically, Shane must deny his heterosexual attraction to Marion in order to preserve his own code of manliness. Meanwhile, Schaefer considers but finally refutes the idea

A scene from the film, in which Shane (Alan Ladd) and Joe (Van Heflin) chip away at the stump. (Courtesy Academy of Motion Picture Arts and Sciences. © 1995 by Paramount Pictures. All rights reserved.)

that the hero's friendship with Joe might be homosexual. In one scene, the men compete with each other to remove a stump from Joe's land. The stump simultaneously unites Shane and Joe, who join in the task of removing it, and separates the two men, who engage in a contest to see who can lift his end first. In the middle of the ordeal, Joe looks across the tree stump at Shane, as if there were "some unspoken thought between them that bothered him" (24). But at the end of the day, with the work now completed, the two men "looked up and their eyes met and held." Although the silence that greets them when they lay down their axes is both "clean and wholesome" (26), the sounds of grunting and "blowing" (25), the squatting and thrusting that the men perform audibly, and the "sucking" noise that the stump makes when it releases its roots from the soil (24), seemingly articulate something the two men can't say.

The bond between Shane and Joe is tested and strengthened by their mutual affection for Marion. The task of removing the stump merely redirects the men's sexual energy. When Marion comes outdoors to model a hat, she only briefly distracts the two laborers. "Stop bothering us. Can't you see we're busy?" says Joe, who then goes back to work (20). The triangular relationship among the three characters generates what Eve Kosofsky Sedgwick has called "homosocial desire."[8] In the process of competing for Marion, Shane and Joe establish an erotic rivalry that binds them to each other as well as to the woman they love. Unlike the narrator in *The Virginian*, who imaginarily impersonates the woman whom the cowboy desires, Shane and Joe use Marion as a medium through which to channel their own same-sex love.

The mediating presence of women enables readers to interpret male same-sex relationships as manifestations of homosocial desire. In the absence of women, however, certain acts intervene, filtering male same-sex relationships and thus removing the tainted suggestion that these dangerous friendships are sexual. Violent acts of disruption in westerns always function cathartically, first dramatizing intimate, complex relations between heroes and villains, then climactically purging them, terminating relations that might have become homosexual by means of a deadly fist fight, shoot-out, or hanging.

In *The Virginian*, the hero hangs Steve for rustling Judge Henry's stock. After the hanging, which Steve endures silently, the Virginian breaks down and cries, overcome by remorse for having killed his best friend. "It was the first [sob] I had ever heard from him," the narrator writes. "I had no sooner touched him than he was utterly overcome. 'I knew Steve awful well,' he said" (250). This scene not only reveals that the hero has feelings for Steve; it also suggests that the two men enjoyed an exclusive relationship. The reader learns that Steve called him "Jeff" (264), a name which no one else (not even Molly) knows. The Virginian's friendship with Steve—and his association with the narrator, who is privileged to hear the intimate confession that was intended for Steve—distinguish the Virginian's same-sex friendship from his relations with Molly, which never achieve a similar emotional expressiveness, passionate depth, or intensity.

The hanging precipitates—and also resolves—the crisis at the center of this same-sex relationship. Steve, the cattle rustler, is the cowboy's personal friend and at the same time his professional enemy. Forced to punish the criminal, the Virginian demonstrates how much he cares for Steve in the process of killing him. His sorrow over the death of his former companion finally enables the hero to confess the emotions that he could never acknowledge to Steve. The hanging, a retributive act of violence, leads to an indirect admission of love, addressed to the third-party narrator; at the same time, it makes the reciprocation of feeling between the lover and his love-object no longer possible. The imposition of punishment—the lynching of a cowboy for having stolen a rancher's stock, and the perceived justice of that act in a vigilante society—cancels out the hypothetical impropriety of the Virginian's affection for Steve. Sacrificing his best friend would seem to prove his emotional invulnerablity. It suggests that the Virginian is "hard, isolate, stoic," like other mythic figures in American literature whom D. H. Lawrence identifies.[9]

In the case of Shane's fist fight with Chris, a violent crisis also leads to a subdued denouement. In a saloon brawl, the hero beats up one of the cattleman's hands, who has attempted to terrorize the Starretts into leaving their land. After pummeling the cowboy into a state of unconsciousness, Shane lifts "the sprawling figure up in his arms." Carrying the body to one of the tables, he gently "set it down, the legs falling limp over the edge." Using a bartender's rag, he "tenderly cleared the blood from the face. He felt carefully along the broken arm and nodded to himself at what he felt" (61–62). Although Shane now feels compassion for Chris, the language used to describe that compassion also neuters the love-object. Shane lavishes care not on a man but on an ungendered object—on "it," not on Chris; on "the face," not on "his face."

The words "he felt" begin and end the last sentence. But instead of lending emphasis, the repetition creates ambiguity. At first, Shane physically (clinically, unemotionally) "felt" Chris's arm, examining his opponent for injuries. After touching the wounded man, however, Schaefer indicates that Shane "felt" something else, either unexpressed sorrow or unspoken sympathy.

If Shane's emotional response to this violent encounter is controlled or subdued, his physical actions during the encounter are explicitly and erotically charged. After the fist fight with Chris, Shane wrestles three more of Fletcher's men. Choreographed as a perverse kind of foreplay, the match simulates castration and graphic acts of arousal. After kneeing one of Fletcher's men in the groin (71), Shane escapes the embrace of another man who "hugs" him too tightly (72), who engorges Shane, causing him to rise "straight and superb, the blood on his face bright like a badge" (74). At the end of the scene, Shane stands free and alone, erect with his gun cocked: "the man and the tool, a good man and a good tool," finally safe from assault (118).

One might expect westerns to give audiences "masculine" heroes with whom to identify, since the audience for westerns is primarily heterosexual males. Instead, although they exhibit some "macho" tendencies, heroes are actually more dandified and effeminate than most other characters. The typical hero—a killer, an outcast, a loner—may exist outside society. But in the process of protecting "civilization" from "savagery," he is often absorbed by society. The traditional villain, however, has an unregenerate status that codes him as "masculine." He is crude, ungroomed, and uncivilized, whereas the hero, in his role as protector or rescuer, possesses at least a rough sense of decorum and romantic chivalry. The Virginian, for example, decorates his hat band with flowers when he pays court to Molly (84). After observing that he wears a petunia in his hat band and grooms himself carefully (4), Marion asks Shane about the latest fashions in town. "You're the kind of man [who] would notice them" (11).

In spite of each man's refinement, no one questions the Virginian's or Shane's masculinity. Violence simultaneously consummates and terminates their same-sex relationships. At the same time, it confuses and clarifies their own sexuality. Victories over their enemies signify that the heroes are physically stronger than their seemingly more masculine foes. In the aftermath of their triumphs, however, the heroes also reveal themselves as delicate and emotionally sensitive characters.

II

Early westerns, such as *The Virginian* and *Shane*, feature homosocial relationships that become erotically charged. More recent experimental
works, in the process of straying from formula, explore the extent to
which these relationships become overtly sexual. In these works, the
hero's orientation, his relations with men, and his status in society are
more complexly analyzed. Here, although the hero is often portrayed
sympathetically, he is stigmatized by society because of his sexual
activities or because of some equal "crime."

In the 1940s, Jean Genet began writing about similarities between
homosexuals and criminals, noting that both groups of men are traditionally scorned by society. (The temporary sexual liaisons that homosexuals and criminals sometimes establish in prison only serve to
express the deeper sense of alienation that the two groups share philosophically.[10]) Genet's theory—that gay men bear a criminal stigma, a
liminal status in mainstream society—anticipates Leslie A. Fiedler's idea
that men, if they consummate same-sex relationships, are "guilty" of
having committed improper acts. In the 1950s, when Fiedler's work first
achieved prominence, artists began more frequently casting western
heroes as sexually ambiguous, socially marginal characters. Although
heroes in the past had been portrayed as outsiders, they had often been
romanticized because of their liminality and eventually reintegrated
within their communities. Now they were permanently exiled, having
broken certain sexual taboos.

Gore Vidal's teleplay, *The Death of Billy the Kid* (1955); the subsequent
feature film, entitled *The Left-Handed Gun* (1958); James Leo Herlihy's
novel, *Midnight Cowboy* (1965); and the film of same name (1969) depict
their protagonists as male hustlers and/or repressed homosexuals[11].
In Cold Blood (1966), Truman Capote's bestseller, offers perhaps the most
complex example during this period of "queer frontier" literature.
In Cold Blood reconstructs the crimes of Perry Smith and Dick Hickock,
two small-time convicts who become famous mass murderers. In 1959,
while serving time for theft in the Kansas state prison, Dick learns that
his cell mate once worked for a farmer named Clutter. When he hears
that Clutter stores his money at home in an office safe, Dick imagines
the secluded farm as the perfect site for a robbery. After his release,
Dick contacts Perry, a former inmate now on parole, and the two men
make plans. On the night of November 14, they break into the Clutter
household, look in vain for the safe, slit Clutter's throat in frustration,

and then kill his wife, son, and daughter. Three years later, Dick and Perry are tried and convicted of first-degree murder. On April 14, 1965, after three years of Supreme Court appeals, the men finally hang.

In Cold Blood echoes the western in certain characteristic details. The Clutter farm is situated in westernmost Kansas, not far from Dodge City, where Wyatt Earp and Bat Masterson once sent men to their graves.[12] Curly and Dewey, FBI agents who arrest Dick and Perry, are respectively known for being a quick "draw" and for rounding up cattle thieves.[13] Somewhat facetiously, Capote notes that the hangman who executes Dick and Perry wears a green cowboy hat (378, 380).

In addition to exploiting recognizable settings and leitmotifs, In Cold Blood resembles the western, according to Leslie A. Fiedler, because it features an inter-racial, same-sex relationship.[14] However, the union between Dick, who is white, and Perry, who is half-Cherokee Indian, is more "perverse" than the simple friendship between Natty Bumppo and Chingachgook. Despite protestations of innocence—"I'm a normal," Dick claims repeatedly (111, 128)—the ex-convict would rather rape Clutter's daughter than rob Clutter's home. Perry, a paranoid schizophrenic and repressed homosexual, also unconvincingly defends his normality. Referring to his time in the Merchant Marines, he says that although "I wouldn't roll over," "the queens wouldn't leave me alone" (156). Their sexual abnormalities and their criminal status as killers link Dick and Perry together in a same-sex union of miscreants.

Although they never have intercourse,[15] the two men enjoy a relationship that appears homosexual. Perry admires Dick because he seems "pragmatic," "practical," "masculine" (27, 57). "That Dick had been married—married twice—and had fathered three sons was something he envied. A wife, children—those were experiences 'a man ought to have'" (117). While Dick packs a gun, Perry strums a guitar and projects femininity. His tiny feet belong in a "lady's dancing slippers" (26). His eyes, "with their moist, dreamy expression," seem "rather pretty" (189). His handwriting, with its "feminine flourishes" (169), and his tendency to lisp (202) with a darting "pink" tongue (254), cause women to question his manliness. Dick's mother tells an FBI agent that she always loathed Perry. "No, sir, I wouldn't have him in the house. One look and I saw what he was. With his perfume. And his oily hair. It was clear as day where Dick had met him," she says, condemning Perry for being an ex-convict and/or an effete homosexual (194).

Dick and Perry are equally stigmatized because of their criminal actions and "perverse" sexuality. Dick calls his co–conspirator "honey," "baby," and "sugar" (26, 60, 106). By fatal coincidence, Clutter mistakes the two men for his wife when he hears noises downstairs. "Is that you, honey?" he says, echoing one of the terms of endearment that the two men bestow on each other (268). On their way to the Clutter farm, Dick and Perry behave like "two dudes" on a "date" (44). But their date with death results in a marriage between two hardened killers. (In the 1967 film adaptation, Dick jokes: "I'm the best friend you got." Perry: "'Til death do us part?" Dick: "All we need is the ring, sugar."[16]) After the killings, Dick forges checks in order to buy Perry clothes, telling the clerk at one men's store that Perry is about to get married and that Dick has agreed to pay for "what you might [call] his—ha–ha—trousseau" (115). At the small county courthouse, the two reenact their relationship (284). In the "men's" cell, Dick reads men's magazines. In the "women's" cell, Perry flips through *Good Housekeeping*, buffs his nails, and combs his "lotion–soaked" hair (286). While the cells divide Dick and Perry, the labeled compartments symbolically unite the two criminals, stereotyping the men as gendered partners in crime.

Although he was "aggressively heterosexual,"[17] as Capote stated in interviews, Dick found himself attracted to Perry because of his friend's violent tendencies. In the novel, a story that Perry narrates about having killed a black man named King persuades Dick that the two men would make great accomplices. King, who once lived with Perry in a Las Vegas boarding house, had done "roadwork and other outdoor stuff—he had a good build." Every time he passed by King's door, Perry saw the man lying naked in bed, reading "cowboy junk." Aroused by this exhibition in some dangerous way, Perry invited King to go for a drink with him. Instead, stopping his car in the desert, he says that he suddenly attacked King and left him on the roadside to die. "Maybe nobody ever found him. Just buzzards," he says somewhat boastfully (132). In the tradition of westerns (or "cowboy junk," as Perry calls it derisively), the killing eliminates not only King but the threatening homosexual love–object whom King represents. However, at the same time that the killing ends a complex connection with King, it initiates an even more problematic friendship with Dick. Perry lies about having killed King, as he later admits to authorities. By portraying himself as a cold–blooded, "masculine" criminal, Perry hoped to seduce Dick, he says (131).

However, events finally force Perry to prove he can kill. At the Clutter farm, although Dick picks up a knife, he hesitates to slit Clutter's throat. Perry grabs the knife and screams, "All right, Dick. Here goes." Explaining that "it was something between me and Dick," Perry says his threat was a test. "I meant to call his bluff, make him argue me out of it" (276). Instead, realizing that the man he has idolized is afraid to kill Clutter, Perry also discovers that he, who has lied about having killed King, can prove himself by sacrificing four people now. In an "exclusive" interview, Dick later confessed that he felt the need to test his bravado. "When I got into that house I was going to show who was boss. Although my partner had never said so I knew he was thinking I didn't have the guts to go through with it.... What would my partner think if I chickened out? These thoughts raced through my mind."[18] Dick's manhood is challenged by his refusal to commit violent acts. In a reversal of roles, the "effeminate" Perry succeeds where the "macho" Dick fails. Perry now understands that, instead of being "pragmatic" and "virile," Dick is "pretty weak and shallow," "a coward" (292).

Analyzing the events at the Clutter farm, a doctor at the Menninger Clinic, specializing in forensic psychiatry, claimed that Clutter's death, the first murder, was the only one that mattered to Perry, at least psychologically (338). Clutter, an older man and an authority figure in Holcomb society, represented the father with whom Perry had shared a love–hate relationship. After the separation of his parents (a rodeo cowboy and a full-blooded Cherokee Indian), Perry had gone to live with his father. But when his father had threatened to shoot him one day, in the midst of an argument, Perry had abruptly left home (158). Eventually, the abused boy developed his father's quick temper. His temper, in turn, may have triggered his violent assault on the Clutters. "I thought [Clutter] was a very nice gentleman.... I thought so right up to the moment I cut his throat," Perry testified (275).

The murder therefore reconstructed while at the same time revising acts from his past. (The psychiatrist believed that Perry killed Clutter in order to reverse the fact that Perry's father had once almost shot him.) In the same complex fashion, Perry uses violence both to distance himself from Dick and to draw himself more deeply into a love–hate relationship. By murdering Clutter, Perry hopes to shame Dick, calling attention to his ruthless audacity and Dick's false bravado. But instead of distinguishing them from each other, the murder and the subsequent killings make the two men accomplices. Regardless of who killed the family, the law holds

both men responsible. The criminal acts link Dick to a cold–blooded murderer. Unable to escape his fate, which Perry has effectively sealed, Dick
finds himself stuck with an unwanted "wife" (244).

III

Because of their differences, the white man and colored man, in the
frontier tradition, represent two distinct worlds, racially coded as "civilization" and "savagery." Because of their same sex, however, these types
also share similarities. Thus, Dick and Perry—as white man and half-
breed, as man and "wife"—serve as two halves of one pair. As mirror
images of each other, they reverse but reflect one identity. In their
adjoining cells, Dick and Perry—different yet double, individual yet
joined—seem like strange "Siamese twins" (355).

Narcissistic tendencies hint at their preference for same–sex relationships. "Every time you see a mirror you go into a trance.... Like you
was looking at some gorgeous piece of butt," Dick teases Perry (26). The
repressed homosexual also gazes at "sweaty studies" of men in weight-
lifting magazines (204). Capote suggests that this activity allows Perry to
redirect his libido. Because Perry, the weight lifter, sees his own muscled
form reflected in images, the magazines take on the same masturbatory
function as soft–core pornography.[19]

After killing the Clutters, Dick and Perry escape and drive down to
Mexico. In Acapulco, they spend time with Otto, a wealthy gay tourist,
and his Mexican gigolo. Otto sketches Dick while he lies in the nude, in
exchange for money and favors that the host lavishes on his two new
acquaintances (140). Like Perry, who identifies himself in the pages of
weight–lifting magazines, Dick narcissistically transforms himself into a
series of eroticized images. Replacing the Cowboy (as Otto nicknames
the gigolo), Dick becomes a paid "cowboy" substitute, honoring his end
of an unseemly transaction by striking a nude "macho" pose.

Robert Warshow suggests that "a certain image of man" expresses
itself in most western films. Audiences like to see how a man looks
"when he shoots or is shot. A hero is one who looks like a hero," the
critic claims.[20] In westerns, heroes function not as unique individuals,
acting out their personal histories, but as archetypes, working out our
shared mythic destiny. When we identify with heroes, we narcissistically project ourselves into those roles, doing so with some degree of
self-consciousness. *In Cold Blood* observes Dick and Perry acting those

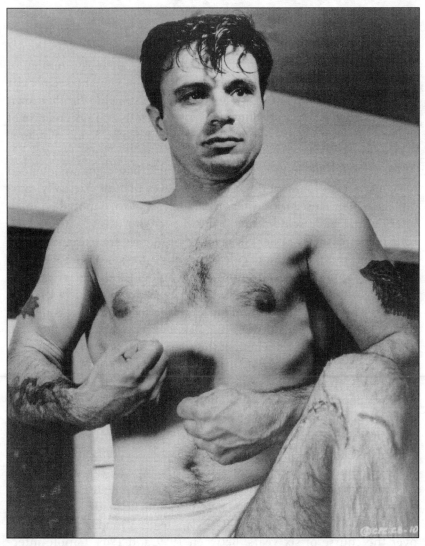

Perry (Robert Blake) looks in the mirror, admiring his muscles, scars, and tattoos. (*In Cold Blood*. 1967 © Pax Enterprises, Inc. Courtesy Columbia Pictures.)

parts, not so successfully although just as self-consciously. Dick plays
the "cowboy" while Perry flexes his muscles, gazing into the mirror to
see if he looks like a "man." (Perry's screen persona, Robert Blake,
reflects his counterpart's qualities. Blake interprets Perry as a sensitive
psychopath, a variation on the misfits and rebels that James Dean and

Marlon Brando made popular. Like Perry, Blake has Brando's squat legs and well-muscled torso, his soft skin, curly forelock, and melting dark eyes—all of which hint, more strongly than in the case of Brando, at a potential bisexuality.) If Dick and Perry were "gay," their assumptions of stereotypical heterosexual roles (their "voguing") might seem subversive or camp. But since Dick and Perry are "straight"—in their own minds, at least—their modeling represents a serious and sincere form of flattery. Dick and Perry aspire, and fail, to become icons of "pure" masculinity.

The friends both sport tattoos. But although these signs are intended to signify a man's masculinity, Capote believes that they actually camouflage a man's insecurity. After writing *In Cold Blood*, Capote said in an interview; "I have seldom met a murderer who wasn't tattooed. Of course, the reason is rather clear; most murderers are extremely weak men who are sexually undecided and quite frequently impotent."[21] Whether Capote's generalization is psychologically valid or not, his characterization of Dick and Perry supports his hypothesis. When Dick and Perry gaze into mirrors and view their tattoos (42, 26), it is unclear whether they see colorful scars that acknowledge their initiation into tough prison gangs or whether they see cosmetic ornaments that enhance them romantically. Dick and Perry reflect provocative but ambiguous images. They undermine, while attempting to reinforce, representations of "straight" sexuality. When Perry buys a pair of dark glasses, "fancy ones" with "mirrored lenses," for instance, Dick seems uncomfortable. He feels embarrassed to be seen with someone who wears "that kind of flit stuff," he says. For when he looks in his friend's mirrored lenses, Dick sees himself unexpectedly (128–29).

While researching and writing *In Cold Blood*, Capote tried to suspend judgment and sympathy. But in spite of claims he made later, alleging that he had kept himself "out of it,"[22] Capote grew fond of the two men over the course of six years. Between 1959 and 1965, Capote interviewed the men hundreds of times and painstakingly studied their histories. The two men became "very good friends of mine (I mean ... very close friends, very very close intimates in every conceivable way)," he conceded.[23] "It wasn't a question of my *liking* Dick and Perry.... That's like saying 'Do you like yourself?' What mattered was that I knew them, as well as I know myself," he maintained.[24]

Because Perry and Capote looked alike, in certain ways felt the same, and shared the same destiny, Capote identified with Perry especially.

Both men were social misfits who had come from broken families and foster homes; both were superstitious, boyish, and short; both were artists (a writer and a would-be musician, respectively). Harper Lee—who came to interview subjects, take notes, and keep her friend company— remembered the time at the county courthouse when Capote first noticed Perry's short legs. "Look, his feet don't touch the floor!" Capote exclaimed, as Perry sat patiently, waiting to be arraigned by the judge. "This is the beginning of a great love affair," thought Lee at the time, although she later understood the relationship between Capote and Perry to be more complex than that. Each man "looked at the other and saw, or thought he saw, the man he might have been," explained Lee.[25] While Perry had the self-destructive criminal tendencies that Capote (the drug addict, the alcoholic) also exhibited, Capote represented the successful artist and practicing homosexual whom Perry both aspired to be and feared he might one day become.

Sigmund Freud has argued that narcissism plays a role in determining certain same-sex relationships. According to Freud, a man who seeks other men may be yearning, on some deeper level, to embrace his own self-reflection.[26] Although Capote and Perry never consummated their relationship sexually, their bond certainly seemed homosexual. Their tendency to find themselves drawn to, and at the same time repulsed by, facets of themselves that they saw in each other gave the friendship an intense, self-absorbed quality.

Capote loved Perry and, at the same time, craved his demise. In choosing his title, a grim double entendre, Capote assumed that just as the two men had murdered the Clutters, in cold blood, so the law would execute them. But the Supreme Court appeals, which lasted three years, postponed the men's execution date. Eager to deliver the book to his publisher, Capote waited for Dick and Perry to die so he could write his conclusion. After the third appeal failed, Capote resisted the temptation to celebrate. He wrote to a friend, "I've been disappointed so many times I hardly dare hope. But keep your fingers crossed." When Dick and Perry tried to contact Capote, to see if he could help them win a reprieve, Capote refused to answer their telephone calls or respond to their messages. In the meantime, he outlined the book's ending, planning to fill in the details once the two men had hanged. "Hope this doesn't sound insane, ... but the way I've constructed things, I will be able to complete the entire manuscript within hours after [the execution]. Keep *everything* crossed."[27]

In the western tradition, Perry's death, which was staged as a hanging, finalized the relationship between the outlaw/half–breed and his
white male counterpart. Minutes before dying, in the courtyard at the
Kansas state prison, Perry surprised Capote by asking to speak to him.
In a farewell speech, he forgave Capote for not having answered his
messages. "Good–bye. I love you and I always have," he said lispingly.
Capote remembered the scene in an interview. "I was standing there at
the foot of the gallows. There were about fifty people surrounding me.
They couldn't hear what he said to me because he was whispering. I
was very upset. . . . I didn't love [Dick or Perry], but I had a great understanding for both of them, and for Perry I had a tremendous amount of
sympathy," he said, qualifying his feelings in retrospect.[28]

The friendship between Capote (the representative of "civilization")
and Perry (the unredeemed "savage") resembles other same–sex relationships in frontier American literature. At the same time, it suggests a
correspondence between homosexuality and criminality, which exists
outside as well as within the western tradition. Capote, the self–destructive gay writer, and Perry, the convicted mass murderer, share their
"guilty" love secretly in an intimate moment, in a whispered confession,
that prison officials and public spectators can't hear. This episode reenacts a familiar western scenario. Here, as in *The Virginian*, violence acts
as a catalyst, forcing the victim to realize that he loves his own executioner. At the same time, the executioner, who loves his victim but
won't save his life, belatedly expresses his feelings by mourning the
absent beloved. Before the hanging, Capote restrains himself as Perry
confesses his love. ("I spent the entire two days before the execution
throwing up . . . but somehow when the time came I got myself together
and went there and spoke to [him]."[29]) After the hanging, however, the
stoic who passively willed Perry's death now feels implicated, guilty,
regretful. Perry's death, for which Capote feels partly responsible,
causes the author to mourn and do penance. At the height of his success, after publishing *In Cold Blood*, the writer begins to act self–destruc-
tively, turning more frequently to narcotics and alcohol. Capote the
narcissist, having eliminated his love–object, tries to kill himself too. "It
really killed me. I think, in a way, it *did* kill me," he said in an interview,
explaining how the emotional crisis exhausted him.[30]

While it is true that westerns privilege male friendships and rivalries,
minimizing the roles played by female characters, westerns also restrict

men by qualifying the nature of their same-sex relationships. Leslie A. Fiedler and Jane Tompkins suggest that men escape to the wilderness in order to free themselves from the civilizing influence of women.[31] Seeking out each other's company, men form alternative relationships outside the bounds of society. But although they have complex interactions, men can't express themselves sexually. If they were to couple, their same-sex partnerships would resemble the "marriages"—the civilized unions with women—that they seek not to make.

Westerns, concerned almost exclusively with the actions and feelings of men, by definition possess homosocial and homoerotic components. Actual homosexual behavior, however, appears only in western send-ups and parodies. Members of the Village People perform as cowboys and Indians. In leather bars, men wear western clothes, enacting self-conscious fantasies. The Waco Kid and his black male lover ride into the sunset at the end of *Blazing Saddles* (1974), a western film farce. An artist covers John Wayne's mouth with red lipstick and produces "camp" art.

Capote never acknowledged having borrowed from westerns in order to create an artistic hybrid. Having claimed that *In Cold Blood* was the first nonfiction novel, Capote was forced to deny his indebtedness to other genres in American literature. In private life, however, he demonstrated an awareness of westerns, one that was informed by his sly sense of humor. Near the end of his life, having concluded a love affair, Capote, depressed and addicted to narcotics and alcohol, entered Roosevelt Hospital. Because he dreaded publicity, Capote adopted a pseudonym. Facetiously comparing his own failed love affair to the "friendship" between Theodore Roosevelt and Owen Wister, the gay writer signed Wister's name in the register. (The doctor attending him, thinking that Capote had written *The Virginian*, innocently asked for his autograph.[32])

In Cold Blood has more in common with westerns than the author's superficial acquaintance with Wister might indicate. Separately and together, as members of a same-sex relationship, Dick and Perry resemble mythic archetypes in frontier American literature. (Like other members of their generation, however, Dick and Perry are decidedly antiheroic. They resemble James Dean and Sal Mineo more than Natty Bumppo and Chingachgook.) The book's resemblance to westerns, rather than its uniqueness as a nonfiction novel—its familiarity, rather than its bizarre topicality—partly explains why *In Cold Blood* remains enormously popular. At the same time, however, *In Cold Blood* flirts with western conventions. With a text that acknowledges a homoerotic friendship between two hardened criminals, and a subtext that reveals a narcissistic attraction between the author and one of his characters, *In Cold Blood* explores homosexuality more boldly than any previous western-themed literature.

TEN

Welcome to Twin Peaks

ince the publication of "The Significance of the Frontier in American History" in 1893, scholars have amended and rejected numerous claims made by Frederick Jackson Turner in his now famous argument. Most historians, however, have tended to agree with at least one notion central to Turner's hypothesis. In his essay Turner defined westward movement as process. For Turner the historical process of exploration, conquest, and settlement meant that the West was a continually moving place that constantly changed shape geographically. At various times during the course of national expansion, New England, the Midwest, the Great Plains, the Southwest, and the Pacific Northwest each represented western frontiers. The physical process of taming successive frontiers coincided with the psychological process of developing America's collective identity. Clearing the forest, crossing the desert, and farming the prairie: according to Turner, these acts helped to form the American character, fostering confidence, optimism, independence, and fortitude. For those who never took part in the movement of Manifest Destiny but who sympathize with the notions of frontier "progress" and "enterprise," these are characterisitics that many still identify as uniquely American.

Turner feared that the frontier process would end when America ran out of land. He wouldn't have worried if he had realized that America never runs out of literature. For, more than 100 years after Turner claimed that the frontier had closed, people continue to discover the West through the works of such prolific writers as Zane Grey, Max Brand, and Louis L'Amour. Pulp westerns, produced quickly according to formulas, are consumed in mass quantities. The ongoing, unending process of reading allows audiences to experience the frontier repeatedly. Westerns give pleasure not only because they reopen the frontier but also because they make that frontier, and the imaginative process of exploring it, seem unending, unlimited. Readers can defer closure by reading an infinite number of generically identical, interchangeable narratives, producing an effect that is continuous, repetitious, and pleasurable.

Consumers of popular culture experience this "process" of pleasure in films and on television as well as in literature. In the early years of American cinema, westerns enjoyed great popularity. In the 1950s and 1960s, television condensed westerns into weekly, hour–long dramas, exposing them to a new and much wider audience. Shows such as *Gunsmoke* (1955–75), *Bonanza* (1959–73), *Rawhide* (1959–65), and *Wagon Train* (1957–61) reenacted the process of westward movement—week after week, year after year—in a seemingly unending series of episodes.

Westerns began to disappear from television in the early and mid–1970s. Beginning several years later, *Dallas* (1978–91), *Dynasty* (1981–89), *Knots Landing* (1979–92), and *Falcon Crest* (1981–90) filled a void in the marketplace. At the height of their popularity during the early and mid–1980s, when the notion that "greed is good" competed with an increasing awareness of the destructive effect that the pursuit of profit and pleasure had on individuals, on society, and on nature's environment, nighttime soaps such as *Dallas* captialized on both the positive and negative aspects of Turner's philosophy. Presenting their heroes as villains, nighttime soaps defined J. R., Blake and Alexis, and others, as ruthless entrepreneurs, admitting that their plundering of the West was deplorable. At the same time these shows encouraged viewers to share vicariously in the triumph of business people whose transactions in cattle, oil, vineyards, and real estate enriched individuals at the expense of their once pristine environment.

Neither the characters nor the audience realized what toll on the environment these human transactions might take. For the most part, nighttime soaps glossed over the fact that settlement, urbanization, and competitive enterprise led to the misuse, exploitation, and depletion of the West's finite resources. Not until David Lynch's *Twin Peaks* (1990–91) would a nighttime soap finally consider—in seriocomic, creepy, and surrealistic detail—the inter-relationship between environmental destruction and human corruption in one eerie, make-believe, western frontier community.

I

Daytime soaps almost always take place in the East or Midwest. Currently all of ABC's soaps are set in the eastern United States *General Hospital* occurs in Port Charles, New York, not far from Albany. *All My Children* is located in one of the mid-Atlantic states, in the fictional town of Pine Valley. Nearby, *One Life to Live* takes place in Llanview. On NBC and CBS, most soaps are set in the Midwest, in fictional mid-sized communities. Oakdale, a town in an unnamed Midwestern state, provides the setting for *As the World Turns*. Near Oakdale, *Another World* unfolds in Bay City. *The Guiding Light* emanates from Springfield, in what is "perhaps" Illinois. *The Young and the Restless* is based in Genoa City, a generic Midwestern town.

With the exception of CBS's *The Bold and the Beautiful*, which is set in Los Angeles, daytime soaps that take place in the West—usually in real-life locales, such as NBC's *Santa Barbara*—tend to fail. However, the longest running and most popular nighttime soaps invariably staked out the West as their turf. *Dallas* moved between the Southfork Ranch and the city that lent its name to the show; *Dynasty* took place in Denver; *Falcon Crest* was set in the valleys and vineyards near San Francisco; and *Knots Landing* identified a fictional suburb in a northern California community.

The reasons nighttime soaps moved West were at least partly logistical. Daytime soaps, originating as radio serials, initially broadcast from Chicago in the 1930s and from New York City in the 1940s and afterwards. Since they first transmitted from the Midwest and East, radio and television tended to create shows for audiences that were fictionally set in the same local areas.[1] However, when they began airing in the late 1970s, nighttime soaps were filmed in Los Angeles, like most prime-time shows. It was tempting to set nighttime soaps in the West in part because it was less expensive and more convenient to film western exteriors and outdoor location shots. In addition, political, economic, and cultural factors may explain why western soaps thrived, albeit for a relatively short length of time. Critics have noted that the shows experienced their greatest popularity during Ronald Reagan's two terms as president. Celebrating personal wealth and economic growth, at a cost to the environment and at the expense of society, the shows reflected a 1980s' philosophy that some critics claim glorified the ex-California governor's own public policies.[2]

Nighttime soaps exploited the West in order to boost their ratings as well. Because they were produced relatively cheaply, daytime soaps could afford to attract a smaller, predominately female audience. But prime-time shows such as *Dallas* and *Dynasty*, because they had larger budgets, had to stimulate much greater revenue. Seeking to expand the marketplace, and to capture male as well as female viewers, nighttime soaps therefore moved westward in course. Reinventing the soap-opera formula, nighttime soaps interwove traditional plots dealing with family relationships, set in the familiar domestic sphere, with new kinds of story lines. In these plots the professional, middle-class characters found on most daytime soaps—housewives, lawyers, doctors, and business folk, who appeared mainly inside their households and offices[3]—were replaced by wealthy, self-made entrepreneurs and industrialists, who fought over property in western showdowns that ended each week in cliffhangers. Believing that male viewers preferred corporate melodramas, staged against scenic backdrops that featured the rugged outdoors,[4] nighttime soaps staged long-running feuds between the Ewings and Barneses of *Dallas*, between the Carringtons and Colbys of *Dynasty*, and between the Channings and Giobertis of *Falcon Crest*. (*Knots Landing*, although originally more suburban and domestic in emphasis, was eventually refashioned to resemble other nighttime soaps in an effort to win the ratings war with NBC's *Hill Street Blues*.[5])

As soon as it premiered on April 8, 1990, viewers noticed that *Twin Peaks* imitated and to some extent parodied the conventions of soaps. The show's melodramatic and sometimes comic intrigues—narrated in multiple, intersecting, and ongoing story lines—often mirrored the antics that occur on "Invitation to Love," the fictional soap that airs in the town of Twin Peaks. (In episode seven of *Twin Peaks*,[6] when Leo is shot in his living room, the television next to him shows a similar character being shot by his adversary on an installment of "Invitation to Love.") The fact that *Twin Peaks* resembles nighttime soaps as well as daytime dramas perhaps explains why its counterpart, "Invitation to Love," broadcasts on the town's local network both night and day.

In the early 1990s, just as the once popular prime-time soaps of the

1980s were ending their rule, *Twin Peaks* began its short, two-season run. Like a daytime soap, it examined the personal heartaches and domestic disturbances of the show's central characters. But like a nighttime soap, it interwove stories about the private lives of the region's inhabitants with tall tales about the exploits of people in western business and industry. Twin Peaks is governed, like the cities in all nighttime soaps, by members of a tightknit but dysfunctional family who scheme for control of a dynasty. Instead of contending for range land, vineyards, or oil fields, the members of the Packard family fight for ownership of the town's only lumber mill. Living in the forests of northeastern Washington, the people of Twin Peaks depend for economic survival on their access to timber land. Hence Josie Packard, her sister-in-law Catherine Packard Martell, and Catherine's husband Pete, each week on *Twin Peaks*, in a series of shifting alliances and rivalries, seek ownership of the lumber mill through legal or illegal means. At the same time, they scheme either to sell or to avoid selling the mill to Benjamin Horne, the town's villainous but charismatic real estate mogul and hotel entrepreneur, who wants to raze the mill and clear the site so he can build a suburban development called Ghost Wood Estates.

If it followed strictly in the tradition of nighttime soaps, *Twin Peaks* would focus almost exclusively on the plot to control the town's central dynasty. Instead, it subordinates this story line in most weekly episodes. Rather than showcasing the actions of the town's few wealthy characters, *Twin Peaks* concentrates on the lives of all of its citizens. Rather than glorifying the titans of local business and industry, who seek to acquire timber land for their own selfish purposes, *Twin Peaks* questions the relationship between the community and the western environment. On most nighttime soaps, people profit from nature in one-sided, exploitative relationships, appropriating land, livestock, crops, and other valuable resources. *Twin Peaks* differs from these prime-time shows in that it often represents people interacting and contending with nature instead of exploiting it. In the logging community—and in the fog-filled, dark, silent forests enshrouding it—there lurks an unknown (super)natural entity, dominating, potentially threatening, and perhaps uncontrollable.

The show's central story line, in the first season and in part of the second one, deals with the circumstances surrounding the death of the local high school homecoming queen. In trying to discover who murdered her, Special Agent Dale Cooper, sent by the FBI to investigate, learns that Laura Palmer, a seeming ingenue, was involved in prostitution, incest, and drugs. In addition to discovering proof of illegal drug use and sexual activity, Agent Cooper finds evidence of blackmailing schemes, gambling rings, UFOs, and inexplicable paranormal phenomena, which seem directly or indirectly to implicate everyone—*except* members of the logging and real estate dynasties—in a cross-town conspiracy. However, shortly after Laura's ravaged body is found in the show's premiere episode, Benjamin Horne tells a group of potential investors in Ghost Wood Estates that "here in Twin Peaks health and industry go hand in hand." Story lines tracing the threatened "health" of the Twin Peaks community run parallel to story lines concerning the unregulated, unfettered growth of the town's local "industry." In the first shot of Laura's stiff oblong corpse, floating like a piece of driftwood downstream, and throughout later episodes, in words and in images, viewers learn to relate the corruption, degeneration, and death of particular characters to the pollution, deforestation, and environmental devastation of northeastern Washington.

The process of producing and consuming timber complements the process of viewing and interpreting the soap opera's narrative. Pictures of forests, shots of lumber in logging trucks, images of wood planks being cut by noisy sawmill machinery, and scenes of fireplaces crackling with small sticks and kindling, edited into the narrative, call attention to representative stages in the production and consumption of forest land. Establishing shots—showing a grove of trees, a buzz saw, or a wood-burning fireplace—punctuate the otherwise continuous and unending narrative, reminding viewers that the process of deforestation parallels the evolution of the show's weekly mysteries. The association of those mysteries with a series of iconic images gives the establishing shots the power to evoke feelings of fear and anxiety, at the same time relieving viewers by helping them to distinguish and separate a series of overlapping, intersecting, and bewildering story lines. The establishing shots not only depict the process of deforestation (in its various sequential stages) but also participate structurally in the process of narrative, since the shots flash between scenes and therefore transition them. Each time one of four or five repeated stock images appears on the screen it creates a pause in the action, signaling viewers that the show is once more about to switch scenes or story lines.

On *Twin Peaks*, the majority of scenes take place indoors. But the interior settings and decor remind viewers of the show's exterior setting and the town's outdoor industry. Sheriff Harry Truman, Deputies Andy Brennan and Hawk, and Agent Cooper discuss their detective work in a pine-paneled conference room. Above them, in a bark picture frame, hangs the portrait of a tall Douglas fir. (The picture of a tree in a room made of trees, surrounded by a forest of trees, has the same comic impact as "The Far Side" cartoons, in which amoebas live in houses and hang pictures of other amoebas on the walls of their living rooms.) The Packards and Martells uneasily coexist in the Blue Pine Lodge, the Packard family's aptly named ancestral home. Benjamin Horne, their nemesis and arch-rival, owns and operates the Great Northern Hotel, which is built out of wood beams and rough-hewn log walls. The Log Lady decorates her cabin with log tables, log chairs, and other handmade log furniture, while Leo and Shelly live in a sparsely furnished house still under construction outside of town. Through wooden columns, support beams, and joists, they view the great western wilderness.

The woodsy sets and decor provide concrete texture, making the mysterious evil that resides in Twin Peaks seem palpable, tangible. Each of the episodes demonstrates that evil, in both spirit and human form, issues forth from the wilderness. The domestication of wilderness enables evil to relocate indoors. In episode five, Deputy Hawk warns the Log Lady that "the woods hold many spirits." In episode seventeen, Sheriff Truman echoes this superstition: "I've lived in these old woods most of my life. I've seen some strange things." While stationed in the forest in episode nine, manning deep-space monitors that transmit data from extraterrestrials, Major Briggs decodes a message that reads: "The owls are not what they seem." Wooden interiors insinuate the presence of nature, allowing evil to appear to inhabit the characters as well as their dwelling space. Like "Bob," who lives in the forest but who enters the Palmer home, and who repeatedly rapes Laura and invades Leland's body, evil originates in nature but penetrates everywhere, transgressing all human boundaries.

On most nighttime soaps, homes allow unrestricted movement within seemingly unlimited space. Oil barons, cattle kings, and wine-valley matriarchs—who maintain their wealth by controlling the external western environment—build personal monuments featuring equally expansive interiors: multiroom mansions, characterized by royal entranceways and wide sweeping staircases. On *Twin Peaks*, however, the transformation of buildings and homes into sets that resemble the wilderness tends not to open and help circulate space but to enclose, suffocate, and almost extinguish it. In surroundings where vision is narrowly telescoped and movement is circumscribed, people look through peepholes, enter and exit through secret doors, and use hidden passageways.

These secret doors, peepholes, and passageways, because they allow people to eavesdrop and spy, thus involve characters and viewers in tacit conspiracies as they seek each week to solve mysteries, bizarre crimes, and other fantastic perplexities. In the forest, deprived of light and all landmarks, surrounded by darkness and trees, one travels constantly yet never seems to go anywhere. As enclosed yet unlimited and seemingly undifferentiated terrain, the forest paradoxically, according to Gaston Bachelard, represents both finite space and immensity.[7] *Twin Peaks* creates that same contradictory feeling of confinement and

The lobby of the Great Northern Hotel: logs (stacked and upright) by the fireplace; wood floors and walls, shelves, vases, and ornaments; Native American art, upholstery, and haphazard insignia. Even with the lights on, the claustrophobic, window-less room appears dark and enclosed. (Courtesy Lynch/Frost Productions.)

movement by recreating the forest as an assortment of dark, cramped interiors. Covered peepholes, disguised doors, and mazes of passageways permit censored vision and unhampered but covert activity. One-way but not two-way vision, stealthy individual action rather than open interaction with characters, take place on *Twin Peaks*, which represents the Pacific Northwest as a brooding, gothic frontier.

The fact that people have cleared and settled the wilderness is offset by the disturbing notion that no one in Twin Peaks can quite conquer nature. Log-beamed ceilings and wood-paneled walls shelter human beings from the elements while at the same time reminding them of the outdoors that they have sought to defeat. Like trophies, the mounted dead timbers signify civilization's capture and destruction of forest land. But *Twin Peaks* also imagines that the forest is (re)animated by a mysterious natural or supernatural force and by an active intelligence, one that takes human shape in the form of the forest's evil inhabitants. Because the wilderness surrounds Twin Peaks, seeming even to prey on it, the log-built enclosures—with their claustrophobic interiors—not only protect but also menace people who dwell in them. Although people contain nature, they are also contained by it.

These sets are like galleries, displaying painted or embalmed replicas of the forest's inhabitants. Wood-framed portraits of trees—on the staircase landing of the Palmer home, in the local town hall, in the hospital—constitute "natural" still-life reminders of that which is animate. Sketches of Northwest Native American totems, on the walls in the lobby of the Great Northern Hotel, call attention to those who once lived in the wilderness. (In the American imagination, as Philip Fisher has noted, chopping down a tree is equivalent to killing an Indian.[8]) At Blue Pine Lodge, the stuffed and mounted heads of deer and other dead animals, like the owls in the forest, give the impression of being not what they seem. As the camera fixes its gaze on these creatures, whose dull glassy eyes stare back at viewers unnervingly, one experiences the uneasy sensation that nature, though temporarily defeated, waits to take its revenge. The fixtures—like ancestral portraits and gothic statues of gargoyles—have eyes that seem to be watching us, turning us paranoid, making us wonder about nature and whether we have conquered it. As we travel through *Twin Peaks*, we come to understand what Agent Cooper means when he says in episode five: "Once a traveler leaves home he loses almost one hundred percent of his ability to control his environment."

II

Unlike most nighttime soaps, *Twin Peaks* suggests that its characters can never successfully subdue their environment. Nature sends forth spirits, madmen, and extraterrestrials, all of whom challenge human authority, frontier progress, and enterprise. Even vanquished nature—still, lifeless objects such as dead wood and animals—has a haunting presence, a latent power to terrorize. *Twin Peaks* disputes the success of the frontier endeavor to tame and harness the wilderness. It also questions, however, whether people can practice the only alternative; whether they can coexist with nature, learning to understand, respect, and hence value the wilderness.

Interacting with nature instead of controlling it, and working to preserve nature instead of despoiling it, are notions that have been embraced by twentieth-century environmental philosophers. In *A Sand County Almanac* (1949), the bible of environmental ecologists, Aldo Leopold defines conservation as "a state of harmony between men and land." In order to achieve and maintain that harmony, Leopold exhorts members of the conservation movement to uphold what he calls "The Land Ethic," a belief that human beings belong to an interdependent community, "a biotic team," comprised of people, plant life, and animals.[9] In *Silent Spring* (1962), another powerful testament, Rachel Carson echoes this sentiment, claiming that the "earth's vegetation is part of a web of life in which there are intimate and essential relations between plants and the earth, between plants and other plants, between plants and animals." Rather than ruling over this kingdom, human beings merely participate in "a complex, precise, and highly integrated system of relationships between living things."[10]

During the 1960s, when Carson's work attained prominence, another way of viewing the relationship between human beings and their environment gained popularity. The counterculture movement of the mid- and late 1960s now perceived the union between "man and not-man" as romantic or mystical. "From that 'superstitious perception,'" according to Theodore Roszak, "there derive[d] a sense of the world as our house, in which we reside with the ease, if not always the comfort, of creatures who trust the earth that raised them ... and nurtures them."[11] Rachel Carson might demonstrate that herbicides and insecticides pollute the environment, proving the damage caused by chlorinated hydrocarbons and organic phosphates. But the representation of nature, and its alien components, as so many chemicals, having fixed classifications and properties, serves to reduce the workings of the environment to a series of "formal relationships" (252). While the scientist learns "by scrutinizing the trees and ignoring the forest" (251), the shaman—the mystic—gains wisdom by "experiencing" the forest in its entirety. "Such experience yields no sense of accomplished and rounded-off knowledge." On the contrary, claims Roszak, it produces the feeling of having been "awed, not informed" (253). This mystic, holistic vision, absent in Carson's work, sometimes occurs in contemporary Native American literature, which began in the 1960s to experience an artistic renaissance; in Edward Abbey's western romances; and in Gary Snyder's poetry, which preaches the tenets of environmental philosophy as well as the teachings of Buddhism.

The theory that the scientific universe can be understood, ordered, and improved by human intelligence, and the opposing belief that the world can best be experienced as supernatural, transcendental, or mystical, are both comically challenged as ideas on David Lynch's *Twin Peaks*. Born in 1946, Lynch grew up in Montana, Idaho, and Washington state. As a child he sometimes accompanied his father on expeditions involving research outdoors. On these occasions his father, who worked as a scientist for the Forest Service in Washington, usually wandered off to work by himself, leaving Lynch to play in the wilderness. In an interview, Lynch once spoke of his memories of Washington—of tall trees, bright shafts of sunlight, and streams stocked with trout. "It was a weird, comforting feeling being in the woods," he recalled. "There were odd, mysterious things. That's the kind of world I grew up in."[12]

The "odd, mysterious things" that lurk in the wilderness constantly threaten to disrupt the rational universe on Lynch's *Twin Peaks*. Long before he invented his soap opera, Lynch—who came of age in the 1960s—fantasized about creating a show that would feature the Log Lady. Each weekly episode of the imaginary series, entitled *I'll Test My Log with Every Branch of Knowledge*, would comically examine scientific efforts to make sense of nature. Lynch imagined that the Log Lady "takes the Log to various experts in various fields of science or whatever. Like, if she goes to the dentist, the Log would get put into the chair. With a little bib on it. The dentist would X-ray the Log, even to find out where its teeth were. So through the Log, through this kind of absurdity, you would learn, you'd be gaining so much knowledge," he theorized.[13] On *Twin Peaks*, the quest for knowledge extends not only into the physical wilderness (into the forest's internal "cavities") but also into the outer realms of the universe. Like the Log Lady's log, extraterrestrials are nonhuman life forms that can allegedly communicate and interact with the town's local citizens. But in episode nine, when Major Briggs tries to translate extraterrestrial messages, he ends up with "gibberish." Lynch exposes the folly of attempting to explain nature's mysteries either by resorting to scientific technology or by practicing a particular religious creed. Agent Cooper's reliance on Buddhist teachings to help solve the puzzle of Laura's death, for example, in episode two inspires the Tibetan rock–throwing contest, an exercise in slapstick absurdity.

Certain characters on *Twin Peaks* believe that they are links in a great chain of being, one that includes human as well as nonhuman life forms. Because they coexist and interact with elements in their earthly and cosmic environments, it might be tempting to argue that these characters express Lynch's belief in peaceful cohabitation, one of the tenets of environmental philosophy. But the failure of those who try (either rationally or mystically) to relate to the elements suggests the inappropriateness of looking in *Twin Peaks* for didactic messages. "I'm of the Western Union school. If you want to send a message, go to Western Union," Lynch once said in an interview, ridiculing the critical impulse to look for overt meaning in art.[14] Environmentalism on *Twin Peaks* is portrayed inconsistently. After losing control of his real estate project, for example, Benjamin Horne tries to stop Catherine Packard Martell from building Ghost Wood Estates. In episode twenty–six, posing as a developer–turned–conservationist, Horne alleges that the "pine weasel" (*Twin Peaks*'s equivalent of the spotted owl) will become extinct if Martell disrupts its habitat. By episode twenty–eight, however, Benjamin—who suffers from bouts of insanity—seems to have become a real conservationist and sincere vegetarian. While plotting with a group of environmentalists to stop Martell from building Ghost Wood Estates, he nibbles earnestly on carrots and celery. Instead of imparting a distinct and consistent philosophy, *Twin Peaks* demonstrates a unique sensibility. Concerned less with the content of its programming than with the attitude towards its material, the show often treats serious issues with sophomoric humor.

Crusaders such as Rachel Carson, however, view human action in strict moral terms. Pollution, according to Carson, is an "evil" (6) that corrupts nature's food chain, contaminating human beings, plant life, and animals. Carson argues that people have allowed herbicides and insecticides to harm with impunity, in a world as "weird" as "The

Addams Family" (33), she claims, invoking an unexpected analogy. While it seems odd for a scientific writer to resort to fanciful metaphor, Carson does so in order to contrast a humane world with an unjust environment. For Carson, the cartoon series is a popular contemporary example of chaos run wild. "The Addams Family," appearing during the 1960s in *The New Yorker* magazine, depicts a bizarre amoral universe, one in which monsters play pranks on unsuspecting humans in a decent but bland middle-class neighborhood. The characters in "The Addams Family" and the people on *Twin Peaks* inhabit the same anarchic zone, in which evil triumphs subversively. From David Lynch's perspective, victimization and suffering have morbid entertainment value rather than moral meaning or real human poignancy. The closest thing to an environmental "message" that *Twin Peaks* delivers in episode eight is Ed Hurley's zany soliloquy. Explaining why he no longer hunts, Ed says that once, when he shot at a pheasant, the bullet ricocheted off a tree and put out his wife's eye. The story ends with a punchline instead of a moral, for providing this context ensures that, whenever Nadine appears in subsequent episodes, her eye patch serves as a sight gag rather than as a symbol of tragedy.

If a disregard for wildlife generates consequences that are humorous, although humanly grave, an appreciation for nature creates situations that are just as often ridiculous. As someone new to Twin Peaks, Agent Cooper appreciates the Pacific Northwestern wilderness. But as an investigator, he subjects nature, like the people and clues in his case, to trained objective analysis. Unlike Agent Cooper—who has a comic obsession with classifying animals (snowshoe rabbits) and trees (Douglas firs)—the irrational Icelandic businessmen, who come to Twin Peaks to invest in Ghost Wood Estates, have a folk sense, a blood instinct, a mythic yearning for forest land. Having left the arctic tundra, the Icelanders worship this new western landscape without quite knowing why. They become born-again, tree-hugging maniacs, meeting in episode five in "The Timber Room" at the Great Northern Hotel, where they get drunk and incoherently sing a translated Icelandic version of "Home on the Range."

The Log Lady is nature's most zealous worshipper. Cradling her log, whispering to it, treating it as though it were a personified crystal ball, the Log Lady demonstrates the apparent truth of Agent Cooper's remark—made in episode three, when he first comes to Twin Peaks—that "all life has meaning here." The log has neither purpose nor mean-

The Log Lady. (Courtesy Lynch/Frost Productions.)

ing, however. As a device, like everything else on *Twin Peaks*, it turns out to be mostly nonsensical. The Log Lady opens the show's premiere episode, holding her log on her lap and sitting in a log chair in front of a log–burning fireplace. In her introductory monologue, she alludes to "the mystery of the woods, the woods surrounding Twin Peaks." In the subsequent episode, referring to the "mystery" that might explain Laura's death, she tells Agent Cooper, "One day my log will have some–

thing to say." Agent Cooper, hoping that the log might have information, says, "Really, what did it see?" When the Log Lady tells him to ask it, Agent Cooper puts his ear to the log, listens, and then says, "I thought so." The Log Lady doesn't reveal the log's secret message to viewers, although she suggests in the introduction to episode nine that it might have something to do with "creamed corn."

Does the log, like nature itself, contain answers to life's deepest mysteries? Or is the log what it seems to be, an insensate object that the Log Lady has comically fetishized? *Twin Peaks* acknowledges the mystery and beauty of the Pacific Northwestern wilderness. But it also humorously celebrates the exploitation, objectification, and commodification of nature by the town's crazy residents. In episode twenty–eight, the image of Benjamin Horne's mentally retarded son Johnny, wearing an Indian headdress and shooting rubber–tipped arrows at cardboard cut-outs of buffalo, may suggest the predatory nature of people who dwell in the wilderness. But the inspired lunacy of this scene softens the message's impact on viewers. Killing may not be a good thing, but it is often a fun thing on Lynch's *Twin Peaks*. The deer–antler door handles in the Great Northern Hotel; the television in Leo's home, supporting a squirrel figurine; the log bed in which Agent Cooper sleeps, next to a nightstand on which his gun and a ceramic Indian rest side by side: these various objects memorialize the progress that civilization has made in the wilderness. Rather than lamenting the deforestation of mountain land, the extermination of wildlife species, and the passing of Indians, the show sometimes amuses viewers by reminding them of the human resourcefulness, the tacky inventiveness, and the marvelously poor taste that has made the production and consumption of these kitsch objects possible. The notion that a whole herd of deer has to die so their antlers can be turned into a chandelier that will hang in the lobby of the Great Northern Hotel, for example, has a let–them–eat-cake quality about it, a decadent ring to it, in tune with the consumerism of the 1980s, which the hip *Twin Peaks* comments on. Instead of judging this phenomenon critically, Lynch actively participates in the process of mass exploitation, collaborating with his writers and producers to transform the show itself into a brand–name commodity. While the town of Twin Peaks traffics in fetishized objects, the show of the same name produces, markets, and distributes a series of twenty-nine disposable soap–opera episodes, to be consumed by a cult audience eager to view the work of a well–known *auteur*.

The environmental activist and writer Edward Abbey once claimed that the human race's destruction of its natural habitat would make for a "mighty book worthy of a modern Melville or Tolstoy. But our best fictioneers confine themselves to domestic drama—soap opera with literary trimmings," he noted sarcastically.[15] The forest has inspired works in American literature that one might call soap operas. As a space filled with ancient trees that have grown through the centuries, it lends itself to the creation of generational sagas that span great lengths of time. The deforestation of timber land—a time-consuming, sequential act—lends itself to the production of episodic, ongoing narratives. Set in Wisconsin and spanning the course of twenty-five years, Edna Ferber's *Come And Get It* (1935), a sudsy bestseller, demonstrates how the logging industry in the early twentieth century affects the fortunes of one family dynasty. Even Ken Kesey's *Sometimes a Great Notion* (1964), a complex stream-of-consciousness narrative, in spite of its artsy pretensions can't disguise its soap-opera origins. Taking place during a strike at a family-owned lumber mill, located in the contemporary backwoods of Oregon, the novel narrates the story of a woman who loves and has to choose between two rival brothers.

Twin Peaks, like these western soap operas, celebrates the process of frontier expansion while at the same time mourning the outcome of that process, the loss of northwestern forest land. This fundamental ambivalence helps explain the show's ambiguity. At different times on *Twin Peaks*, the forest instills human terror, vaguely morbid forebodings, and mystical feelings of reverence. In particular instances, the process of deforestation results in a boost to the local economy, in environmental catastrophe, or in the production of aesthetic objects that the show values for their outrageous tastelessness. Although the show itself ceased production after less than two years, *Twin Peaks*, like the frontier, never ended or closed. The availability of reruns on television and the reproduction of *Twin Peaks* on video make lasting access to the soap opera possible. Like the frontier, *Twin Peaks* is a process, one that has a repeated, incantatory, magic power to tantalize. Its promise of renewal is summoned by the repetition of the talismanic phrase that closes each episode: "To be continued . . ."

Permissions

A modified and condensed version of "Little House on the Rice Paddy" first appeared in *American Literary History* vol. 10 (1998). It reappears here by permission of Oxford University Press. "Anastasia of Oregon" first appeared in *Arizona Quarterly* vol. 51 (1995). It is reprinted by permission of the Regents of The University of Arizona. An early version of "The White Open Spaces," published under the title "Deadwood Dick: The Black Cowboy as Cultural Timber," first appeared in the *Journal of American Culture* vol. 16 (1993).

The author gratefully acknowledges the following sources for permission to reprint images in this book: p. 49, The Museum of Modern Art, Film Stills Archive; p. 53, © The Church of Jesus Christ of Latter-Day Saints, used by permission; p. 56, Denver Public Library, Western History Department; p. 68–69, reproduced by permission of the Henry E. Huntington Library and Art Gallery, San Marino, CA; p. 70, Reproduced by permission of the Henry E. Huntington Library and Art Gallery, San Marino, CA; p. 82, Massachusetts Historical Society; p. 85, Image #CN83, Opal Whiteley Collection PH204, Special Collections, University of Oregon Library; p. 90, Image #CN2, Opal Whiteley Collection PH204, Special Collections, University of Oregon Library; p. 91, Massachusetts Historical Society; p. 92, Image #CN82, Opal Whiteley Collection PH204, Special Collections, University of Oregon Library; p. 110, Manuscript Collection, Indiana Historical Society Library, Negative No. C5741; p. 115, © Turner Entertainment Co., all rights reserved; p. 124, © R. Marsh

Starks; p. 142, The Denver Public Library, Western History Department; p. 149, courtesy Academy of Motion Picture Arts and Sciences, © 1937 Turner Entertainment Co., all rights reserved; p. 156, courtesy Academy of Motion Picture Arts and Sciences, © 1995 by Paramount Pictures, all rights reserved; p. 165, courtesy Columbia Pictures, © 1967 by Pax Enterprises, Inc.; p. 178, courtesy Lynch/Frost Productions; p. 184, courtesy Lynch/Frost Productions.

Notes

INTRODUCTION

1. Lee Clark Mitchell begins his acknowledgments facetiously by thanking his friends for indulging his interest in "popular culture." See *Westerns: Making the Man in Fiction and Film* (Chicago: University of Chicago Press, 1996), xv.
2. Elizabeth Cook-Lynn, "Why I Can't Read Wallace Stegner," in *Why I Can't Read Wallace Stegner and Other Essays: A Tribal Voice* (Madison: University of Wisconsin Press, 1996), 29–40.
3. Wallace Stegner, "Born a Square," in *The Sound of Mountain Water* (Garden City, NY: Doubleday, 1969), 174–75.
4. Stegner, "History, Myth, and the Western Writer," in ibid., 195.
5. The Western History Association and the Western Literature Association claim approximately 2,000 and 700 members, respectively. Numbers based on 1997 estimates.
6. In 1997, Melody Graulich replaced Thomas J. Lyon as editor of *Western American Literature*. It remains to be seen whether this is a temporary or permanent change. In the past, Mr. Lyon has stepped aside, allowing others to edit the journal, only to reassume his position after a year or so.
7. *Western American Literature* 32 (1997): 65–69.
8. Annete Kolodny, "Letting Go Our Grand Obsessions: Notes Toward a New Literary History of the American Frontiers," *American Literature* 64 (March 1992): 3.
9. Ibid., 13.
10. Ibid., 9.

ONE: The White Open Spaces

1. Frederick Jackson Turner, "The Significance of the Frontier in American History," in *The Significance of the Frontier in American History*, ed. Harold P. Simonson (New York: Continuum, 1991 rpt.), 44.

2. In 1995, the University of Nebraska Press issued Love's book in paperback, printing a facsimile of the first edition of 1907.

3. In "Negro Art and Literature," W.E.B. DuBois established the precedent, excluding Love from a discussion of important black writers [*The Gift of Black Folk: The Negroes in the Making of America* (Boston: Stratford, 1924 rpt.), 287–319]. Since then, only two histories of blacks in the West have mentioned Love's name: William Loren Katz, *The Black West* (Seattle: Open Hand, 1987), 150–52; and W. Sherman Savage, *Blacks in the West* (Westport, CT: Greenwood, 1976), 90–91. Each work curtly summarizes *The Life and Adventures*, failing to provide an in–depth analysis of Love's autobiography. Three recent articles mention Love's work in passing: "Black Rodeos: Once Locked Out of Big–Time Rodeos, Blacks Still Compete Mainly Against Each Other," *Black Enterprise* 2 (1972): 39–41 (no author cited); H. Lloyd Gaines and Edith Gaines, "Land of the Black Cowboys," *Sepia* 23 (1974): 35–40; and Gloria Mushonge, "Blacks in the Old West," *Journal of Intergroup Relations* 37 (1980): 55–57. These brief articles treat Love's work superficially.

4. Nat Love, *The Life and Adventures of Nat Love, Better Known in the Cattle Country as "Deadwood Dick,"* ed. William Loren Katz (New York: Arno, 1968 rpt.), 7. Subsequent references to this edition appear in the text.

5. Turner, 46.

6. Elsewhere, Love writes: "I was not the wild blood thirsty savage and all around bad man many writers have pictured me" (70). It is unclear which writers Love is referring to, since no other author is known to have mentioned him. Some critics argue that Love took his nickname from "Deadwood Dick," the dime novel hero who disguised himself in a black mask and costume. [See, for example, Philip Durham and Everett L. Jones, *The Adventures of the Negro Cowboys* (New York: Dodd, Mead, 1965), 103; and Richard Slatta, *Cowboys of the Americas* (New Haven: Yale University Press, 1990), 169.] Edward Wheeler, however, didn't publish the first Deadwood Dick novel until a year after Love claimed the name. [Christine Bold, *Selling the West: Popular Western Fiction, 1860 to 1960* (Bloomington: Indiana University Press, 1987), 13.] At this time, no evidence documents Wheeler's influence on Love or vice versa. Perhaps it is merely coincidence that the black cowboy and the dime novel hero share the same name, given the fact that Deadwood, Dakota Territory—a popular hangout like Abilene and Dodge City, Kansas—was a cultural reference point for cowboys and a source of nicknames as well.

7. Durham and Jones claim that approximately 5,000 black men, comprising one–fifth to one–fourth of all working cowboys, passed through the U.S. frontier in the late nineteenth century [*The Negro Cowboys* (Lincoln: University of Nebraska Press, 1983 rpt.), 44]. Katz echoes this claim (146), as do the following: Savage (2); Slatta (168); Kenneth Wiggins Porter, *The Negro on the American Frontier* (New York: Arno, 1971), 521; and Lawrence D. Rice, *The Negro in Texas, 1874–1900* (Baton Rouge: Louisiana State University Press, 1971), 196. William W. Savage Jr. criticizes scholars who repeat these statistics without verifying them, noting that a lack of evidence makes it impossible to prove or disprove these claims [*The Cowboy Hero: His Image in*

American History and Culture (Norman: University of Oklahoma Press, 1979), 6–7].

8. U.S. census figures show that 384 blacks lived in Kansas in 1840; 2,179 in 1850; 7,689 in 1860; and 33,109 in 1870, the year after Love first appeared.

9. In *Cowboys of the Americas*, Slatta mistakenly claims that the celebration took place in Deadwood, Arizona–not in Deadwood, Dakota Territory. He also states incorrectly that Love was born in Ohio (169).

10. For a discussion of train traveling as bondage, see Michel de Certeau, "Railway Navigation and Incarceration," in *The Practice of Everyday Life*, trans. Steven F. Rendall (Berkeley: University of California Press, 1984), 111.

11. Slatta, 159.

12. Jack Santino, *Miles of Smiles, Years of Struggle: Stories of Black Pullman Porters* (Urbana: University of Illinois Press, 1989), 6, 8.

13. Ibid., 18–19, 23.

14. Ibid., 68.

15. Sidonie Smith, *Where I'm Bound: Patterns of Slavery and Freedom in Black American Autobiography* (Westport, CT: Greenwood, 1974), 8.

16. Robert B. Stepto defines the "primary pregeneric myth for Afro–America [as] the quest for freedom and literacy" [*From Behind the Veil: A Study of Afro-American Narrative* (Urbana: University of Illinois Press, 1979), ix]. Valerie Smith examines a similar quest in Frederick Douglass's work [*Self-Discovery and Authority in Afro-American Narrative* (Cambridge: Harvard University Press, 1987), 24–25].

17. Henry Louis Gates Jr., *The Signifying Monkey: A Theory of Afro-American Literary Criticism* (New York: Oxford University Press, 1988), xxv–xxvii.

18. Ishmael Reed, *Yellow Back Radio Broke-Down* (New York: Atheneum, 1988 rpt.). For similar representations, see "The Jackal–Headed Cowboy," "I am a Cowboy in the Boat of Ra," and "Loup Garou Means Change Into," in Reed, *New and Collected Poems* (New York: Atheneum, 1988), 5–7, 17–18, 125–26.

19. Richard Yarborough, "Race, Violence, and Manhood: The Masculine Ideal in Frederick Douglass's 'The Heroic Slave'," in *Frederick Douglass: New Literary and Historical Essays*, ed. Eric J. Sundquist (Cambridge: Cambridge University Press, 1990), 174. For a related discussion, see Yarborough, "Strategies of Black Characterization in *Uncle Tom's Cabin* and the Early Afro–American Novel," in *New Essays on "Uncle Tom's Cabin,"* ed. Eric J. Sundquist, (Cambridge: Cambridge University Press, 1986), 52.

20. William L. Andrews claims that "the politics of literary interpretation in the 1960s" explains the ascendance of Frederick Douglass over Booker T. Washington. Andrews notes that autobiographies published during this period had an "apocalyptic tone or revolutionary message" that resonated with Frederick Douglass's work more than with Washington's. Since the 1960s, Douglass's work has represented "the epitome of and model for the slave narrative in most early studies of black autobiography" ["Towards a Poetics of Afro–American Autobiography," in *Afro-American Literary Study in the 1990s*, ed. Houston A. Baker, Jr., and Patricia Redmond (Chicago: University of Chicago Press, 1989), 82].

21. Howard W. Felton, *Nat Love, Negro Cowboy* (New York: Dodd, Mead, 1969), 11.

22. Houston A. Baker, Jr., *Long Black Song: Essays in Black American Literature and Culture* (Charlottesville: University Press of Virginia, 1972), 2.

TWO: Less Than Zorro

1. David Farmer and Rennard Strickland claim that Ridge was the "first truly professional Indian writer" in their introduction, "John Rollin Ridge," in Farmer and Strickland, comps. and eds., *A Trumpet of Our Own: Yellow Bird's Essays on the North American Indian* (San Francisco: Book Club of California, 1981), 31. To date no one has challenged this claim.

2. See A. LaVonne Brown Ruoff, "American Indian Literatures: A Guide to Anthologies, Texts, and Research," in *Studies in American Indian Literature: Critical Essays and Course Designs*, ed. Paula Gunn Allen (New York: Modern Language Association of America, 1983), 305; and Peter G. Christensen, "Minority Interaction in John Rollin Ridge's *The Life and Adventures of Joaquín Murieta*," *MELUS* 17 (Summer 1991–92): 61. Charles R. Larson incorrectly identifies Chief Simon Pokagon's *Queen of the Woods* (1899) as the first Native American novel, in *American Indian Fiction* (Albuquerque: University of New Mexico Press, 1978), 2. In fact, *The Life and Adventures of Joaquín Murieta* preceded Chief Pokagon's novel by forty–five years.

3. Christensen, 61.

4. Leonard Pitt writes that Joaquín Murieta became "California's foremost folk legend," in *The Decline of the Californios: A Social History of the Spanish-Speaking Californians, 1846–1890* (Berkeley: University of California Press, 1968), 81. Joseph Henry Jackson states that Ridge "produced the right fiction at the right moment and in the right place. California badly needed a folk hero and had none." See Jackson, "Introduction," in Ridge, *The Life and Adventures of Joaquín Murieta* (Norman: University of Oklahoma Press, 1986 rpt.), xii.

5. For formal definitions as well as impressionistic accounts of what it means to live in the "borderlands," see Gloria Anzaldúa, "La Prieta," in *This Bridge Called My Back: Writings By Radical Women of Color*, ed. Cherríe Moraga and Gloria Anzaldúa (New York: Kitchen Table, 1983 rpt.), 205–06; and Anzaldúa, *Borderlands/La Frontera: The New Mestiza* (San Francisco: spinsters/aunt lute, 1987), i–ii, 3.

6. For more information concerning the discovery of gold in the Cherokee Nation, the resulting efforts of the U.S. government to purchase Cherokee land, the intertribal disputes about whether to sell to the government, and the fatalities that occurred because of government policies and intertribal disputes, see Farmer and Strickland, 15–19; James W. Parins, *John Rollin Ridge: His Life and Works* (Lincoln: University of Nebraska Press, 1991), 18–29; Lucy Maddox, *Removals: Nineteenth-Century American Literature and the Politics of Indian Affairs* (New York: Oxford University Press, 1991), 17–18; and William G. McLoughlin, *The Cherokees and Christianity, 1794–1870: Essays on Acculturation and Cultural Persistance*, ed. Walter H. Conser Jr. (Athens: University of Georgia Press, 1994), 113.

7. For a full account of the events in Ridge's life during this period, see Parins, 32–60.

8. Richard Griswold del Castillo, *The Treaty of Guadalupe Hidalgo: A Legacy of Conflict* (Norman: University of Oklahoma Press, 1990), 190.

9. For an analysis of the tax law and its impact on foreigners, see Parins, 98; and Jackson, "Introduction, " xv–xvi. Reasons for targeting Hispanics, especially Mexicans, are cited in Remi Nadeau, *The Real Joaquín Murieta: California's Gold Rush Bandit: Truth vs. Myth* (Santa Barbara: Crest, 1974), 22; and in Douglas Monroy, *Thrown Among Strangers: The Making of Mexican Culture in Frontier California* (Berkeley: University of California Press, 1990), 201–02.

10. Although California historians tend to agree that Ridge's hero was based on a composite of real-life bandits and outlaws, Nadeau suggests that he was based on one man specifically. Nadeau claims that the character was named after a real-life "Joaquín," who "terrorized Armador, Calaveras, and probably Mariposa counties for just two months—January to early March, 1853. In that short period he ran up such a fearful catalogue of crimes that the local population began to flee and the Legislature was forced by aroused opinion to raise a company against him" (20).

11. Ridge, *The Life and Adventures of Joaquín Murieta*, 9. Subsequent references to the 1986 reprint of the first edition appear in the text. The first edition of the novel was published in 1854. A pirated version, printed by the California *Police Gazette*, ran in ten weekly installments, from September 3 to November 5, 1859. Because of its similarity to Ridge's work, this version is often referred to as the second edition, although Ridge received neither authorship credit nor royalties. In 1871 Ridge issued a revised version of his novel, which divided the work into chapters and added some new material. In order not to confuse it with the California *Police Gazette* version, Ridge's second edition of *The Life and Adventures of Joaquín Murieta* is usually referred to by scholars as the third edition. For more information on the novel's various incarnations and publishing history, see Franklin Walker, "Ridge's Life of Joaquín Murieta: The First and Revised Editions Compared," *California Historical Society Quarterly* 16 (1937): 256–62.

12. Parins writes: In "some ways Joaquín's early history was much like that of the writer who was to immortalize him; his later career had to appeal to Ridge's deep thirst for revenge" (103). This thought is echoed by Farmer and Strickland, 25; by Nadeau, 120; by Pitt, 81; by Franklin Walker, in *San Francisco's Literary Frontier* (New York: Knopf, 1939), 53; by Andrew Wiget, in *Native American Literature* (Boston: Twayne, 1985), 63–64; by Chris Burchfield, in "The Sweet, Sad Song of Yellow Bird, California's Confederate Cherokee," *The Californians* 8 (November–December, 1990): 20; and by Louis Owens, in *Other Destinies: Understanding the American Indian Novel* (Norman: University of Oklahoma Press, 1992), 8, 39. Firsthand evidence of Ridge's "thirst for revenge" can be found in some of his nonfiction writings. See, for example, personal letters republished in Edward Everett Dale and Gaston Litton, eds., *Cherokee Cavaliers: Forty Years of Cherokee History as Told in the Correspondence of the Ridge-*

Watie-Boudinot Family (Norman: University of Oklahoma Press, 1939), 64, 77; and newspaper editorials reprinted in Farmer and Strickland, 76.

13. Krupat, *For Those Who Come After: A Study of Native American Autobiography* (Berkeley: University of California Press, 1989 rpt.), 48.

14. Parins, 76.

15. For example, see Walker, 53; Burchfield, 20, 23; and Pitt, 81.

16. Those who speculate about why Ridge "sold out" include Christensen, 63; Owens, 33; and A. LaVonne Brown Ruoff, "On Literature in English: American Indian Authors, 1774–1899," in *Critical Essays on Native American Literature*, ed. Andrew Wiget (Boston: Hall, 1985), 198.

17. A more extensive catalog of Cherokee accomplishments can be found in McLoughlin, 3–4; in Brian W. Dippie, *The Vanishing American: White Attitudes and U.S. Indian Policy* (Middletown: Wesleyan University Press, 1982), 57; and in Arnold Krupat, *Ethnocriticism: Ethnography, History, Literature* (Berkeley: University of California Press, 1992), 149–50.

18. McLoughlin, 132.

19. As quoted in Parins, 54. For more information about the slave holdings of Ridge's father and grandfather, see McLoughlin, 12, 18.

20. Ridge's poem, "The Atlantic Cable," addresses both themes [*Poems*, San Francisco: Payot, 1868), 17–21].

21. Ridge's opinions on such subjects as social Darwinism, scientific racism, Manifest Destiny, and nineteenth–century technology are revealed and interpreted in Parins, 124–39, 146–55.

22. Karl Kroeber, "American Indian Persistence and Resurgence," *boundary 2* 19 (Fall 1992): 9.

23. Krupat, *For Those Who Come After*, 31.

24. Ibid., 52. Krupat returns to this notion of the text as "frontier" in *Ethnocriticism*, 5.

25. See, respectively, Farmer and Strickland, 31; and Angie Debo, "John Rollin Ridge," *Southwest Review* 17 (Autumn 1931): 67.

26. Krupat, *Ethnocriticism*, 153.

27. Owens suggests that "the internally persuasive discourse of the oppressed and marginalized minority continually subverts the authority of the dominant discourse" (34). This reading supports the notion once expressed by Roberto Fernández Retamar: "Prospero invaded the islands, killed our ancestors, enslaved Caliban, and taught him his language to make himself understood. What else can Caliban do but use that same language—today he has no other—to curse him . . . ?" See *Caliban and Other Essays*, trans. Edward Baker (Minneapolis: University of Minnesota Press, 1989), 14.

28. The "eloquent" noble savage is a fixture in nineteenth–century American literature. See Roy Harvey Pearce, *Savagism and Civilization: A Study of the Indian and the American Mind* (Baltimore: Johns Hopkins University Press, 1967 rpt.), 78–79; Louise K. Barnett, *The Ignoble Savage: American Literary Racism, 1790–1890* (Westport, CT: Greenwood, 1975), 75; and David Murray, *Forked Tongues: Speech, Writing and Representation in North American Indian Texts* (London: Pinter, 1991), 41–42.

29. As Christensen points out, Ridge was less ambivalent and more critical in

his representation of Indians, certain ones of which he felt belonged to debased western tribes (64–65, 70).

30. My thinking about Indian captivity narratives has been influenced by Richard Slotkin, *Regeneration Through Violence: The Mythology of the Frontier, 1600–1860* (Middletown: Wesleyan University Press, 1987 rpt.), 94, 99, 101–102, 109, 269. Barnett writes about the way in which the stereotype of the "bad Indian" alternates with the representation of the "noble savage" in nineteenth–century literature (48–49, 85–87).

31. Robert F. Berkhofer Jr. offers reasons for the development of the romantic cult of the Indian, in *The White Man's Indian: Images of the American Indian from Columbus to the Present* (New York: Vintage, 1979 rpt.), 86–88. In a related observation, Pitt claims that by "worshiping a Joaquín motivated by revenge at Yankee injustices, the Yankees admitted at least partial responsibility for the early struggles with the Spanish–American miners" (285).

32. Ronald Takaki, *A Different Mirror: A History of Multicultural America* (Boston: Little, Brown, 1993), 178.

33. For a discussion of the relation of the Indian to the development of a national literature, see Barnett, 21–24; and Maddox, 36–38.

34. Slotkin, *The Fatal Environment: The Myth of the Frontier in the Age of Industrialization, 1800–1890* (Middletown: Wesleyan University Press, 1986 rpt.), 32. For Slotkin, Custer's Last Stand presents American history as a race war in which the losers are Cowboys, not Indians. For more on the appeal of this particular paradigm, see 17, 47.

35. Parins argues convincingly that "Mount Shasta" follows Shelley's "Mont Blanc" in terms of theme, description, diction, and meter (87).

36. In a later collection of poetry, an additional break is printed before the poem's final nine lines. See Ridge, *Poems*, 16.

37. Arthur Francis Eichorn Sr., *The Mt. Shasta Story* (Mount Shasta: Mount Shasta Herald, 1957), 21.

38. Werner Sollors, *Beyond Ethnicity: Consent and Descent in American Culture* (New York: Oxford University Press, 1986), 126.

39. Homi Bhabha, "Introduction: Narrating the Nation," in *Nation and Narration*, ed. H. Bhabha (London: Routledge, 1991 rpt.), 3, 5.

40. Pitt, 7–8, 214–16.

41. John Lowe argues that the "expulsion from Eden/home is a constant theme" in the novel, in "Space and Freedom in the Golden Republic: Yellow Bird's *The Life and Adventures of Joaquín Murieta, The Celebrated California Bandit*," *Studies in American Indian Literature* 4 (Fall 1992): 107. Speaking more generally, Debo claims that the author's bent "was all Christian" (71).

42. In a letter dated October 9, 1854, Ridge claims that his book has sold only 7,000 copies, due to the fact that his publishers have quit business and left California (reprinted in Dale and Litton, 82). Parins questions this claim, noting that public court documents fail to list Ridge's publishers among businesses filing for bankruptcy. Parins believes that Ridge, embarrassed by the book's meager sales, may have been making excuses and "trying to put the best face on … affairs" (106).

43. Pitt, 284; Nadeau, 14.

44. For comparisons between Joaquín Murieta and Robin Hood, see Jackson, xxvii; and Walker, 51. Nadeau denies the validity of this comparison, pointing out that Murieta was a selfish, bloodthirsty murderer (22, 144–45). Distinguishing between "noble robbers," such as Robin Hood, and "avengers," such as Ridge's Mexican character, Eric Hobsbawm writes that avengers are "exerters of power" rather than "men who right wrongs ... their appeal is not that of the agents of justice, but of men who prove that even the poor and weak can be terrible." See *Bandits* (New York: Delacorte, 1969), 50.

45. Other versions of the story, however, have interpreted Joaquín Murieta as a defender of Latino and Chicano societies. See, for example, Pablo Neruda, *Splendor and Death of Joaquín Murieta*, trans. Ben Belitt (New York: Farrar, Straus and Giroux, 1972 rpt.); and Rodolpho Gonzales, "I am Joaquín" (N.p.: n.p., 1967), an epic poem which became an anthem of the Chicano movement in the late 1960s.

46. Later versions of the story have sought to make Murieta resemble Zorro and thus appear more like Robin Hood. In a popular account written by Walter Nobel Burns, Murieta uses a knife to cut an "M" on his victims' foreheads, just as Zorro slashes a "Z" with his sword. The resemblance is superficial, however, since Murieta is a murderer who cuts up his victims, unlike Zorro, who leaves his signature on wanted posters, walls of build-ings, etc. [See *The Robin Hood of El Dorado: The Saga of Joaquín Murieta, Famous Outlaw of California's Age of Gold* (New York: Coward–McCann, 1932), 37.] In 1936, MGM released *Robin Hood of El Dorado*, based on Burns's book, star-ring Warner Baxter and Ann Loring. Four years later, 20th Century–Fox issued *The Mark of Zorro*, starring Tyrone Power and Linda Darnell.

THREE: Wife #19, Etc.

1. Leonard J. Arrington and Jon Haupt, "Intolerable Zion: The Image of Mormonism in Nineteenth–Century American Literature," *Western Humanities Review* 22 (1968): 244.

2. Jessie L. Embry, *Mormon Polygamous Families: Life in the Principle* (Salt Lake City: University of Utah Press, 1987), 8.

3. For information concerning the first four antipolygamy novels, which appeared in 1855–56, see Arrington and Haupt, 244–53.

4. Harriet Beecher Stowe, "Preface," in Mrs. T.B.H. (Fanny) Stenhouse, *"Tell It All": The Story of a Life's Experience in Mormonism: An Autobiography* (Hartford, CT: Worthington, 1874), vi.

5. Ann Eliza Young, *Wife No. 19, or the Story of a Life in Bondage, Being a Complete Exposé of Mormonism, and Revealing the Sorrows, Sacrifices and Sufferings of Women in Polygamy* (Hartford, CT: Dustin, Gilman, 1876), 32.

6. For a discussion of Ann Eliza Young's performance on tour, see Irving Wallace, *The Twenty-seventh Wife* (New York: Simon and Schuster, 1961), 291–304.

7. Richard S. Van Wagoner, *Mormon Polygamy: A History* (Salt Lake City: Signature, 1989), 85–86.

8. Ray R. Canning and Beverly Beeton summarize the political situation that led to the Mormon War in their introduction to *The Genteel Gentile: Letters of Elizabeth Cumming, 1857–1858* (Salt Lake City: Tanner, 1977), xiii–xiv. See also Norman F. Furniss, *The Mormon Conflict 1850–1859* (New Haven: Yale University Press, 1966 rpt.), 87.

9. The Book of Mormon's genealogical history of American Indians is explained in greater detail in Van Wagoner, 224; Nels Anderson, *Desert Saints: The Mormon Frontier in Utah* (Chicago: University of Chicago Press, 1942), 11; Dean C. Jessee, comp. and ed., *The Personal Writings of Joseph Smith* (Salt Lake City: Deseret, 1984), 211, 273; Leonard J. Arrington, *Brigham Young: American Moses* (New York: Knopf, 1985), 211; and Scott H. Faulring, ed., *An American Prophet's Record: The Diaries and Journals of Joseph Smith* (Salt Lake City: Signature, 1989), 57.

10. Leonard J. Arrington and Davis Bitton, *The Mormon Experience: A History of the Latter-Day Saints* (New York: Knopf, 1979), 147.

11. Ibid., 146; Furniss, 33.

12. Arrington, 210.

13. The Mormons' methods for dealing with Indians are outlined in Arrington, 210, 219, 221; Arrington and Bitton, 149, 151, 153; and Austin and Alta Fife, *Saints of Sage and Saddle: Folklore Among the Mormons* (Bloomington: Indiana University Press, 1956), 155.

14. Arrington and Bitton, 156.

15. Wallace Stegner, *Mormon Country* (New York: Duell, Sloan, and Pearce, 1942), 31.

16. Arrington, 256; Arrington and Bitton, 148.

17. See Wallace Stegner, *The Gathering of Zion: The Story of the Mormon Trail* (New York: McGraw-Hill, 1964), for a book-length study of the way in which nineteenth-century Mormons used Christian typology.

18. John Doyle Lee offered one of the most lively, though highly suspect, accounts of the Danites in his 1877 autobiography, *The Mormon Menace; Being the Confession of John Doyle Lee, Danite* (New York: Home Protection, 1905 rpt.).

19. Historians still debate whether Mormons played a role in this tragedy. The recognized authority on the subject, however, argues that a group of Mormons, probably acting without Brigham Young's knowledge, indeed were responsible. See Juanita Brooks, *The Mountain Meadows Massacre* (Stanford, CA: Stanford University Press, 1950).

20. Arrington, 257.

21. For information concerning men whom Buchanan appointed to serve in the Mormon War, see Canning and Beeton, xiii–xiv.

22. See Arrington and Bitton, 186, for an account of Mormon theology, including a discussion of the reproduction of spirits in heaven.

23. As cited in D. Carmon Hardy, *Solemn Covenant: The Mormon Polygamous Passage* (Urbana: University of Illinois Press, 1992), 15.

24. Charles A. Cannon, "The Awesome Power of Sex: The Polemical Campaign Against Mormon Polygamy," *Pacific Historical Review* 43 (1974): 71.
25. Richard Slotkin, *Regeneration Through Violence: The Mythology of the American Frontier, 1600–1860* (Middletown: Wesleyan University Press, 1973), 95.
26. Ibid., 109, 135.
27. Roy Harvey Pearce, "The Significance of the Captivity Narrative," *American Literature* 19 (1947): 9.
28. See, for example, *In the Toils; or, Martyrs of the Latter Days* (Chicago: Dixon and Shepard, 1879), in which Mrs. A. G. Paddock writes that her heroine was terrorized by a mysterious stranger whose eyes "repelled while they mastered you" (11).
29. Maria Ward (pseud.), "The Editor's Design," in Austin N. Ward (pseud.), *The Husband in Utah; or, Sights and Scenes among the Mormons*, ed. Maria Ward (New York: Derby and Jackson, 1857), ix.
30. Richard F. Burton, *The City of the Saints, and Across the Rocky Mountains to California* (New York: Harper, 1862), 116.
31. J. H. Beadle attests that Indians are, "by nature, habit and religion, thoroughgoing polygamists." See *Life in Utah; or, the Mysteries and Crimes of Mormonism. Being an Exposé of the Secret Rites and Ceremonies of the Latter-Day Saints* (Philadelphia: National, 1870), 357.
32. Mrs. B. G. Ferris, *The Mormons at Home; with Some Incidents of Travel from Missouri to California, 1852–3* (New York: Dix and Edwards, 1856), 167.
33. Jennie Anderson Froiseth, ed., *The Women of Mormonism; or, the Story of Polygamy as Told by the Victims Themselves* (Detroit: Paine, 1882), 319.
34. Ibid., 59.
35. Young, 352.
36. Mrs. T.B.H. (Fanny) Stenhouse, *Exposé of Polygamy in Utah–A Lady's Life among the Mormons: A Record of Personal Experiences as One of the Wives of a Mormon Elder during a Period of More than Twenty Years*, 2d ed. (New York: American News, 1872), 65. Marilyn Warenski explains nineteenth–century theological reasons for "sealing" women in marriage; see *Patriarchs and Politics: The Plight of the Mormon Woman* (New York: McGraw–Hill, 1978), 35.
37. Mark Twain, *Roughing It* (Berkeley: University of California Press, 1973 rpt.), 115.
38. Ferris, 108, 145, 111, 117.
39. Froiseth, 136–37.
40. A. Jennie Bartlett (Switzer), *Elder Northfield's Home; or, Sacrificed on the Mormon Altar* (New York: Brown, 1882), 67, 70.
41. Sandra L. Myres, *Westering Women and the Frontier Experience 1800–1915* (Albuquerque: University of New Mexico Press, 1982), 92.
42. Cannon, 71.
43. Ward, *Female Life among the Mormons: A Narrative of Many Years' Personal Experience* (New York: Derby and Jackson, 1859 rpt.), 221. Subsequent references to this edition appear in the text.
44. For more information about Mormon women who wrote in the mid- and late nineteenth century, see Janet Peterson and LaRene Gaunt, *Elect Ladies* (Salt Lake City: Deseret, 1990).

45. Elizabeth Wood Kane, *Twelve Mormon Homes, Visited in Succession on a Journey through Utah to Arizona* (Salt Lake City: Tanner, 1974 rpt.), 40.
46. Arrington and Haupt, 256, 244.
47. Leslie Fiedler, *The Return of the Vanishing American* (New York: Stein and Day, 1968), 50.
48. Jane Tompkins, *West of Everything: The Inner Life of Westerns* (New York: Oxford University Press, 1992), 38–39.
49. Myres, 89.
50. Stowe, vi.
51. Richard Slotkin, *The Fatal Environment: The Myth of the Frontier in the Age of Industrialization, 1800–1890* (Middletown: Wesleyan University Press, 1986 rpt.), 15.
52. For a list of political acts, amendments, and bills that attempted to outlaw polygamy in the mid– and late nineteenth century, see Embry, 8–10.

FOUR: Mother Lode

1. For information concerning the final years of Louise A.K.S. Clappe, also known as "Dame Shirley," see Rodman Wilson Paul, "In Search of 'Dame Shirley'," *Pacific Historical Review* 33 (1964): 146. Paul's article is one of the few works of scholarship dealing with "Dame Shirley's" life.
2. Cowboys, who also formed homosocial communities on the early frontier, like miners performed both traditional male and female roles. See Blake Allmendinger, *The Cowboy: Representations of Labor in an American Work Culture* (New York: Oxford University Press, 1992), 48–75.
3. As quoted in Kevin Starr, *Americans and the California Dream, 1850–1915* (New York: Oxford University Press, 1973), 61.
4. David Goodman delineates two ideologies: one that associated the hearth and home with the feminine and one that equated the western mines with the masculine. See *Gold Seeking: Victoria and California in the 1850s* (Stanford: Stanford University Press, 1994), 180.
5. Goodman, 179.
6. Numerous historical records of the Gold Rush document male cohabitation. For example, see Alfred T. Jackson, *The Diary of a Forty-Niner*, ed. Chauncey L. Canfield (Boston: Houghton Mifflin, 1920), 152–53; and Enos Christman, *One Man's Gold: The Letters and Journals of a Forty-Niner*, comp. and ed. Florence Morrow Christman (New York: Whittlesey, 1930), 132.
7. Richard A. Dwyer and Richard E. Lingenfelter, eds., *The Songs of the Gold Rush* (Berkeley: University of California Press, 1964), 97.
8. Theodore H. Hittell, *History of California*, vol. 3 (San Francisco: N. J. Stone, 1897), 186.
9. Susan Lee Johnson, "Bulls, Bears, and Dancing Boys: Race, Gender, and Leisure in the California Gold Rush," *Radical History Review* 60 (1994): 32.
10. Charles Howard Shinn, *Mining Camps: A Study in American Frontier Government*, ed. Rodman Wilson Paul (Gloucester: Smith, 1970), 11–12.
11. For more information on this first phase of mining, see Rodman Wilson Paul, *California Gold: The Beginning of Mining in the Far West* (Cambridge:

Harvard University Press, 1947), 16–17, 50; and Jay Ellis Ransom, *The Gold Hunter's Field Book* (New York: Harper and Row, 1975), 11–12.

12. W. A. Chalfant, *Outposts of Civilization* (Boston: Christopher, 1928 rpt.), 170.

13. Walter Colton, *Three Years in California* (New York: Barnes, 1850), 298.

14. Many early accounts of the Gold Rush acknowledge the double meaning of "washing." See, for example, Elisabeth L. Egenhoff, comp., *The Elephant as They Saw It: A Collection of Contemporary Pictures and Statements on Gold Mining in California* (San Francisco: n.p., 1949), 19, 62.

15. John Walton Caughey, *Gold Is the Cornerstone* (Berkeley: University of California Press, 1948), 26. The "dry-washing" method is also reported in Bayard Taylor, *El Dorado, or Adventures in the Path of Empire* (New York: Putnam's, 1850), 89.

16. J. D. Borthwick, *The Gold Hunters: A First-Hand Picture of Life in California Mining Camps in the Early Fifties*, Horace Kephart, ed. (New York: Book League of America, 1929 rpt.), 334.

17. Philip Ross May provides an etymology of the term "mother lode" in his work, *On the Mother Lode* (Christchurch: University of Canterbury Press, 1971), 13.

18. For technical definitions of the typical "rocker" or "cradle," see Ransom, 35; and Paul, *California Gold*, 52–53. Women as well as men recognized the comparison between ministering to a child and mining for gold. In a camp on "Negrobar," on October 30, 1852, Mary Ballou wrote in her journal that it was "harder to rock the cradle to wash out gold than it is to rock the cradle for the Babies in the States" [Ballou, "'I Hear the Hogs in My Kitchen': A Woman's View of the Gold Rush," excerpted and reprinted in Christiane Fischer, ed., *Let Them Speak for Themselves: Women in the American West, 1849–1900* (Hamden: Archon, 1990), 45]. And in the mid–1850s, this advertisement appeared in the Marysville newspaper: "A HUSBAND WANTED ... BY A LADY WHO can wash, cook, scour, sew, milk, spin, weave, hoe (can't plow), cut wood, make fires, feed the pigs, raise chickens, rock the cradle, (gold-rocker, I thank you, Sir!), saw a plank, drive nails, etc." [reprinted in Joseph Henry Jackson, *Anybody's Gold: The Story of California's Mining Towns* (New York: Appleton–Century, 1941), 101].

19. Annette Kolodny, *The Lay of the Land: Metaphor as Experience and History in American Life and Letters* (Chapel Hill: University of North Carolina Press, 1975), 71.

20. For contemporary accounts of subsurface mining, see the anonymously written *How We Get Gold in California, By a Miner of the Year '49* (New York: n. p., 1860); the anonymously written *The Miner's Own Book, Containing Correct Illustrations and Descriptions of the Various Modes of California Mining* (San Francisco: Hutchings and Rosenfield, 1858); David T. Ansted, *The Gold-Seeker's Manual, Being a Practical and Instructive Guide to All Persons Emigrating to the Newly Discovered Gold Regions of California* (New York: Appleton, 1849); Augustus J. Bowie Jr., *Hydraulic Mining in California* (Easton: privately printed, 1878); and Bowie, *A Practical Treatise on Hydraulic Mining in California* (New York: Van Nostrand, 1885).

21. Shinn, 5.
22. C. Grant Loomis has demonstrated that the Mother Lode country was the setting for "The Luck of Roaring Camp," even though Harte never refers to the region by name in his text ["Bret Harte's Folklore," *Western Folklore* 15 (1956): 19–22].
23. Bret Harte, "The Luck of Roaring Camp," in *Selected Stories and Sketches*, ed. David Wyatt (New York: Oxford University Press, 1995 rpt.), 8. Further references to this edition appear in the text.
24. Winfred Blevins, *Dictionary of the American West* (New York: Facts on File, 1993), 83.
25. Richard O'Connor, *Bret Harte: A Biography* (Boston: Little, Brown, 1966), 5, 94.
26. From "The Argonauts of '49," first delivered at the Martin Opera House in Albany, New York, on December 3, 1872. Reprinted in *The Lectures of Bret Harte*, ed. Charles Meeker Kozlay (Brooklyn: self-published, 1909), 13.
27. For a more expansive account of the writer's life during this period, see Paul, 134–40.
28. "Dame Shirley" (Louise Amelia Knapp Smith Clappe), *The Shirley Letters, Being Letters Written in 1851–52 from the California Mines* (Salt Lake City: Peregrine Smith, 1992 rpt.), 95. Further references to this edition appear in the text.
29. Eliza W. Farnham, *California, In-Doors and Out; or, How We Farm, Mine, and Live Generally in the Golden State* (New York: Dix, Edwards, 1856), 345–46.
30. Among those who speculate that the fifth letter is the source of Harte's story, without giving reasons, are Hubert Howe Bancroft, *History of California, 1860–1890*, vol. 7, *The Works of Hubert Howe Bancroft*, vol. 24 (San Francisco: History, 1890), 724; and Van Wyck Brooks, *The Times of Melville and Whitman* (New York: Dutton, 1947), 111–12.
31. Gary Scharnhorst, "Introduction," *Bret Harte's California: Letters to the 'Springfield Republican' and 'Christian Register,' 1866–67*, ed. G. Scharnhorst (Albuquerque: University of New Mexico Press, 1990), 78.
32. Patrick D. Morrow, *Bret Harte: Literary Critic* (Bowling Green, KY: Bowling Green State University Press, 1979), 8.

FIVE: Anastasia of Oregon

1. Elizabeth Hampsten discusses the fact that "adults [on the early frontier] did not usually describe their children at length in the letters, diaries, and other private documents that have survived" [see *Settlers' Children: Growing Up on the Great Plains* (Norman: University of Oklahoma Press, 1991), 6]. Lillian Schlissel suggests that women may have privately shared information concerning menstruation, pregnancy, childbirth, and other subjects that were considered taboo, in *Women's Diaries of the Westward Journey* (New York: Schocken, 1982), 82.
2. Christiane Fischer, ed., *Let Them Speak for Themselves: Women in the American West, 1849–1900* (Hamden: Archon, 1977 rpt.), 20.

3. Ellery Sedgwick, "Preface," in Opal Whiteley, *The Story of Opal: The Journal of an Understanding Heart* (Boston: Atlantic Monthly, 1920), v–vi.

4. For detailed information about the writing, destruction, and reconstruction of Opal's diary, see ibid., vi–vii; Benjamin Hoff, "Magical Opal Whiteley," in Opal Whiteley, *The Singing Creek Where the Willows Grow: The Rediscovered Diary of Opal Whiteley* (New York: Ticknor and Fields, 1986), 7, 18; and Jane Boulton, "Afterword," in Opal Whiteley, *The Story of Opal: The Journal of an Understanding Heart* (Palo Alto: Tioga, 1984), 176–77. Hoff has assigned titles to the chapters and has retitled the manuscript, while at the same time providing an annotated bibliography, introduction, and afterword. Boulton has also written an introduction and afterword and has adapted Opal's original diary, selecting certain passages, rearranging their order, and arranging the prose on the page so that it reads as stanzas of poetry.

5. Whiteley, 112. Subsequent references to this edition appear in the text.

6. For information concerning Opal's alleged ancestry and history, see Hoff, 15; Boulton, 179, 181; and E. S. Bradburne, *Opal Whiteley: The Unsolved Mystery* (London: Putnam, 1962), 17–18, 26. In addition to reviewing Opal's life history, Bradburne reprints the 1920 American edition of Opal's journal.

7. Aspects of Opal's childhood and adolescence, education, and early teaching and writing careers are discussed in Hoff, 5, 11–12, 17–18, 20, 22, 27–29, 37.

8. Ibid., 36–37.

9. No one who has written about Opal extensively has been able to answer any of these questions with certainty. Hoff believes, but cannot prove, that Opal was a schizophrenic girl, born to the Whiteleys in Oregon, who wrote the diary when she claimed she did, while at the same time sincerely believing that she was a member of the French aristocracy [see ibid., 15, 41, 45]. Bradburne also contends that the diary was written by a young girl who was born and raised in America. But she is careful not to state that Opal was mad—only that her literature was the product of a "sensitive and unusual mind" (29, 50–51, 61–62, 68). Boulton writes that Opal seemed to believe in her "obsessive dream" (186). Sedgwick himself attested to the "rightness and honesty of the manuscript as the *Atlantic* published it," but added: "Who can say that here or here runs the boundary line of sanity and verity? . . . The child who wrote Opal's diary believed in it" [*The Happy Profession* (Boston: Little, Brown, 1946), 263]. Elbert Bede, who knew Opal while he edited a local newspaper in Cottage Grove, Oregon, thinks that Opal probably wrote a version of the diary as a child and later amended it. He doesn't enter into the dispute regarding her sanity [see Bede, *Fabulous Opal Whiteley: From Oregon Logging Camp to Princess in India* (Portland: Binfords and Mort, 1954), 151–55, 165].

10. For a summary of the evidence against Opal, both factual and circumstantial, see Hoff, 7, 9, 16, 38–39; and Bede, 48, 79–80, 95–97, 155.

11. A history of the debate over the use of foreign languages and anagrams in Opal's work is provided by Hoff, 43, 48; Boulton, 183–85; and Bradburne, 39, 63.

12. For an account of Opal's belief in her Indian heritage and her travels to India, see Hoff, 17, 52–54; and Bede, 127, 137.

13. From a letter written by Opal to "a girlhood friend" in 1929, as cited in Bede, 80.

14. Facts and rumors about Opal's last years are recounted in Hoff, 55–56, 59. In a telephone conversation with Jane Boulton, conducted on March 14, 1994, I learned about Opal's death and the off–Broadway musical based on her life.

15. Elliot West examines the function and significance of "exploration" play for children who lived in early America, in *Growing Up with the Country: Childhood on the Far Western Frontier* (Albuquerque: University of New Mexico Press, 1989), 101.

16. White, *"It's Your Misfortune and None of My Own": A New History of the American West* (Norman: University of Oklahoma Press, 1993 rpt.), 181. The desire to re-create older forms of civilization on the western frontier was especially strong among women. See Fischer, 13.

17. Marx, *The Machine in the Garden: Technology and the Pastoral Ideal in America* (New York: Oxford University Press, 1979 rpt.), 22–23.

18. One of the most heavily forested states in America, Oregon had become one of the targeted sites of the timber industry by the late nineteenth century. See Richard L. Williams, *The Loggers* (New York: Time-Life, 1976), 195; and Thomas R. Cox, *Mills and Markets: A History of the Pacific Coast Lumber Industry to 1900* (Seattle: University of Washington Press, 1974), 301.

19. Kolodny, *The Land Before Her: Fantasy and Experience of the American Frontier, 1630–1860* (Chapel Hill: University of North Carolina Press, 1984), xiii.

20. Lewis, *The American Adam: Innocence, Tragedy and Tradition in the Nineteenth Century* (Chicago: University of Chicago Press, 1955), 5.

21. For accounts of the reasons for which western men and women wrote journals and diaries, see Steven E. Kagle, *Early Nineteenth-Century American Diary Literature* (Boston: Twayne, 1986), 24; John Mack Faragher, *Women and Men on the Overland Trail* (New Haven: Yale University Press, 1979), 12–13; Schlissel, 11; West, 26; and Fischer, 15.

22. Coles, *Uprooted Children: The Early Life of Migrant Farm Workers* (Pittsburgh: University of Pittsburgh Press, 1970), 58–59.

23. Schlissel, "Family on the Western Frontier," in *Western Women: Their Land, Their Lives*, ed. Schlissel, Vicki L. Ruiz, and Janice Monk (Albuquerque: University of New Mexico Press, 1988), 86–87.

24. Bixby-Smith, *Adobe Days* (Cedar Rapids: Torch, 1925). As quoted in Fischer, 250.

25. Sigmund Freud, "Family Romances," James Strachey, trans., *The Standard Edition of the Complete Psychological Works of Sigmund Freud*, vol. 9 (London: Hogarth, 1973 rpt.), 238; Bruno Bettelheim, *The Uses of Enchantment: The Meaning and Importance of Fairy Tales* (New York: Knopf, 1976), 236–37, 241.

26. Emerson, "Nature," in *Selected Essays, Lectures, and Poems*, ed. Robert D. Richardson Jr. (New York: Bantam, 1990 rpt.), 17–18.

27. Fuller, *Summer on the Lakes, in 1843* (Urbana: University of Illinois Press, 1991 rpt.), 18.

28. Nash, *Wilderness and the American Mind* (New Haven: Yale University Press, 1982 rpt.), 2.

29. Williams states that when the first colonists came to America, "they found

themselves engulfed in trees. Approximately one third of the virgin continent was heavily wooded, and the whole of the Northeast was practically a single forest, stretching 1,000 miles north and south, and extending more than 1,000 miles inland, with only a few sizable open tracts of prairie land" visible (22).

30. Daniel G. Hoffman, *Paul Bunyan: Last of the Frontier Demigods* (Philadelphia: Temple University Press, 1952), 25.

31. Constance Rourke, *American Humor: A Study of the National Character* (Tallahassee: Florida State University Press, 1959 rpt.), 232–33.

32. Nathaniel Hawthorne, *The Scarlet Letter* (New York: Signet, 1980 rpt.), 97.

33. Lawrence, *Studies in Classic American Literature* (Harmondsworth, UK: Penguin, 1983 rpt.), 60.

34. Alexis de Tocqueville, *Democracy in America*, vol. 1, ed. Phillips Bradley (New York: Vintage, 1990 rpt.), 322.

SIX: Toga! Toga!

1. Robert Epstein, "The Search for DeMille's Lost City," *Los Angeles Times*, March 11, 1993: F12.

2. Lew Wallace, *Lew Wallace: An Autobiography* (New York: Harper, 1906), 16. A summary of the war and its effect on Wallace appears here and in Robert M. Morsberger and Katherine M. Morsberger, *Lew Wallace: Militant Romantic* (New York: McGraw–Hill, 1980), 5.

2. Wallace, *Lew Wallace*, 188.

3. Wallace's years with the Juáristas are dealt with in detail in Irving McKee, *"Ben-Hur" Wallace: The Life of General Lew Wallace* (Berkeley: University of California Press, 1947), 90–110.

5. My understanding of *The Fair God* is based on the reading of the novel given in Morsberger and Morsberger, 224–37. For an account of the 1838 removal of the Potawatomi Indians, see ibid., 12.

6. Susan Wallace, *The Land of the Pueblos* (New York: Alden, 1890 rpt.), 16, 131.

7. Cited in Morsberger and Morsberger, 215.

8. Edward H. Spicer believes that, in the territories of Arizona and New Mexico, the United States "thought in terms of extermination or forcible isolation, rather than Christian conversion." The concept of the reservation, he claims, "developed out of the policy of isolation" and offered a practical alternative to killing the Indians [*Cycles of Conquest: The Impact of Spain, Mexico, and the United States on the Indians of the Southwest, 1533–1960* (Tucson: University of Arizona Press, 1962), 344–45, 347]. At the same time, the religious conversion and political containment of the Indians in the southwestern United States have been seen as equally controlling strategies designed to cope with the "other." One western historian argues, for instance, that General Kearney's 1846 triumphal march into New Mexico and Bishop Lamy's 1852 arrival in Santa Fe both constituted invasions, although one was sponsored by the U.S. government and one was decreed by the Church. [See Howard Roberts Lamar, *The Far Southwest 1846–1912: A Territorial History* (New Haven: Yale University Press, 1966), 102–103.] For

information on Jean Baptiste Lamy, who was appointed to reform the Catholic Church in New Mexico, see Paul Horgan, *Lamy of Santa Fe: His Life and Times* (New York: Farrar, Straus and Giroux, 1975). Willa Cather's novel, *Death Comes for the Archbishop* (1927), is a thinly disguised account of his career in New Mexico.

9. The war against Victorio is chronicled in C. L. Sonnichsen, *The Mescalero Apaches* (Norman: University of Oklahoma Press, 1958), 160–64; in Dan L. Thrapp, *Victorio and the Mimbres Apaches* (Norman: University of Oklahoma Press, 1974); in McKee, 155–56; and in Morsberger and Morsberger, 282–87.

10. Morsberger and Morsberger, 916, 918.

11. As one would imagine, there have been numerous works written on the Lincoln Country War and on Billy the Kid. For the best account of Billy's role in the feud, see Stephen Tatum, *Inventing Billy The Kid: Visions of the Outlaw in America, 1881–1981* (Albuquerque: University of New Mexico Press, 1985 rpt.), 15–34; for an explanation of Wallace's role, see Morsberger and Morsberger, 257–81.

12. The complete correspondence between the two men is traced in Morsberger and Morsberger, 274–77.

13. John G. Cawelti, *The Six-Gun Mystique* (Bowling Green, KY: Bowling Green University Popular Press, 1971), 35. Subsequent references to this edition appear in the text.

14. Lew Wallace made this observation in a letter that he wrote, quoted in Morsberger and Morsberger, 291. Susan Wallace commented on the western landscape in *The Land of the Pueblos* as well (51).

15. Lew Wallace, *Ben-Hur: A Tale of the Christ* (New York: Grosset and Dunlap, 1922 rpt.), 319. Subsequent references to this edition appear in the text.

16. Will Wright, *Six Guns and Society: A Structural Study of the Western* (Berkeley: University of California Press, 1975), 69. Subsequent references to this edition appear in the text.

17. Some critics feel that *Ben-Hur* is a revenge tragedy disguised as a historical religious romance. These critics, including Carl Van Doren, argue that Ben-Hur's thirst for revenge overpowers his hunger for Christ and that his thirst lingers at the end of the book, even after Christ dies. See *The American Novel 1789–1939* (New York: Macmillan, 1940), 114.

18. In addition, the chariot race scene, as it has been staged in the theater and later on screen, has involved a number of western directors, actors, and props. In the popular 1899 stage version, the future cowboy movie star William S. Hart played Messala. His expertise with horses enabled him to prevent a serious mishap in the theater on opening night, when the horses veered out of control and almost ran off the stage. In MGM's 1925 silent film version, directed by Fred Niblo and starring Ramon Navarro, the race scene was directed, not by Niblo, but by the second unit director, B. Reaves Eason, who later directed the land rush scene in *Cimarron* (1930) and the stallion scenes in *Duel in the Sun* (1946). In MGM's follow-up 1959 film version, directed by William Wyler, Charlton Heston (Ben-Hur) and Stephen Boyd (Messala)–amazingly–raced their own chariots. Professional rodeo riders drove the rest of them. For more information, see William S.

Hart, *My Life East and West* (Boston: Houghton Mifflin, 1929), 149; Morsberger and Morsberger, 464–66, 475–76, 483.

19. For a discussion of the relationship between the historical romance and the dime novel, see Tatum, 43. In a retrospective review of *Ben-Hur*, written twenty–five years after the book first appeared, Hammond Lamont claimed that the book's characters and incidents "make a dime novel about bandits and beauties seem dull and lifeless.... Jesse James is a divinity student in a white choker when compared with Messala.... And for your high–souled, dauntless hero, we back Ben Hur [sic] against any combination of Old Sleuth and Crimson Dick yet presented to the world." In "The Winner in the Chariot Race," *The Nation* 80 (February 23, 1905): 148.

20. Writing from Crawfordsville, Indiana, on May 6, 1890, Wallace informed A. J. Wissler that he composed the last three books of *Ben-Hur* while he lived in New Mexico. Wallace Papers, New Mexico Records Center and Archives, Santa Fe.

21. Wallace, "How I Came to Write *Ben-Hur*," *Youth's Companion* 66 (February 2, 1893): 57. Later the essay was reprinted in Wallace's autobiography, where it was placed near the end.

22. De-emphasizing the hero's quest for revenge in the second half of *Ben-Hur*, the 1959 film makes no mention of the hero's attempt to gather and train Jewish troops. After the race the film concerns itself only with Ben–Hur's reunion with his mother and sister and with his conversion to Christianity.

23. Wallace, *Lew Wallace*, 1–2.

24. Morsberger and Morsberger, 296.

25. As quoted in ibid., 267.

26. Morsberger and Morsberger, 450. Noting that the subject of religion was "one of perennial importance in the making of best sellers" in America in the middle and late nineteenth century, James D. Hart claims that Wallace's novel "combined the historical values of Scott and the moral worth of Mrs. Stowe, the two previous novelists who had battered down almost the last prejudices against fiction. *Ben-Hur* was endorsed on all sides by clergymen and leaders of public opinion." See *The Popular Book: A History of America's Literary Taste* (Berkeley: University of California Press, 1950), 163–64.

SEVEN: X Marks the Spot

1. Robert Louis Stevenson, *The Silverado Squatters* (New York: Scribner's, 1899 rpt.), 70. Subsequent references to this edition appear in the text.

2. Richard Aldington argues that Stevenson ignored empirical evidence in order to make the camp seem more picturesque [*Portrait of a Rebel: The Life and Work of Robert Louis Stevenson* (London: Evans, 1957), 122–23]. At "many points the description of people and places is plain enough," James D. Hart adds. But Stevenson's "arch and amused manner makes even the most forthright remarks appear [more] agreeable" [*From Scotland to Silverado* (Cambridge: Belknap, 1966), xiv].

3. For information concerning Fanny's life before meeting Stevenson, see Nellie Van de Grift Sanchez, *The Life of Mrs. Robert Louis Stevenson* (London: Chatto and Windus, 1920), 28–32; Laura L. Hinkley, *The Stevensons: Louis and Fanny* (New York: Hastings, 1950), 71–74; Margaret Mackay, *The Violent Friend: The Story of Mrs. Robert Louis Stevenson* (Garden City, NY: Doubleday, 1968), 11–12; and James Pope Hennessy, *Robert Louis Stevenson* (London: Cape, 1974), 91–96.

4. Mackay, 118.

5. As cited in John E. Jordan, ed., *Robert Louis Stevenson's Journal* (San Francisco: Book Club of California, 1954), xviii.

6. For accounts of mining activities at Silverado in the mid- and late nineteenth century, see Hubert Howe Bancroft, *The Works of Hubert Howe Bancroft*, vol. 24, *History of California*, vol. 7 (San Francisco: History, 1890), 650; Anne Roller Issler, *Stevenson at Silverado* (Caldwell: Caxton, 1939), 150–52, 202–03; Hart, xxxiii–iv; and Jordan, xvi.

7. Jordan reproduces the first draft of Stevenson's travelog, discussing additions and deletions made in Stevenson's hand. I cite some of those passages as they appear in the 1899 published edition.

8. Stevenson, "My First Book—Treasure Island," *The Works of Robert Louis Stevenson*, vol. 16 (London: Chatto and Windus, 1912), 333–39.

9. Regarding correspondences between the "mythical" Treasure Island and the "real" Mount St. Helena, see Roy Nickerson, *Robert Louis Stevenson in California: A Remarkable Courtship* (San Francisco: Chronicle, 1982), 112–13; Katharine D. Osbourne, *Robert Louis Stevenson in California* (Chicago: McClurg, 1911), 28–29; Lawrence Clark Powell, *California Classics: The Creative Literature of the Golden State* (Los Angeles: Ritchie, 1971), 164; Harold Francis Watson, *Coasts of Treasure Island: A Study of the Backgrounds and Sources for Robert Louis Stevenson's Romance of the Sea* (San Antonio: Naylor, 1969), 120, 160; Hart, xliii; and Issler, 235–36.

10. Stevenson, *Treasure Island* (New York: Bantam, 1981 rpt.), 177, 186. Subsequent references to this edition appear in the text.

11. As quoted in Sidney Colvin, ed., *Letters from Robert Louis Stevenson to His Family and Friends*, vol. 1 (New York: Scribner's, 1902 rpt.), 257, 261.

12. David Angus, "Youth on the Prow: The First Publication of *Treasure Island*," ed. G. Ross Roy, *Studies in Scottish Literature* 25 (1990): 83.

13. Roger G. Swearingen, *The Prose Writings of Robert Louis Stevenson: A Guide* (Hamden: Archon, 1980), 66.

14. Stevenson, "Letter to a Young Gentleman Who Proposes to Embrace the Career of Art," *The Works of Robert Louis Stevenson*, vol. 27, 7.

15. Stevenson, "Henry David Thoreau: His Character and Opinions," *The Works of Robert Louis Stevenson*, vol. 5, 116.

16. Colvin, vol. 1, 347.

17. Ibid., 353.

18. Swearingen, 76.

19. Stevenson, "El Dorado," *The Works of Robert Louis Stevenson*, vol. 25, 82–83.

EIGHT: Little House on the Rice Paddy

1. Buck first recounted this anecdote in *The Kennedy Women: A Personal Appraisal* (New York: Cowles, 1970), 55. Nora Stirling claims that it was an unnamed elderly woman who made this comment to Buck [*Pearl Buck: A Woman in Conflict* (Piscataway: New Century, 1983), 279].
2. As cited in Stirling, ibid.
3. Peter Conn, "Introduction: Rediscovering Pearl S. Buck," in *The Several Worlds of Pearl S. Buck*, ed. Elizabeth J. Lipscomb, Frances E. Webb, and Peter Conn (Westport, CT: Greenwood, 1994), 2.
4. John F. Kennedy's acceptance speech was delivered at the Democratic National Convention in Los Angeles on July 15, 1960. It is reprinted in Theodore C. Sorenson, ed., *"Let the Word Go Forth": The Speeches, Statements, and Writings of John F. Kennedy* (New York: Delacorte, 1988), 100–101.
5. Conn, "Introduction," in Lipscomb et al., 2.
6. James D. Hart, *The Popular Book: A History of America's Literary Taste* (Berkeley: University of California Press, 1950), 253. In "Pearl Buck," Dody Weston Thompson argues that *The Good Earth* "spoke to the poverty and uncertainty of the times" [see Warren G. French and Walter E. Kidd, eds., *American Winners of the Nobel Literary Prize* (Norman: University of Oklahoma Press, 1968), 91]. W. J. Stuckey, sharing this opinion, wonders rhetorically: "Weren't the poverty and suffering of the 1930s a result of the extravagence of the 1920s, when America had strayed from the rocky path along which Americans had traditionally traveled, abandoning the old virtues–thrift, hard work, and sobriety?" [in *The Pulitzer Prize Novels: A Critical Backward Look* (Norman: University of Oklahoma Press, 1981), 91]. Recently other critics have echoed these sentiments. See James C. Thomson Jr., "Pearl S. Buck and the American Quest for China"; Charles W. Hayford, "*The Good Earth*, Revolution, and the American Raj in China"; and Peter Conn, "Pearl S. Buck and American Literary Culture," in Lipscomb et al., 13, 23, 111.
7. For a brief explanation of why works such as *The Good Earth, The Grapes of Wrath, Tobacco Road*, and *Gone With the Wind* appealed to American audiences during this period, see Peter Conn, *Pearl S. Buck: A Cultural Biography* (Cambridge: Cambridge University Press, 1996), 131.
8. Smith, *Virgin Land: The American West as Symbol and Myth* (Cambridge: Harvard University Press, 1971 rpt.), 176–77.
9. In his eighth annual message to Congress on December 8, 1908, Theodore Roosevelt stressed the need to conserve America's forests by reminding Congress how deforestation had environmentally destroyed parts of China [Roosevelt, *State Papers as Governor and President: 1899–1909* (New York: Scribners, 1925), 607–15]. Roosevelt "had no intimation of what would soon happen to the grasslands of mid–America," Paul Russell Cutright points out ironically, in *Theodore Roosevelt: The Making of a Conservationist* (Urbana: University of Illinois Press, 1985), 219.

    John King Fairbank has recorded the annual rainfall amounts in parts of China in the first part of the twentieth century, in *The United States and China* (Cambridge: Harvard University Press, 1983 rpt.), 5. See also John Lossing Buck, who compares the dust storms in China to those on the Great Plains, in *Chinese Farm Economy: A Study of 2866 Farms in Seventeen Localities and Seven Provinces in China* (Chicago: University of Chicago Press, 1930), 9.

10. Smith, *Virgin Land*, 179–82; and Rodman W. Paul, *The Far West and the Great Plains in Transition: 1859–1900* (New York: Harper and Row, 1988), 222.

11. Smith, *Chinese Characteristics* (New York: Revell, 1894), 27–34, 115–24.

12. R. H. Tawney, *Land and Labor in China* (London: Allen and Unwin, 1932), 46–47. For equally critical accounts of Chinese systems of farming, see Harry A. Franck, *Wandering in China* (New York: Century, 1923), 332; and Hubert Freyn, *Free China's New Deal* (New York: Macmillan, 1943), 11–12, 23–26.

13. Walter LaFeber, *The New Empire: An Interpretation of American Expansion, 1860–1898* (Ithaca, NY: Cornell University Press, 1963), 9.

14. Freyn, 11.

15. Justification for the 1899 "Open Door" Policy is usually phrased using rhetoric borrowed from the movement of westward expansion. See, for example, LaFeber, 5, 83–84; Marilyn Blatt Young, *The Rhetoric of Empire: American China Policy, 1895–1901* (Cambridge: Harvard University Press, 1968), 2, 95–96, 223; Robert McClellan, *The Heathen Chinee: A Study of American Attitudes Toward China, 1890–1905* (Columbus: Ohio State University Press, 1971), 134; Delber L. McKee, *Chinese Exclusion Versus the Open Door Policy, 1900–1906: Clashes Over China Policy in the Roosevelt Era* (Detroit: Wayne State University Press, 1977), 19–21; and Randall E. Stross, *The Stubborn Earth: American Agriculturalists on Chinese Soil, 1898–1937* (Berkeley: University of California Press, 1986), 15.

16. Speer, *The Oldest and the Newest Empire: China and the United States* (Chicago: National Publishing, 1870), 24. Richard Drinnon discusses comparisons between Chinese and Indians at the turn of the century, in *Facing West: The Metaphysics of Indian-Hating and Empire-Building* (Minneapolis: University of Minnesota Press, 1980), 271, 275.

17. Richard Slotkin, *Gunfighter Nation: The Myth of the Frontier in Twentieth-Century America* (New York: Harper Perennial, 1993 rpt.), 86.

18. For information concerning Roosevelt's efforts to conquer China nonmilitarily, see Murray R. Benedict, *Farm Policies of the United States, 1790–1950: A Study of their Origins and Development* (New York: Twentieth Century Fund, 1953), 122; Jane Hunter, *The Gospel of Gentility: American Women Missionaries in Turn-of-the-Century China* (New Haven: Yale University Press, 1984), 8; and Fairbank, *The United States and China*, 311.

19. The following works explain the history, growth, and purpose of U.S. missions in China: McClellan, 102, 134; McKee, 17–18; Stross, 92; Fairbank, *The United States and China*, 310–11; Fairbank, *Chinese-American Interactions: A Historical Survey* (New Brunswick, NJ: Rutgers University Press, 1975), 45–46; and Michael H. Hunt, *The Making of a Special Relationship: The United States and China to 1914* (New York: Columbia University Press, 1983), 285.

20. Stross recapitulates Buck's early life and career, 111–15, 161–62.

21. Scholarship on the history of farming in the United States in the years leading up to the Dust Bowl is both extensive and extremely diverse. For thorough yet succinct introductions, see Vance Johnson, *Heaven's Tableland:*

The Dust Bowl Story (New York: Farrar, Strauss, 1947), 119–132, 145–52; R. Douglas Hurt, *The Dust Bowl: An Agricultural and Social History* (Chicago: Nelson-Hall, 1981), 19–35; Theodore Saloutos, *The American Farmer and the New Deal* (Ames: Iowa State University Press, 1982), 3–14; and Donald Worster, *Dust Bowl: The Southern Plains in the 1930s* (New York: Oxford University Press, 1982 rpt.), 83–93.

22. Buck, *Chinese Farm Economy*, 421.

23. Stross, 175, 187.

24. Jonathan D. Spence, "Chinese Fiction in the Twentieth Century," in *Asia in Western Fiction*, ed. Robin W. Winks and James R. Rush (Manchester: Manchester University Press, 1990), 102.

25. Irvin Block, *The Lives of Pearl Buck: A Tale of China and America* (New York: Crowell, 1973), 74. For less speculation and more information, see Thomson, in Lipscomb et al., 9.

26. Buck, *My Several Worlds: A Personal Record* (New York: Day, 1954), 139.

27. As cited in Theodore F. Harris, *Pearl S. Buck: A Biography*, vol. 1 (New York: Day, 1969), 143.

28. Buck, *The Good Earth* (New York: Pocket, 1973 rpt.), 37. Subsequent references to this edition appear in the text.

29. White, "'Are You an Environmentalist or Do You Work for a Living?': Work and Nature," in *Uncommon Ground: Toward Reinventing Nature*, ed. William Cronon (New York: Norton, 1995), 171, 178.

30. Buck, *Chinese Farm Economy*, 178. For details concerning double-cropping, see Philip C.C. Huang, *The Peasant Economy and Social Change in North China* (Stanford, CA: Stanford University Press, 1985), 58–61.

31. The Great Plains Committee, *The Future of the Great Plains* (Washington, DC: House of Representatives, 75th Congress, 1st Session, Document No. 144, 1937), 5.

32. Worster, *Nature's Economy: The Roots of Ecology* (San Francisco: Sierra Club, 1977), 226.

33. Tawney, 44.

34. See Buck's statistics on tenant rates in north and south China (*Chinese Farm Economy*, 145). For confirmation, see Tawney, 32–36; and Dwight H. Perkins, *Agricultural Development in China, 1368–1968* (Chicago: Aldine, 1969), 87–89.

35. For a definition and discussion of naturalism, as it appears in Buck's fiction, see Kidd, "Introduction," in French and Kidd, 6, 8; Yu Yuh-choo, "Chinese Influences on Pearl S. Buck," *Tamkang Review* 11 (Fall 1980): 36; and Hayford, in Lipscomb et al., 23–24.

36. White, *Metahistory: The Historical Imagination in Nineteenth-Century Europe* (Baltimore: Johns Hopkins University Press, 1985 rpt.), 7.

37. Webb, *The Great Plains* (Lincoln: University of Nebraska Press, 1981 rpt.), 3, 10.

38. Ibid., 331.

39. The Great Plains Committee, 63.

40. "'The Good Earth' and Other Recent Work," *New York Times Book Review* (March 15, 1931): 6.

41. Florence Ayscough, "The Real China," *Saturday Review of Literature* 7 (March 21, 1931): 676.

42. This view, expressed frequently by reviewers and critics, is summed up in Harold R. Isaacs, *Scratches on Our Minds: American Views of China and India* (White Plains, NY: M. E. Sharpe, 1980 rpt.), 155–56. For a dissenting opinion, see Gianna Quach, "Chinese Fictions and the American Alternative: Pearl Buck and Emily Hahn," *Tamkang Review* 24 (Fall 1993): 75–116.

43. Said defines Orientalism as a "discourse" or system of representation that includes, among "a complex array of 'Oriental' ideas," stereotypes of sensual splendor, decadence, and despotic cruelty. In *Orientalism* (New York: Vintage, 1979 rpt.), 3–4.

44. Interestingly, when she dies O–lan turns "as shrivelled and yellow as the Old Mistress" in the great House of Hwang (231).

45. Conn, "Pearl S. Buck and American Literary Culture," in Lipscomb et al., 113. In 1945 Buck, writing under the pseudonym "John Sedges," published a historical novel set in Kansas at the turn of the century. See *The Townsman* (New York: Day, 1945). For her thoughts on the novel, see Buck, "Forward," in *American Triptych: Three "John Sedges" Novels* (New York: Day, 1958), vii.

46. Kevin Brownlow recounts the film's troubled production in "Sidney Franklin and 'The Good Earth'," *Historical Journal of Film, Radio and Television* 9 (1989): 80–84. See also the review of "The Good Earth," *Time* (February 15, 1937): 55.

47. Conn notes the parallels between the two films in *Pearl S. Buck*, 194.

48. Billington, *America's Frontier Expansion* (Albuquerque: University of New Mexico Press, 1978 rpt.), 47–48.

49. For an account of MGM's expeditions to China in 1933–34, see Brownlow, 81–82; and "When a Little Child Fell Ill ... an Epic Was Born," MGM press-clipping file, Academy of Motion Picture Arts and Sciences, Los Angeles, CA.

50. My account of the preparations for filming *The Good Earth* is based, almost verbatim, on the following sources: Brownlow, 82–83; "The Good Earth: A Preview of Scenes from One of the Most Daring Film Experiments Ever Attempted in Screen History," *Movie Classic* (October 1936): 88; "On Location with 'The Good Earth'," *Motion Picture* (October 1936): 40; "China Rises out of Hollywood," *Picturegoer* (December 18, 1937): 3; and anonymously written and untitled accounts of the filming of Buck's novel, contained in the MGM press-clipping file.

51. Brownlow, 81.

52. James L. Hoban Jr. discusses Thalberg's reputed fascination with spectacle and his plans for *The Good Earth* in particular. See "Scripting *The Good Earth*: Versions of the Novel for the Screen," in Lipscomb et al., 138.

53. The filming of the plague scene is cited in Jerome Lawrence, *Actor: The Life and Times of Paul Muni* (New York: Putnam's, 1974), 225–26; Brownlow, 84; and the MGM press-clipping file.

54. Brownlow, 88.

55. *The Good Earth*, MGM, 1937, dir. Sidney Franklin with Paul Muni and Luise Rainer. Hoban summarizes the changes that were contemplated and/or made in the film, in Lipscomb et al., 128–39.

56. As quoted in Bob Thomas, *Thalberg: Life and Legend* (Garden City, NY: Doubleday, 1969), 303.

57. Robert L. Snyder, *Pare Lorentz and the Documentary Film* (Norman: University of Oklahoma Press, 1968), 42–48.

58. Richard Lowitt refers to the plague of 1937 as the "greatest grasshopper menace 'in modern times,'" in *The New Deal and the West* (Bloomington: Indiana University Press, 1984), 56. Worster, citing statistics provided by the Soil Conservation Service, writes that there were fourteen major dust storms on the Great Plains in 1932; 38 in 1933; 22 in 1934; 40 in 1935; 68 in 1936; 72 in 1937; 61 in 1938; 30 in 1939; 17 in 1940; and 17 in 1941; thus, making 1937 the worst year for dust storms on record. See *Dust Bowl*, 15.

59. Terry Ramsaye, "'Good Earth' Opens East and West After Four Years in the Making," *Motion Picture Herald* (February 6, 1937): 19.

NINE: The Queer Frontier

1. Lawrence, *Studies in Classic American Literature* (Harmondsworth, UK: Penguin, 1983 rpt.), 59.

2. Fiedler, *Love and Death in the American Novel* (New York: Criterion, 1960), 210. Also, see Fiedler, "Come Back to the Raft Ag'in, Huck Honey!" (1955), in which Fiedler defines male same-sex relationships in nineteenth-century American literature as examples of "chaste male love." In *The Collected Essays of Leslie Fiedler*, vol. 1 (New York: Stein and Day, 1971), 144.

3. Fiedler, *Love and Death in the American Novel*, 539.

4. Ibid. Fiedler also uses the term "Western" to describe this literary phenomenon in *The Return of the Vanishing American* (New York: Stein and Day, 1969 rpt.), 21, 24.

5. Fiedler, *Love and Death in the American Novel*, 210.

6. Wister, *The Virginian* (New York: Signet, 1979 rpt.), 3. Subsequent references to this edition appear in the text.

7. Schaefer, *Shane* (New York: Bantam, 1983 rpt.), 104. Subsequent references to this edition appear in the text.

8. Sedgwick, *Between Men: English Literature and Male Homosocial Desire* (New York: Columbia University Press, 1985), 21.

9. Lawrence, 68.

10. The comparison of homosexuals with criminals occurs throughout Genet's literature. For example, see *The Thief's Journal*, trans. Bernard Frechtman (New York: Grove, 1964 rpt.), 9–10, 149, 171, 243. Also, see Edmund White's biography, *Genet* (London: Chatto and Windus, 1993), 38, 197–99, 291.

11. For an interpretation of Billy the Kid as a "repressed homosexual," see Stephen Tatum, *Inventing Billy the Kid: Visions of the Outlaw in America, 1881–1981* (Albuquerque: University of New Mexico Press, 1985 rpt.), 139.

12. Gerald Clarke, *Capote: A Biography* (New York: Simon and Schuster, 1988), 320.

13. Capote, *In Cold Blood* (New York: Signet, 1980 rpt.), 102, 382. Subsequent references to this edition appear in the text.

14. Fiedler, *The Return of the Vanishing American*, 14.

15. In an interview, Capote later clarified that "there was no homosexual rela-

tionship between Hickock and Smith; Perry once had an affair with a man and had definite homosexual fixations, but he had nothing to do with Hickock; they were completely frank about such matters and would have told me like a shot." Eric Norden, "Playboy Interview: Truman Capote," *Playboy* 15 (March 1968). Reprinted in M. Thomas Inge, ed., *Truman Capote: Conversations* (Jackson: University Press of Mississippi, 1987), 130.

16. *In Cold Blood*, 1967, Columbia, dir. Richard Brooks, with Robert Blake and Scott Wilson.

17. George Plimpton, "The Story Behind a Nonfiction Novel," *The New York Times Book Review* (January 16, 1966). Reprinted in Inge, *Truman Capote*, 60.

18. Richard Eugene Hickock, as told to Mack Nations, "America's Worst Crime in Twenty Years," *Male* (December 1961). Reprinted in Irving Malin, ed., *Truman Capote's "In Cold Blood": A Critical Handbook* (Belmont: Wadsworth, 1968), 10.

19. For an analysis of weight–lifting as a means of deflecting and redirecting male homosexual tendencies, see Mark Simpson, *Male Impersonators: Men Performing Masculinity* (London: Cassell, 1994), 32.

20. Warshow, "Movie Chronicle: The Western," in *Focus on the Western*, ed. Jack Nachbar (Englewood Cliffs: Prentice-Hall, 1974), 56.

21. Norden, 131. In another interview, Capote said: "Most people who are tattooed, it's a sign of some feeling of inferiority, they're trying to establish some macho identification for themselves." See Lawrence Grobel, *Conversations with Capote* (New York: Plume, 1985), 126.

22. Capote, "Preface," *Music for Chameleons* (New York: Signet, 1981 rpt.), xviii. See also Grobel, 116.

23. Haskell Frankel, "The Author," *Saturday Review* 49 (January 22, 1966). Reprinted in Inge, 71.

24. Jane Howard, "How the 'Smart Rascal' Brought It Off," *Life* (February 18, 1966). Reprinted in William L. Nance, *The Worlds of Truman Capote* (New York: Stein and Day, 1970), 72.

25. As quoted in Clarke, 326.

26. It is not my intention to explore or debate Freud's ideas in this essay. On the relationship between male homosexuality and narcissism, see Freud, "The Sexual Aberrations" (1905), in James Strachey, trans. and ed., *Three Essays on the Theory of Sexuality* (New York: Basic Books, 1962 rpt.), 11n., 12n; Freud, "On Narcissism: An Introduction" (1914), and "Instincts and Their Vicissitudes" (1915), in Strachey, trans., *The Standard Edition of the Complete Psychological Works of Sigmund Freud*, vol. 14 (London: Hogarth, 1957 rpt.).

27. As quoted in Clarke, 352–55.

28. As quoted in Grobel, 118.

29. Shana Alexander, "A Nonfictional Visit with Truman Capote," *Life* (February 18, 1966). Reprinted in Kenneth T. Reed, *Truman Capote* (Boston: Twayne, 1981), 103.

30. As quoted in Clarke, 398.

31. Fiedler, *Love and Death in the American Novel*, 210; Jane Tompkins, *West of Everything: The Inner Life of Westerns* (New York: Oxford University Press, 1992), 66.

32. Jack Dunphy, *"Dear Genius . . . "*: *A Memoir of My Life with Truman Capote* (New York: McGraw–Hill, 1987), 25.

TEN: Welcome to Twin Peaks

1. For an account of the transition from radio serials to daytime soap operas, see Robert LaGuardia, *Soap World* (New York: Arbor, 1983), 22–23.
2. See Christine Geraghty, *Women and Soap Opera: A Study of Prime Time Soaps* (Cambridge: Polity, 1991), 121–22; and Ien Ang, *Watching Dallas: Soap Opera and the Melodramatic Imagination*, trans. Della Couling (London: Metheun, 1985), 19.
3. Madeleine Edmondson and David Rounds, *From Mary Noble to Mary Hartman: The Complete Soap Opera Book* (New York: Stein and Day, 1976), 15, 78, 148; Robert C. Allen, *Speaking of Soap Operas* (Chapel Hill: University of North Carolina Press, 1985), 74; and Rodney Andrew Carveth, "Exploring the Effects of 'Love in the Afternoon': Does Soap Opera Viewing Create Perceptions of a Promiscuous World?" in Suzanne Frentz, ed., *Staying Tuned: Contemporary Soap Opera Criticism* (Bowling Green, KY: Bowling Green State University Popular Press, 1992), 6.
4. Muriel G. Cantor and Suzanne Pingree, *The Soap Opera* (Beverly Hills: Sage, 1983), 26–27; and George Comstock, "A Social Scientist's View of Daytime Serial Drama," in Mary Cassata and Thomas Skill, eds., *Life on Daytime Television: Tuning-In American Serial Drama* (Norwood: Ablex, 1983), xxiv.
5. According to David Jacobs, who created the show, *Knots Landing* started "making [its] characters richer. We took them out of the cul–de–sac and put them in the corridors of power. People got threatened, blackmailed, murdered." See Jacobs, "Introduction," in Laura Van Wormer, *Knots Landing: The Saga of Seaview Circle* (Garden City, NY: Dolphin, 1986), viii.
6. For the sake of consistency I refer to the episodes as they are numbered on video, since this is the medium that anyone is likely to resort to in order to review certain episodes. The pilot for *Twin Peaks* (the unnumbered, premiere, two–hour episode) is followed by twenty–nine (mostly one–hour) episodes, which are numbered accordingly. Hence the first installment is treated as a two–hour movie in its own right; the first subsequent one–hour episode is episode one, followed by episode two, and so forth. This essay reproduces that form of citation.
7. "We do not have to be long in the woods to experience the always rather anxious impression of 'going deeper and deeper' into a limitless world," claims Bachelard in *The Poetics of Space*, trans. Maria Jolas (Boston: Beacon, 1969 rpt.), 185.
8. Philip Fisher, *Hard Facts: Setting and Form in the American Novel* (New York: Oxford University Press, 1985), 11.
9. Aldo Leopold, "The Land Ethic," in *A Sand County Almanac* (New York: Oxford University Press, 1966 rpt.), 219–20.
10. Rachel Carson, *Silent Spring* (Boston: Houghton Mifflin, 1962), 64, 246. Subsequent references to this edition appear in the text.

11. Theodore Roszak, *The Making of a Counter Culture: Reflections on the Technocratic Society and Its Youthful Opposition* (Garden City, NY: Doubleday, 1968), 248–49. Subsequent references to this edition appear in the text.

12. As quoted in Richard Corliss, "Czar of Bizarre," *Time* (October 1, 1990): 87. For further information relating to Lynch's experiences in the forests of Washington, see David Chute, "Out to Lynch," *Film Comment* 22 (October 1986): 32.

13. As quoted in David Breskin, "The Rolling Stone Interview with David Lynch," *Rolling Stone* (September 6, 1990): 98.

14. Ibid., 63.

15. Edward Abbey, *A Voice Crying in the Wilderness (Vox Clamantis in Deserto)* (New York: St. Martin's, 1989), 87.

Index